The Longman Textbook Reader

Compiled by Martha Sledge

LONGMAN

An imprint of Addison Wesley Longman, Inc.

New York · Reading, Massachusetts · Menlo Park, California · Harlow, England
Don Mills, Ontario · Sydney · Mexico City · Madrid · Amsterdam

Acquisitions Editor: Steven Rigolosi
Supplements Editor: Donna Campion
Text Design: Digital Text Construction
Electronic Page Makeup: Digital Text Construction

The Longman Textbook Reader, Compiled by Martha Sledge

ISBN 0-321-04617-X

000102—CRS—98765

Contents

Introduction for Instructors

Reading courses offer college students many opportunities. In addition to helping them increase literal comprehension skills, such courses provide a basis for further college study in a wide variety of disciplines. Students who master the skills taught in their reading courses are well on their way to success in college and in the workplace.

A large part of success in any endeavor involves understanding the expectations of the situation. College students are expected to be independent learners, to take charge of their studies, and to find motivation within. They are expected to attend lectures, take exams, and read their textbooks. Developmental reading texts often stress the importance of attending class and usually offer some tips on how to prepare for and take tests. They also include various excerpts from college texts to prepare students for the material they will encounter in their other college courses.

Unfortunately, such textbook excerpts (which often beautifully illustrate such important concepts as main idea, supporting details, and patterns of organization) tend to be fairly short—no more than a paragraph or two, or three or four pages at most. Such material tends to give ample drill and practice in the all important reading skills, but often does not match the assignments that students will receive in their other courses, where they will be expected to read one or two complete textbook chapters per week.

In the interests of providing students with longer, chapter-length readings, Addison Wesley Longman is pleased to offer *The Longman Textbook Reader.* Prepared in consultation with Addison Wesley Longman's authors, this paperback volume features five complete chapters from freshman textbooks. These five chapters are:

- **Psychology:** Chapter 15, "Psychological Disorders." From Wade, Carole and Carol Tavris. *Psychology,* 5/e. ©1998 by Longman, an imprint of Addison Wesley Longman.
- **Business:** Chapter 2, "The Cultural Environments Facing Business." From Daniels, John D. and Lee H. Radebaugh. *International Business: Environments and Operations,* 8/e. ©1998 by Addison-Wesley.
- **Computers:** Chapter 8, "Security and Privacy: Computers and the Internet." From Capron, H. L. *Computers: Tools for an Information Age,* 5/e. ©1998 by Addison-Wesley.
- **Biology:** Chapter 31, "Plant Structure and Growth." From Campbell, Neil A., *Biology,* 4/c. ©1996 by Benjamin/Cummings.

- **Communications:** Unit 21, "Friends and Lovers." From DeVito, Joseph A. *The Interpersonal Communication Book*, 8/e ©1998 by Longman, an imprint of Addison Wesley Longman.

These five chapters were chosen to reflect the most common majors of community college students across the country: the allied health professions, business administration, the computer and vocational/technical professions, and the social sciences (including sociology, psychology, and communications). Each chapter contains the complete original text, photos, art, and pedagogical features. In addition, a series of additional exercises, group activities, and critical thinking activities have been prepared specially for this edition.

We hope *The Longman Textbook Reader* will be an asset to you and your students. In addition, please visit us at our Web site for additional readings and activities: **http://longman.awl.com/englishpages.**

STEVEN RIGOLOSI
Editor, Developmental English
Addison Wesley Longman
Steven.Rigolosi@awl.com

UNIT I

From

Carole Wade
Carol Tavris

Psychology
Fifth Edition

Chapter 15:
Psychological Disorders

Who in the rainbow can draw the line where the violet tint ends
and the orange tint begins? . . . So with sanity and insanity.
In pronounced cases there is no question about them.
But in [less obvious cases, few people are willing]
to draw the exact line of demarcation
. . . though for a fee some professional experts will.

—Herman Melville, *Billy Budd*

CHAPTER FIFTEEN

Psychological Disorders

Joan of Arc heard voices that inspired her to martyrdom. Was she sane and saintly—or mad?

YOU DON'T HAVE TO BE A PSYCHOLOGIST to recognize extreme forms of abnormal behavior. A homeless woman stands on a street corner every night between midnight and 3:00 A.M., screaming obscenities and curses; by day, she is calm. A man in a shop tells you confidentially that his shoes have been bugged by the FBI, his phone is wiretapped, and his friends are spying on him for the CIA. An old man has kept every one of his daily newspapers going back to 1945, and, although he has no room in his house for anything else, he panics at the thought of giving them up.

When most people think of "mental illness," they think of odd individuals like these, whose stories fill the newspapers. But most of the psychological problems that trouble people are far less dramatic and would never make the nightly news. They occur when an individual cannot cope effectively with the stresses and problems of life. The person may become so anxious and worried that work is impaired, or become severely depressed for months, or begin to abuse drugs. In most cases, as the quote that opens this chapter says, no "exact line of demarcation" indicates when normal behavior ends and abnormal behavior begins.

You will have noticed by now that we have tried to avoid traps of either–or thinking in this book, whether the subject is right-brain versus left-brain differences or nature versus nurture. It is the same with *normality* and *abnormality*, concepts that include a rainbow of behaviors, with many shadings of color and brightness. A given problem is not a fixed point on the rainbow. A person may go through episodes of inability to function, yet get along fine between those episodes. Problems also vary in intensity; they may be mildly uncomfortable, serious but endurable, or completely incapacitating. Psychologists and psychiatrists diagnose and treat a wide range of "abnormal" behavior.

One of the most common worries that people have is "Am I normal?" It is normal to fear being abnormal. We all occasionally have difficulties that seem too much to handle, that make us feel we can't cope. It is also normal to experience "medical students' syndrome": deciding that you suffer from whatever disorder you are reading about. Precisely because many psychological problems are so common, differing only in shades of intensity on the rainbow, you may start thinking that you have them all. (We are tempted to add that this faulty conclusion is a pigment of the imagination.)

DEFINING DISORDER

DEFINE YOUR TERMS

A sect believes that it is being persecuted by nonbelievers, that a secret cabal controls the world, and that World War III is imminent. The group is stockpiling weapons and building bunkers for protection. These beliefs and actions are "normal" to all members of the sect, but would you call them signs of mental disorder? Why or why not?

Many people tend to confuse the terms *abnormal behavior*—behavior that deviates from the norm—and *mental disorder*, but the two are not the same. A person may behave in ways that are statistically rare without having a mental illness. Some of this behavior is destructive, such as murder; some is charmingly unique, such as collecting ceramic pigs; and some is desirable, such as genius. Conversely, some mental difficulties, such as depression or anxiety, can be statistically common in a society; and some thoughts or behaviors that would usually be called disordered, such as paranoid delusions or sadism, may even be considered desirable qualities in certain cults and organizations, such as the neo-Nazi Aryan Nation.

Moreover, the same symptom may be normal in one context but a sign of a disorder in another. For example, it is normal for people to hallucinate when they have a high fever, are isolated from all external sensation (see Chapter 5), are physically and mentally exhausted or stressed, are under the influence of various drugs, or are waking from deep sleep or falling into sleep. These conditions can produce "waking dreams" in which people report seeing ghosts, demons, space aliens, or other terrifying images. These normal hallucinations may be bizarre, but they are not signs of disorder; they arise from reactions of the brain to excessive stimulation or deprivation (Siegel, 1992).

Thus defining mental disorder is not an easy task. It depends in part on who is doing the defining and for what purpose, and it depends on understanding the context of the individual's symptoms and behavior. Here are several criteria in current use:

1. *Violation of cultural standards.* One definition of a mental disorder is that it involves a violation of group standards and cultural rules. Every society sets up standards of behavior that its members are expected to follow, and those who break the rules will be considered deviant or abnormal. Some standards are nearly universal, such as wearing clothes. If you run around naked in New Hampshire, most people (and the police) will think something is the matter with you.

But behavior that reflects normal conformity to a standard in one culture might seem to be abnormal in another setting. For example, seeing visions might be interpreted as a sign of schizophrenia in a twentieth-century farmer, but as a sign of healthy religious fervor in a thirteenth-century monk. For most North American cultural groups, hearing the voice or having visions of a deceased relative is thought to be abnormal; but the Chinese, the Hopi, and several other cultures regard such hallucinations as normal. (Actually, hallucinations are fairly common among whites too during bereavement; it is just that they don't tell anyone because they fear being considered "crazy" [Bentall, 1990].)

2. *Maladaptive behavior.* Many psychologists define mental disorder in terms of behavior that is maladaptive for the individual or society. This definition would ap-

People all over the world paint their bodies, but what is normal in one culture often is abnormal or eccentric in another. Hiromi Nakano (left), whose body has been completely tattooed, has taken body painting to an extreme rare in most societies; but the Samburu tribesman of Kenya (center) is painted and adorned in ways typical of his culture. And the tattoos of the American bikers (right) are abnormal to most Americans but perfectly normal in the biking subculture. How are you reacting to these examples of body decoration? Do you think they are beautiful, amusing, disgusting, or creepy?

You don't need to read a text on abnormal psychology to find cases of psychopathology; just open any magazine or newspaper! You will discover stories of violence, suicide, sexual obsession, delusion ("I was abducted by aliens"), and paranoia ("The government is spying on me from black helicopters"). As you look through an issue of your local paper, ask yourself whether the behavior in such stories seems clearly disturbed, normal, or somewhere in between. What are your criteria: cultural violations, maladaptive behavior, emotional distress, or legal judgments of impaired judgment? Can you identify cases in which it is hard to pinpoint where normality ends and disorder begins?

ply to the behavior of a woman who is so afraid of crowds that she cannot leave her house, the behavior of a man who drinks so much that he cannot keep a job, and the behavior of a student who is so anxious about failure that he cannot write term papers or take exams. It also covers the actions of individuals who say they feel fine and deny that anything is wrong but who behave in ways that are disruptive or dangerous to the community, or who are out of touch with reality—the child who sets fires, the compulsive gambler who loses the family savings, or the man who hears voices telling him to kill.

3. *Emotional distress.* A third definition identifies mental disorder in terms of a person's suffering. A person may conform to the rules of his or her community, working and getting along adequately, yet privately feel unreasonably anxious, afraid, angry, depressed, or guilty. By these criteria, according to a nationwide study of 20,000 randomly selected adults, in any given year about 28 percent of all Americans have one or more disorders—such as depression, anxiety, incapacitating fears, and alcohol or other drug problems (Regier et al., 1993; see also Kessler et al., 1994). The benefit of this definition is that it takes the person's own distress as a measure of disorder instead of imposing a single standard for everyone. A behavior that is unendurable or upsetting for one person, such as lack of interest in sex, may be acceptable and thus not distressful to another. One problem with this definition is that some people may be mentally disturbed and harmful to others, yet not feel troubled or conflicted about their behavior.

4. *The legal definition: impaired judgment and lack of self-control.* In law, the definition of mental disorder rests primarily on whether a person is aware of the consequences of his or her actions and can control his or her behavior. If not, the person may be declared insane—that is, incompetent to stand trial. But *insanity* is a legal term only; psychologists and psychiatrists do not use the terms *sanity* or *insanity* in relation to mental disorders.

Each of these definitions is useful, and no one of them is enough. In this chapter we will define **mental disorder** broadly, as any behavior or emotional state that causes an individual great suffering or worry; is self-defeating or self-destructive; or is maladaptive and disrupts either the person's relationships or the larger community. By these criteria, many people will have some mental-health problem in the course of their lives. This is normal.

mental disorder Any behavior or emotional state that causes an individual great suffering or worry; is self-defeating or self-destructive; or is maladaptive and disrupts the person's relationships or the larger community.

DILEMMAS OF DIAGNOSIS

Even armed with a broad definition of mental disorder, psychologists have found that agreeing on a specific diagnosis is easier said than done. As George Albee (1985), a past president of the American Psychological Association, put it, "Appendicitis, a brain tumor and chicken pox are the same everywhere, regardless of culture or class; mental conditions, it seems, are not." In this section we will examine the difficulties of measuring and diagnosing some of those mental conditions.

MEASURING MENTAL DISORDERS

Clinical and personality psychologists often use psychological tests to help them decide whether a person has a mental disorder. In Chapter 12 we discussed *projective tests*, which are based on the assumption that the test-taker will project his or her unconscious conflicts and motivations onto the stimulus materials. (You may recall the problems with these tests; see pages 478–479.) Most clinicians also rely on *objective tests*, or **inventories,** to diagnose their clients' problems. These tests are standardized questionnaires that require written responses, typically to multiple-choice or true-false items. Usually the test-taker is asked to report how she or he feels or acts in certain circumstances. For example, the Beck Depression Inventory is widely used to measure the severity of depression and distress; the Spielberger State–Trait Anger Inventory and the Taylor Manifest Anxiety Scale assess degrees and expressions of anger and anxiety. Objective tests have better *reliability* (they are more consistent over time) and *validity* (they are more likely to measure what they say they measure) than do projective methods or clinicians' subjective judgments (Anastasi, 1988; Dawes, 1994).

The most famous and widely used objective test of personality is the **Minnesota Multiphasic Personality Inventory (MMPI).** The MMPI was developed in the 1930s by Starke Hathaway and J. Charnley McKinley, who wanted a way to screen people with psychological disorders. They administered 1,000 potential test items to 200 people with various mental disorders and to a control group of 1,500 people who were not in treatment; the two groups differed in their answers to 550 items, and these were retained. The items were then assigned to ten clinical categories, or *scales*, that identified such problems as depression, paranoia, schizophrenia, and introversion. Four *validity scales* indicated whether a test-taker was likely to be lying, careless, defensive, or evasive while answering the items. For example, if a person tried to present an overall favorable but unrealistic image on nearly every item, the person's score on the lie scale would be high.

Since the original MMPI was devised, hundreds of additional scales have been added, and thousands of books and articles have been written on the test (Cronbach, 1990). The inventory has been used in some 50 countries, on everyone from ordinary job applicants to Russian cosmonauts. In 1989, a major revision of the MMPI was released, the MMPI-2, with norms based on a sample that was more representative in terms of region, ethnicity, age, and gender (Butcher et al., 1989).

Despite its popularity, the MMPI has many critics. Some have observed that the test is biased because its standards of normalcy do not reflect cultural differences. Although the sample used for establishing test norms in the MMPI-2 was an improvement, it still underrepresented minorities, the elderly, the poor, and the poorly educated. Some of the scales are still based on inadequate and outdated norms, and some items are affected by the respondent's tendency to give the socially appropriate answer rather than an honest one (Edwards & Edwards, 1991; Helmes & Reddon, 1993). One review concluded that the MMPI is adequate if the test is used for its original purpose—identifying people with emotional disorders (Parker, Hanson, & Hunsley, 1988). Yet in practice, the MMPI is often used in business, industry, and education for inappropriate reasons by persons who are not well trained in testing. Two

Inventories Standardized objective questionnaires requiring written responses; they typically include scales on which people are asked to rate themselves.

Minnesota Multiphasic Personality Inventory (MMPI) A widely used objective personality test.

Harriet Tubman (far left) with some of the people she helped to escape from slavery on her "underground railroad." Slaveholders welcomed the idea that Tubman and others who insisted on their freedom had a "mental disorder" called "drapetomania."

psychologists who reviewed the history and validity of both MMPIs concluded that the correct interpretation of these tests requires "substantial experience and sophistication" by the clinician who administers them (Helmes & Reddon, 1993).

The debate about the MMPI reflects a deeper issue: whether mental disorder can be diagnosed objectively at all. The debate about testing is a whisper compared with the noisy controversy about the diagnosis of mental disorder itself.

DIAGNOSIS: ART OR SCIENCE?

In the early years of the nineteenth century, a physician named Samuel Cartwright argued that many slaves were suffering from two forms of mental illness: *drapetomania*, an uncontrollable urge to escape from slavery, and *dysathesia aethiopica*, the symptoms of which included destroying property on the plantation, being disobedient, talking back, refusing to work, and fighting back when beaten. "Sanity for a slave was synonymous with submission," noted Hope Landrine (1988), "and protest and seeking freedom were the equivalent of psychopathology." Thus doctors could assure slaveowners that a mental illness, not the intolerable condition of slavery, made slaves seek freedom.

Today, "drapetomania" sounds foolish and cruel, and most people assume that the bad old days of psychiatric misdiagnosis are past. Yet cultural factors and subjective interpretations still affect the process of diagnosis, a fact that raises many important issues for those who define and treat mental disorders.

In theory, diagnostic categories must meet a set of solid scientific criteria to be included in the "bible" of psychological and psychiatric diagnosis, the *Diagnostic and Statistical Manual of Mental Disorders* (DSM), which is published by the American Psychiatric Association. The first edition of the DSM, in 1952, was only 128 pages long and contained brief descriptions of organic brain disorders, severe mental disorders, and personality problems. The second edition, the DSM-II, appeared in 1968; it too was short. The third edition, DSM-III, published in 1980, began to include ordinary difficulties such as tobacco dependence, marital conflicts, and sexual problems. The revised third edition, DSM-III-R, in 1987, was 567 pages long and listed more than 200 kinds of mental disorder. The fattest edition yet, the DSM-IV, published in 1994, is nearly 900 pages long and contains more than 300 mental disorders.

The primary aim of the DSM is *descriptive:* to provide clear criteria of diagnostic categories, so that clinicians and researchers can agree on which disorders they are talking about, study them, and treat them. (For a list of its major categories, see Table 15.1.) The DSM makes few assumptions about the causes of the disorders it describes; in many cases, the causes are not known. Where possible, information is provided about typical age of onset, predisposing factors, course of the disorder, prevalence of the disorder, sex ratio of those affected, and cultural issues that might affect diagnosis. The DSM also classifies each disorder on five *axes*, or factors:

1. The primary diagnosis of the problem, such as depression.

2. Ingrained aspects of the client's personality that are likely to affect his or her behavior and ability to be treated, such as narcissism or dependency.

3. General medical conditions that are relevant to the disorder, such as respiratory or digestive problems.

4. Social and environmental problems that can make the disorder worse, such as job and housing troubles or loss of a support group.

_____ TABLE 15.1 *Major Diagnostic Categories*_____
       in the DSM-IV

Disorders usually first diagnosed in infancy, childhood, or adolescence include mental retardation, attention-deficit disorders (such as hyperactivity or an inability to concentrate), eating disorders, and developmental problems.

Delirium, dementia, amnesia, and other cognitive disorders are those resulting from brain damage, degenerative diseases such as syphilis or Alzheimer's, toxic substances, or drugs.

Substance-related disorders are problems associated with excessive use of or withdrawal from alcohol, amphetamines, caffeine, cocaine, hallucinogens, nicotine, opiates, or other drugs.

Schizophrenia and other psychotic disorders are disorders characterized by delusions, hallucinations, and severe disturbances in thinking and emotion.

Mood disorders include major depression, bipolar disorder (manic-depression), and dysthymia (chronic depressed mood).

Anxiety disorders include generalized anxiety disorder, phobias, panic attacks with or without agoraphobia, posttraumatic stress disorder, and obsessive thoughts or compulsive rituals.

Somatoform disorders involve individual reports of physical symptoms (e.g., paralysis, heart palpitations, or dizziness) for which no organic cause can be found. This category includes hypochondria, extreme preoccupation with health and the unfounded conviction that one is ill; and conversion disorder, in which a physical symptom (such as a paralyzed arm or blindness) serves a psychological function.

Dissociative disorders include dissociative amnesia, in which important events cannot be remembered after a traumatic event; and dissociative identity disorder (formerly "multiple personality disorder"), characterized by the presence of two or more distinct identities or personality states.

Sexual and gender identity disorders include problems of sexual (gender) identity, such as transsexualism (wanting to be the other gender); problems of sexual performance (such as premature ejaculation, lack of orgasm, or lack of desire); and paraphilias, which involve unusual or bizarre imagery or acts that are necessary for sexual arousal, as in fetishism, sadomasochism, or exhibitionism.

Impulse control disorders involve an inability to resist an impulse to perform some act that is harmful to the individual or to others, as in pathological gambling, stealing (kleptomania), setting fires (pyromania), or having violent rages.

Personality disorders are inflexible and maladaptive patterns that cause distress to the individual or impair the ability to function; they include paranoid, narcissistic, and antisocial personality disorders.

Additional conditions that may be a focus of clinical attention include "problems in living" such as bereavement, academic difficulties, religious or spiritual problems, and acculturation problems.

5. A global assessment of the client's overall level of functioning in work, relationships, and leisure time, including whether the problem is of recent origin or of long duration, and how incapacitating it is.

The DSM has had an extraordinary impact worldwide. It has standardized the categories of what is, and what is not, a mental disorder. Its categories and terminology have become the common language of most clinicians and researchers. Virtually all textbooks in psychiatry and psychology base their discussions of mental disorders on the DSM. Insurance companies require clinicians to assign their clients the appropriate DSM code number of the diagnosed disorder, which puts pressure on compilers of the manual to add more diagnoses so that physicians and psychologists will be compensated. Attorneys and judges often refer to the manual's list of mental disorders, even though the DSM warns that its categories "may not be wholly relevant to legal judgments."

Because of the power of the DSM to define mental disorders, it is important to know its limitations. Critics point to the following concerns about the scientific basis of diagnosis in general and the DSM in particular:

1. *The fostering of overdiagnosis.* When people have a tool, they will use it, a tendency that Abraham Kaplan (1967) called "The Law of the Instrument." "If you give a small boy a hammer," Kaplan wrote, "it will turn out that everything he runs into needs pounding." So it is, some say, with clinicians. Give them the instruments to diagnose disorders, and everything they run into will need treatment. For example, before 1980, fewer than 200 cases of dissociative identity disorder (commonly known as "multiple personality disorder") had ever been diagnosed. Since 1980, when the DSM-III included new criteria for this diagnosis, thousands and thousands of cases have been reported, most of them in North America (Nathan, 1994; Piper, 1997). Does this mean that the disorder is being better identified, or that it is being overdiagnosed by American and Canadian clinicians who are looking for it? Clinicians are also more likely to diagnose a disorder once they have a treatment for it. As medication was promoted to treat obsessive–compulsive disorder, for example, the rate of diagnosis of this problem rose significantly (Stoll, Tohen, & Baldessarini, 1993).

2. *An increased risk of self-fulfilling prophecies.* The very act of diagnosing a disorder can create a self-fulfilling prophecy for both the client and the clinician: The client tries to conform to the assigned diagnosis, and the clinician interprets everything the client does as further confirmation of the diagnosis (Maddux, 1996; Rosenhan, 1973). Moreover, as we will see in Chapter 17, once a person has acquired a label—for example, once an impulsive, troubled teenager is given the diagnosis of "oppositional defiant disorder"—others often become oblivious to changes in the individual's behavior or to other possible reasons for it, continuing to see him or her only in terms of the diagnosis.

3. *The confounding of serious mental disorders with normal problems in living.* The DSM is not called "The Diagnostic and Statistical Manual of Mental Disorders and a Whole Bunch of Everyday Problems." Yet the compilers of the DSM keep adding everyday problems. The latest version actually contains "disorder of written expression" (having trouble writing clearly), "mathematics disorder" (not doing well in math), and "caffeine-induced sleep disorder." Some critics fear that by lumping together such normal difficulties with true mental illnesses, such as schizophrenia, the DSM implies that everyday problems are comparable to disorders—and equally likely to require professional treatment (Dumont, 1987; Maddux, 1993; Szasz, 1961/1967).

4. *Misuse of diagnoses for social and political purposes.* Some critics are concerned that once people are given a formal diagnosis for their problems, they may feel absolved of responsibility for their behavior or use the label to claim diminished responsibility for criminal acts. This concern was a major reason that the task force revising the DSM-III decided to drop a proposed diagnosis called "paraphilic coercive disorder," describing the behavior of men who rape. The task force agreed with women who were concerned that rapists diagnosed as having such a "disorder" would not be held responsible.

5. *A false implication that diagnosis can be purely objective.* Finally, some critics argue that the whole enterprise of the DSM is a foolhardy effort to impose a veneer of science on the inherently arbitrary process of defining mental disorder. They maintain that the DSM wants to look like an objective set of disorders, as if no bias or choice were involved in deciding what to include and what to leave out (Dumont, 1987; Maddux, 1993; Tiefer, 1995). In fact, say the critics, many such decisions have been based not on empirical evidence, but on group consensus or on the pressure to have more diagnosable categories that insurance companies will compensate (Kirk & Kutchins, 1992).

For example, when the American Psychiatric Association decided in the early 1970s to remove homosexuality from the DSM, it did not base its decision on the research showing that homosexuals were no more disturbed than heterosexuals. Rather, *it took a vote of its members* (Bayer, 1981). Over the years, psychiatrists have quite properly rejected many other "disorders" that reflected cultural prejudices, such as drapetomania, lack of vaginal orgasm, childhood masturbation disorder, masochism, and nymphomania (Wakefield, 1992). But they have also voted in new "disorders" that reflect today's prejudices and values, such as "hypoactive sexual desire disorder"—not wanting to have sex often enough. Compilers of the DSM-III-R, amid much controversy, voted in a diagnosis called "self-defeating personality disorder," which would have applied mainly to women who adopted the extreme self-sacrificing qualities of the female role; compilers of the DSM-IV voted it out. But they kept, in an appendix, "premenstrual dysphoric disorder," even though, as we saw in Chapter 5, this alleged syndrome lacks an agreed-on definition, and men have as many symptoms and mood changes over the month as women do.

The point to underscore is that *as times change, so does the cultural consensus about what is normal—and thus what is abnormal.* And that, in turn, means that clinicians must be aware of how their own beliefs and leanings affect their clinical judgments, even when they are trying to follow objective criteria. In one study, for example, 47 therapists were randomly assigned to view one of two videotapes of a depressed male client. The tapes were identical except for the man's job and family roles: He was portrayed as either a traditional breadwinner or a nontraditional househusband whose wife earned the family income. Later, when the therapists evaluated the man's mental health, assigned a diagnosis, and outlined a proposed treatment, they judged nontraditional men as being more disturbed than traditional men (Robertson & Fitzgerald, 1990).

Advocates of the DSM argue that when the manual is used correctly, diagnoses are more accurate and bias is reduced, and that new field studies are improving the empirical basis of the clinical categories (Barlow, 1991; Spitzer & Williams, 1988; Wittchen et al., 1995). A study of psychiatric patients in Maryland, for instance, found better accuracy in the diagnosis of schizophrenia and mood disorders than other studies had, apparently because the physicians were more closely following DSM criteria (Pulver et al., 1988). Other advocates argue that the correct labeling of a disorder helps people identify the source of their unhappiness and leads them to proper treatment (Kessler et al., 1994). They respond to the criticisms of subjectivity in diagnosis by pointing out that some mental disorders, such as schizophrenia, anxiety, and depression, occur in all societies. The fact, they say, that *some* diagnoses reflect society's biases doesn't mean that *all* diagnoses do (Wakefield, 1992). In cultures around the world, from the Inuit of Alaska to the Yorubas of Nigeria, there are individuals who have delusions, who are severely depressed, or who can't control their behavior; in every culture, they are considered to have mental illnesses (Kleinman, 1988).

We will return to these controversies as we examine some of the major categories of disorder in the DSM.

Your mental health will improve if you can answer these questions.

1. What is the advantage of inventories, compared with clinical judgment and projective tests, in diagnosing mental disorders?

2. The primary purpose of the DSM is to (a) provide descriptive criteria for diagnosing mental disorders, (b) help psychologists assess normal as well as abnormal personality traits, (c) describe the causes of common mental disorders, (d) keep the number of diagnostic categories of mental disorders to a minimum.

3. List five concerns about the DSM and its uses.

 4. Two psychologists are discussing an anxious and depressed Japanese-American man who, along with 112,000 other Japanese-Americans in World War II, lost his job and home and was sent to an internment camp. Dr. Smith diagnoses "posttraumatic stress disorder." Dr. Jones believes that because the man's symptoms resulted from an act of governmental injustice, the diagnosis should be something like "post-oppression disorder" (Loo, 1991). Can you identify the main assumption in the kind of label each psychologist is using and the solution it implies?

Answers:

1. In general, they have better reliability and validity.   2. a   3. Fostering overdiagnosis; increasing the risk of self-fulfilling prophecies; confounding normal problems in living with mental disorders; using diagnoses for undesirable social and political purposes; and creating a scientific veneer to disguise the essentially subjective process of diagnosis.   4. Dr. Smith assumes that the origins of the man's unhappiness lie within him, in his own personal reaction to the trauma of imprisonment; the implied solution is psychotherapy. Dr. Jones assumes that the man's unhappiness is a result of a miscarriage of justice; the implied solution, in addition to psychotherapy, might involve a social remedy, such as reparations.

ANXIETY DISORDERS

The body, sensibly, prepares us to feel anxiety (a general state of apprehension or psychological tension) or fear (apprehension about a specific threat) when we are facing dangerous, unfamiliar, or stressful situations, such as making a first parachute jump or waiting for important news. In the short run, these are adaptive emotions that enable us to cope with danger. But some individuals are prone to irrational fear or to a chronic state of anxiety. In clinical terms, such fear and anxiety can take several forms: *generalized anxiety disorder*, marked by long-lasting, continuous feelings of apprehension and doom; *phobias*, unrealistic fears of specific things or situations; and *obsessive–compulsive disorder*, in which people develop irrational thoughts and rituals designed to ward off anxious feelings.

ANXIETY AND PHOBIAS

The chief characteristic of **generalized anxiety disorder** is continuous, uncontrollable anxiety or worry—a feeling of foreboding and dread—that occurs more days than not in a six-month period and that is not brought on by physical causes such as disease, drugs, or drinking too much coffee. Symptoms include restlessness or feeling keyed up, being easily fatigued, having difficulty concentrating, irritability, muscle tension and jitteriness, and sleep disturbance.

Chronic anxiety has no single cause. *Predisposing factors* include having a hereditary predisposition, having poor coping methods, living through a traumatic event, and having unrealistic goals or unreasonable beliefs that foster worry and fears. *Precipitating factors* are the immediate events that produce anxiety and keep it going. You are likely to feel anxious when you are in a situation in which others continually express their disapproval of you, or when you have to adapt yourself to an environment that doesn't fit your personality, such as being a slow-paced person in a fast-moving job.

When anxiety results from experiencing an uncontrollable and unpredictable danger or a natural disaster, it may produce *posttraumatic stress disorder (PTSD)* or *acute stress disorder.* PTSD consists of emotional symptoms that are common in people who have suffered traumatic experiences such as war, rape, other assaults, and natural disasters such as hurricanes, fire, or earthquake. The reaction might occur immediately or it might be delayed for months. In contrast, acute stress disorder typically occurs right after the traumatic event and subsides within several months. In both disorders, typical symptoms include reliving the trauma in recurrent, intrusive thoughts or dreams; "psychic numbing," a sense of detachment from others and an inability to feel happy or loving; and increased physiological arousal, reflected in difficulty concentrating, insomnia, and irritability. A random survey of 5,877 Americans found that PTSD is more common and more persistent than previously assumed: Nearly 1 in 12 has suffered from PTSD in his or her life, and in more than one-third of the cases, the symptoms lasted for at least ten years (Kessler et al., 1995).

A **phobia** is an unrealistic fear of a specific situation, activity, or thing. Some phobias are extremely common, such as fear of heights (acrophobia); fear of closed spaces (claustrophobia); fear of dirt and germs (mysophobia); and fear of animals, especially snakes, dogs, insects, and mice (zoophobia). Others are rarer, such as fear of purple (porphyrophobia), fear of the number 13 (triskaidekaphobia), and fear of thunder (brontophobia).

Is this woman feeling normal fear or unreasonable panic? (To find out, turn the page.)

generalized anxiety disorder A continuous state of anxiety marked by feelings of worry and dread, apprehension, difficulties in concentration, and signs of motor tension.

phobia An unrealistic fear of a specific situation, activity, or object.

GET INVOLVED

Everyone fears something. Stop for a moment to think about what you fear most. Is it heights? Snakes? Speaking in public? Ask yourself these questions:

- *How long have I feared this thing or situation?*

- *How would I respond if I could not avoid this thing or situation?*

- *How much would I be willing to rearrange my life (my movements, schedule, activities) to avoid this feared thing or situation?*

After considering these questions, would you regard your fear as a full-blown phobia or merely a normal source of apprehension? What are your criteria for deciding?

It is normal to feel afraid when you jump out of a plane for the first time. But people with anxiety disorders feel as if they are jumping out of planes all the time.

People who have a *social phobia* have a persistent, irrational fear of situations in which they will be observed by others. They worry that they will do or say something that will humiliate or embarrass them. Common social phobias are fears of speaking or performing in public, using public restrooms, eating in public, and writing in the presence of others. (Notice that these phobias are more severe forms of the occasional shyness and social anxiety that everyone experiences.)

By far the most disabling fear disorder is **agoraphobia,** which accounts for more than half of the phobia cases for which people seek treatment. Disregard the dictionary and popular definition of agoraphobia as "fear of open spaces." In ancient Greece, the *agora* was the social, political, business, and religious center of town. It was the public meeting place away from home. The essential feature in what agoraphobics fear is being alone in a public place from which escape might be difficult or help unavailable. They may report a great variety of specific fears—of public buses, driving in traffic or tunnels, eating in restaurants, or going to parties—but the underlying fear is of being away from a safe place, usually home, or a safe person, usually a parent or spouse.

Agoraphobia may begin with a series of panic attacks that seem to come out of the blue. A **panic attack** is a sudden onset of intense fear or terror, with feelings of impending doom. It may last from a few minutes to (more rarely) several hours, and it involves such intense symptoms as trembling and shaking; dizziness; chest pain or discomfort; feelings of unreality; hot and cold flashes; sweating; and a fear of dying, going crazy, or losing control. The attack is so unexpected and so scary that the agoraphobic-to-be begins to avoid situations that he or she thinks may provoke another one. After a while, any sort of emotional arousal, from whatever source, feels too much like anxiety, and the person with agoraphobia will try to avoid it. Because so many of the actions associated with this phobia are designed to help the person avoid a panic attack, researchers often describe agoraphobia as a "fear of fear" rather than a fear of places (Chambless, 1988).

People who have panic attacks are found throughout the world, in both industrial and nonindustrial societies (Barlow, 1990). The common symptoms are heart palpitations, dizziness, and faintness, but culture influences the likelihood of other telltale signs. Feelings of choking or being smothered, numbness, and fear of dying are most common in Latin America and southern Europe; fear of public places is most common in northern Europe and America; and a fear of going crazy is more common in the Americas than in Europe. In Greenland, some fishermen suffer from "kayak-angst": a sudden attack of dizziness and fear that occurs while they are fishing in small, one-person kayaks (Amering & Katschnig, 1990).

Studies of twins suggest a heritable component in panic disorder, a tendency for the body to respond to stress with a sudden "alarm" reaction. (For other people, the response may be headaches or hives.) Although panic attacks seem to come from nowhere, they are in fact often related to the physical arousal of stress, prolonged emotion, exercise, drugs such as caffeine or nicotine, or specific worries (Barlow, 1990; Beck, 1988). Panic attacks are not uncommon. The essential difference between people who go on to develop a disorder and those who don't lies in *how they interpret their bodily reactions* (Barlow, 1990; McNally, 1994). Healthy people who have occasional panic attacks see them correctly as a result of a passing crisis or period of stress, comparable to another person's migraines. But people who develop a full-fledged panic disorder regard the attack as a sign of impending death or disaster, and they begin to worry about possible future ones. Agoraphobia develops when they begin to avoid any situation that they fear will set off another attack.

agoraphobia A set of phobias, often set off by a panic attack, involving the basic fear of being away from a safe place or person.

panic attack A brief feeling of intense fear and impending doom or death, accompanied by intense physiological symptoms, such as rapid breathing and pulse, and dizziness.

OBSESSIONS AND COMPULSIONS

Obsessive–compulsive disorder (OCD) is characterized by recurrent, persistent, unwished-for thoughts or images (*obsessions*) and by repetitive, ritualized, stereotyped behaviors that the person feels must be carried out to avoid disaster (*compulsions*). The disorder can begin in childhood, and it occurs in both sexes. Of course, many people have trivial compulsions and superstitious rituals; as we noted in Chapter 7, baseball players are famous for them. Obsessions and compulsions become serious—a disorder—when they trouble the individual and interfere with his or her life.

A person with obsessive thoughts often finds them frightening and repugnant. For example, the person may have repetitive thoughts of killing a child, of becoming contaminated by shaking hands, or of having unknowingly hurt someone in a traffic accident. Obsessive thoughts take many forms, but they are alike in reflecting maladaptive ways of reasoning and processing information. Some people may develop obsessions because they have difficulty managing anger. In one case, a man had repeated images of hitting his 3-year-old son with a hammer. Unable to explain his horrible thoughts about his beloved son, he assumed he was going insane. Most parents, in fact, have occasional negative feelings about their children and may even entertain a fleeting thought of murder, but they recognize that these are not the same as actions. The man, it turned out, felt that his son had usurped his place in his wife's affections, but he was unable to reveal his anger and hurt to his wife directly (Carson, Butcher, & Mineka, 1996).

People who suffer from compulsions likewise feel they have no control over them. For example, a woman *must* check the furnace, lights, locks, oven, and fireplace three times before she can sleep; a man *must* wash his hands and face precisely eight times before he leaves the house. The most common compulsions are hand washing, counting, touching, and checking. Most sufferers of OCD do not enjoy these rituals and realize that the behavior is senseless. But if they try to break the ritual, they feel mounting anxiety that is relieved only by giving in to the compulsion. They are like the man who constantly snaps his fingers to keep tigers away. "But there aren't any tigers here," says a friend. "You see! It works!" answers the man.

PET scans find that several parts of the brain are hyperactive in people with OCD. One area, the orbital cortex (which lies just above the eye sockets), apparently sends messages of impending danger to the caudate nucleus, an area involved in controlling the movement of the limbs, and to other structures involved in preparing the body to feel afraid and respond to external threats. Normally, once danger is past or a person realizes there is no real cause for fear, the caudate nucleus switches off the alarm signals. In people with OCD, however, the orbital cortex sends out repeated false alarms; the emotional networks send out mistaken "fear!" messages, and the caudate nucleus fails to turn them off. The sufferer feels in a constant state of danger and tries repeatedly to reduce the resulting anxiety (Schwartz et al., 1996).

Anxiety disorders, uncomfortable or painful as they can be, are at least a sign of commitment to the future. They mean a person can anticipate the future enough to worry about it. But sometimes people's hopes for the future become extinguished. They are no longer anxious that something may go wrong; they are convinced it *will* go wrong, so there is no point in trying. This belief is a sign of the disorder of depression.

The Disease Germ Is More Dangerous Than the Mad Dog

Lysol Disinfectant

What is a normal concern with hygiene in one culture could seem an abnormal compulsion in another. This Lysol ad played on Americans' fears of disease by warning about the "unseen menace—more threatening, more fatal, more cruel than a million mad dogs—. . . the disease germ."

obsessive–compulsive disorder (OCD) An anxiety disorder in which a person feels trapped in repetitive, persistent thoughts (obsessions) and repetitive, ritualized behaviors (compulsions) designed to reduce anxiety.

MOOD DISORDERS

In everyday talk, we all use the word *depression* to describe sadness, gloom, and loss of pep. By that definition, everyone feels depressed at times. Psychologists, however, consider depression to be a disorder only when it goes beyond normal sadness over life's problems, or even the wild grief that may accompany tragedy or bereavement. Serious depression is so widespread that it has been called the common cold of psychiatric disturbances.

DEPRESSION AND MANIA

Major depression is severe enough to disrupt a person's ordinary functioning. It differs from chronic depressed mood, a condition called *dysthymia* [dis-THIGH-me-a], in the intensity and duration of symptoms. In dysthymia, the depressive symptoms are milder, and they *are* the person's customary way of functioning.

Major depression brings emotional, behavioral, and cognitive changes. Depressed people report despair and hopelessness. They are tearful and weepy. They think often of death or suicide. They lose interest or pleasure in their usual activities. They feel unable to get up and do things; it takes an enormous effort just to get dressed. Their thinking patterns feed their bleak moods. They exaggerate minor failings, ignore or discount positive events ("She didn't mean that compliment; she was only being polite"), and interpret any little thing that goes wrong as evidence that nothing will ever go right. Unlike normal sadness or grief, major depression involves low self-esteem. Emotionally healthy grieving people do not see themselves as completely worthless and unlovable, and they know at some level that grief will pass. Depressed people interpret losses as signs of personal failure and conclude that they will never be happy again.

Depression is accompanied by physical changes as well. The depressed person may stop eating or overeat, have difficulty falling asleep or sleeping through the night, lose sexual desire, have trouble concentrating, and feel tired all the time. Some sufferers have other physical reactions, such as inexplicable pain or headaches. (Anyone with these symptoms should have a medical exam because they can also be signs of physical illness.) About half of all those who go through a period of major depression will do so only once. Others have recurrent bouts. Some people have episodes that are many years apart; others have clusters of depressive episodes over a few years. Alarmingly, depression and suicide rates among young people have increased rapidly in recent years. (See "Taking Psychology with You.")

At the opposite pole from depression is *mania*, an abnormally high state of exhilaration. You might think it's impossible to feel too good, but mania is not the normal

The hallmarks of depression are despair and a sense of isolation.

major depression A mood disorder involving disturbances in emotion (excessive sadness), behavior (loss of interest in one's usual activities), cognition (thoughts of hopelessness), and body function (fatigue and loss of appetite).

joy of being in love or winning the Pulitzer Prize. Someone in a manic phase is expansive to an extent that is out of character. The symptoms are exactly the opposite of those in depression. Instead of feeling fatigued and listless, the manic person is full of energy. Instead of feeling unambitious, hopeless, and powerless, the manic person feels full of ambitions, plans, and power. The depressed person speaks slowly, monotonously, with no inflections. The manic person speaks rapidly, dramatically, often with many jokes and puns. The depressed person has no self-esteem. The manic person has inflated self-esteem. Although people may experience major depressions without manic episodes, they rarely have only manic episodes. Most manic episodes are a sign of **bipolar disorder** (formerly called *manic–depressive disorder*), in which depression alternates with mania.

Although bipolar disorder is equally common in both sexes, major depression is overrepresented among women of all ethnicities (McGrath et al., 1990). Some psychologists think that women actually are more likely to become depressed than men are, but others think the difference is more apparent than real. As we saw in Chapter 10, the sexes often express feelings differently, so men's depression may be overlooked or misdiagnosed. Men, for instance, have higher rates of drug abuse and violent behavior than women do, and some researchers believe that this behavior masks depression or anxiety (Canetto, 1992; Kessler et al., 1994).

THEORIES OF DEPRESSION

Explanations of depression generally fall into five categories, emphasizing biological predispositions, social conditions, problems with close attachments, cognitive habits, or a combination of individual vulnerability and stress.

1. *Biological explanations* account for depression in terms of genetics and brain chemistry. As we saw in Chapter 4, neurotransmitters permit messages to be transmitted from one neuron to another in the brain. Two neurotransmitters that seem to be implicated in depressive disorders are norepinephrine and serotonin. In the view of some researchers, depression is caused by a deficient production of one or both of these neurotransmitters, and manic moods are caused by an excessive production (see Figure 15.1). Biological theories seem especially applicable in cases of depression that do not involve reactions to real-life crises or losses, but which instead seem to come from nowhere or occur in response to minor stresses.

bipolar disorder A mood disorder in which depression alternates with mania (excessive euphoria).

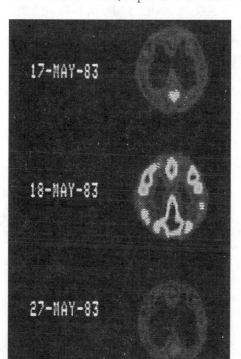

Figure 15.1
The Depressed Brain

These PET scans show changes in the metabolism of glucose, the brain's energy supply, in a patient with bipolar disorder. On May 17 and 27, the patient was depressed, and glucose metabolism throughout the brain was lower than normal. On May 18, the patient became manic, and metabolic activity increased to near normal levels. Keep in mind that such changes do not show the direction of cause and effect: A drop in glucose might bring on depression, but depression might also cause a drop in glucose levels.

Biological theories are supported by studies showing that when animals are given drugs that diminish the body's ability to produce serotonin, the animals become sluggish and inactive—a symptom of depression (Kramer, 1993; Wender & Klein, 1981). Conversely, drugs that increase the levels of serotonin and norepinephrine sometimes alleviate symptoms of depression; hence they are called "antidepressants." The early success of these drugs provoked great interest in the search for the biological origins of depression. However, as we will see in the next chapter, drugs are not universally effective, and even when they help some individuals, this does not necessarily mean that the depression had an organic basis. Studies of adopted twins suggest that major depression and bipolar disorder may have a genetic component, but the search for the gene or genes involved has so far proved fruitless. A decade ago, several highly publicized studies raised the possibility that a specific gene might be linked with bipolar disorder, but subsequent research failed to confirm these results (Faraone, Kremen, & Tsuang, 1990; Kelsoe et al., 1989).

2. *Social explanations* of depression consider the conditions of people's lives. In the social view, for example, the reason that women are more likely than men to suffer from depression is that women are more likely to lack fulfilling jobs or family relations. Men are nearly twice as likely as women to be married and working full time, a combination of activities that is strongly associated with mental health (Brown, 1993; Golding, 1988). In a random sample of 1,111 men and women in Boston, virtually all of the differences between men and women in their reported levels of depression could be accounted for by their different states of marriage and employment (Gore & Mangione, 1983). Mothers are especially vulnerable to depression: The more children they have, the more likely women are to become depressed (McGrath et al., 1990).

Another social factor in the origins of depression may be sexual abuse and other forms of violence. In a study of women in a psychiatric inpatient hospital, over half reported a history of such abuse. Moreover, the number and severity of their depressive symptoms were greater than those of women who reported no sexual trauma (Bryer et al., 1987). A community survey of 3,125 white, Latino, and black women found that depression, anxiety, and panic attacks were significantly more frequent among women who had been sexually molested or raped (Burnam et al., 1988). And in the United States, inner-city adolescents of both sexes who are exposed to high rates of violence report higher levels of depression and more thoughts of, and efforts to commit, suicide than those who are not subjected to violence in their lives or communities (Mazza, Reynolds, & Grover, 1995).

Social and economic explanations may help account for the rise of depression among young people all over the world, many of whom are struggling economically, have delayed making family commitments, or live with violence in their families and communities. Social analyses, though, fail to explain why most people who have these experiences do not become clinically depressed, while others stay locked in the grip of despair. Nor do they explain why some people become depressed even though they seem to "have it all."

3. *Attachment explanations* emphasize the importance to well-being of affiliation and attachment. In this view, depression results from disturbed relationships and separations, both past and present, and from a history of insecure attachments (Roberts, Gotlib, & Kassel, 1996). One important attachment theory, the *interpersonal theory of depression*, recognizes the role of biological and social factors, but it emphasizes the depressed person's disputes, losses, anxieties, feelings of incompetence, and disturbed relationships (Klerman et al., 1984).

The one thing that most often sets off a depressive episode is, in fact, the end of a close relationship, which is hardest on people who lack social support and coping skills (Barnett & Gotlib, 1988). However, attachment theories raise an interesting cause-and-effect problem. Disturbed or broken relationships may make some people severely depressed; but depressed people are also demanding and "depressing" to family and friends, who often feel angry or sad around them and may eventually break away (Gotlib & Hooley, 1988; Joiner & Metalsky, 1995).

4. *Cognitive explanations* propose that depression results from, or is maintained by, particular habits of thinking and interpreting events. Two decades ago, the theory of "learned helplessness" held that people become depressed when their efforts to avoid pain or to control the environment fail (Seligman, 1975). The fatal flaw in this theory was that not all depressed people have actually failed in their lives; many merely believe, without evidence, that nothing they do will be successful. Thus the theory evolved into its current form, which is that some depression results from having a hopeless and *pessimistic explanatory style* (see Chapter 14). People with this habitual way of thinking believe that nothing good will ever happen to them and that they cannot do anything to change this bleak future (Abramson, Metalsky, & Alloy, 1989; Seligman, 1991).

Other cognitive bad habits are associated with depression. People who focus inward and brood endlessly about their negative feelings—who have a "ruminating response style"—tend to have longer and more intense periods of depression than do those who are able to distract themselves, look outward, and seek solutions to problems. Women are more likely than men to develop this introspective style, beginning in adolescence, and this tendency may contribute both to longer-lasting depressions in women and to the sex difference in reported rates (Bromberger & Matthews, 1996; Nolen-Hoeksema, 1991; Nolen-Hoeksema & Girgus, 1994).

Although the evidence is strong that negative thoughts can cause depression, it is also true that depression causes negative thoughts; when you are feeling sad, gloomy ideas come more easily. Negative thinking, therefore, is both a cause and a result of depression (Hilsman & Garber, 1995).

5. *"Vulnerability–stress" explanations* draw on all four explanations just discussed. They hold that depression (and, as we will see throughout this chapter, many other psychological problems and mental disorders) result from an *interaction* between individual vulnerabilities—in personality traits, habits of thinking, genetic predispositions, and so forth—and environmental stress or sad events. In one study of more than 1,000 pairs of female twins, the women most likely to suffer major depression following the death of a close relative, assault, serious marital problems, or divorce were those who had a genetic susceptibility (Kendler et al., 1995).

Interaction models of depression are an improvement over theories implying that everyone is equally vulnerable to depression, given a certain experience or biological disposition. Vulnerability–stress theories try to specify which personality traits interact with which events to produce depression. According to one approach, some depression-prone individuals are excessively dependent on other people for acceptance, understanding, and support. If their relationships fail, they become preoccupied with feelings of loss and abandonment (as the interpersonal theory of depression would predict). Other depression-prone individuals are excessively focused on achievement. If they fail to achieve their goals, they become preoccupied with feelings of inadequacy and incompetence (Coyne & Whiffen, 1995).

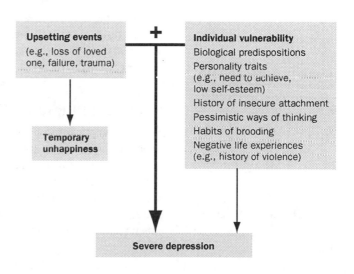

Other vulnerability–stress models are trying to specify which cognitive factors are likely to cause or prolong depression. One study found that students who got worse grades than they expected reported feeling depressed (not a surprise), but this mood persisted only in those who *also* had a depressive attributional style ("I'm stupid and always will be") *and* low self-esteem. In this case, depression resulted from a combination of having a pessimistic explanatory style, low self-esteem, an experience with failure, and a resulting sense of hopelessness (Metalsky et al., 1993).

DON'T OVERSIMPLIFY

Countless studies of depression have been done. What do their contradictory results suggest about the search for a single cause of the disorder? How can we make the most sense of conflicting results and explanations?

In assessing these different approaches, we should keep in mind that depression comes in degrees of severity, from tearful tiredness to an inability to get out of bed. Further, depression may have different causes in different people. One person may have been abandoned in childhood and may therefore feel insecurely attached in current relationships; another may have a pessimistic cognitive style that fosters depressive interpretations of events; a third may have a biological predisposition to respond to stress with depression; a fourth may lack satisfying work or love, or may have been subjected to violence or other trauma. By understanding depression as an interaction between an individual's personality and experiences, we can see why the same precipitating event, such as the loss of a loved one or even a minor setback, might produce different degrees of depression in different people.

Quick Quiz

 A newspaper headline announces that a single gene has been identified as the cause of depression, but when you read the fine print you learn that other studies have failed to support this research. What explanations can you think of to explain these contradictory findings?

Answers:

The conflicting evidence may mean, among other possibilities, that if a genetic predisposition for depression does exist, it is not due to a single specific gene, but involves several genes working in the context of environmental events. It may mean that the right gene has not yet been identified. Or it may mean that genes are not a factor in all forms of depression.

PERSONALITY DISORDERS

Personality disorders involve rigid, maladaptive traits that cause great distress or an inability to get along with others. The DSM-IV describes a personality disorder as "an enduring pattern of inner experience and behavior that deviates markedly from the expectations of the individual's culture." This pattern is not caused by depression, a drug reaction, or a situation that temporarily induces a person to behave in ways that are out of character.

PROBLEM PERSONALITIES

personality disorders Rigid, maladaptive personality patterns that cause personal distress or an inability to get along with others.

paranoid personality disorder A disorder characterized by habitually unreasonable and excessive suspiciousness, jealousy, or mistrust. Paranoid symptoms may also occur in schizophrenia and other psychoses.

narcissistic personality disorder A disorder characterized by an exaggerated sense of self-importance and self-absorption.

People with **paranoid personality disorder** suffer from a pervasive, unfounded suspiciousness and mistrust of other people, irrational jealousy, secretiveness, and doubt about the loyalty of others. They have delusions of being persecuted by everyone from their closest relatives to government agencies, and their beliefs are immune to disconfirming evidence. People who have **narcissistic personality disorder** share an exaggerated sense of self-importance and self-absorption. Narcissism gets its name from the Greek myth of Narcissus, a beautiful boy who fell in love with his own image. Individuals with narcissistic personality disorder are preoccupied with fantasies of unlimited success, power, brilliance, or ideal love. They demand constant attention and admiration and feel entitled to special favors, without being willing to reciprocate. They fall in love quickly and out of love just as fast, when the beloved proves to have some human flaw.

Notice that these descriptions are both specific and vague. They are specific, in that they evoke flashes of recognition ("I know that type!"), but vague in that they involve general qualities that depend on subjective labels and value judgments (Maddux & Mundell, 1997). Culture influences the decision to classify an individual as having one of these disorders. For example, American society often encourages people to pursue dreams of unlimited success and ideal love, but such dreams might be considered signs of serious disturbance in a more group-oriented society. Where would you draw the line between having a "narcissistic personality disorder" and being a normal member of a group or culture that encourages "looking out for number one" and places high values on youth and physical beauty?

One personality disorder in particular has provoked interest and study because of its consequences for society: the disorder of the individual who lacks conscience, morality, and emotional attachments. In the 1830s this disorder was called "moral insanity." By 1900 it had become the "psychopathic personality," a phrase that some researchers and most newspapers still use. More recently the word "sociopath" was coined. The DSM now uses the term *antisocial personality disorder*. By any name, this disorder, which has been around forever, has troubling characteristics.

Narcissus fell in love with his own image, and now he has a personality disorder named after him—just what a narcissist would expect!

THE ANTISOCIAL PERSONALITY

- Two teenage boys held a teacher down while a third poured gasoline over him and set him on fire. Fortunately, another teacher intervened in time for a rescue, but the boys showed no remorse, did not consider their actions wrong, and were disappointed that they had not actually murdered the teacher (whom they did not know). "Next time we'll do it right," said the ringleader, "so there won't be nobody left around to identify us."

- Giovanni Vigliotto was, by all accounts, warm and charming; by too many accounts, in fact. Vigliotto married 105 women in an elaborate con game. He would find a wealthy woman, charm her into marriage, steal her assets, and vanish. Finally, one wife charged him with fraud, and he was convicted. Vigliotto admitted the many marriages, but not deception or theft. He didn't think he had done anything wrong (Carson, Butcher, & Mineka, 1996).

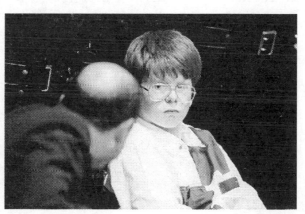

Some people with antisocial personalities use charm and elaborate con tricks to deceive others. Giovanni Vigliotto (left) married 105 women over 33 years, seized their assets, and then abandoned them. But other people with APD are sadistic and violent, starting in childhood. At age 13, Eric Smith (right) bludgeoned and strangled a 4-year-old boy to death. He was tried as an adult and sentenced to a prison term of nine years to life.

People like these, who have **antisocial personality disorder,** are fascinating and frightening because they lack the emotions that link people to one another: empathy, the ability to take another person's perspective; shame for actions that hurt others; and guilt, the ability to feel remorse or sorrow for immoral actions. They have no conscience. They can lie, charm, seduce, and manipulate others, and then drop them without a qualm. If caught in a lie or a crime, they may seem sincerely sorry and promise to make amends, but it is all an act. They are often sexually promiscuous, unable to maintain attachments, and irresponsible in their obligations to others. Some antisocial persons, like the teenagers who set a teacher on fire, are sadistic, with a history of criminal or cruel behavior that began in childhood. They can kill anyone—an intended victim, a child, a bystander—without a twinge of regret. Others direct their energies into con games or career advancement, abusing other people emotionally rather than physically. Understandably, more attention is devoted to the antisocial individuals who commit violent crimes than to those who gain power and fortune while wreaking devastation on their families or employees, but the latter also do great harm.

For unknown reasons, antisocial personality disorder is far more common in males than in females; according to the DSM-IV and survey evidence, it occurs in 3 to 5 percent of all males and fewer than 1 percent of all females (Robins, Tipp, & Przybeck, 1991). Although these percentages are small, antisocial individuals create a lot of havoc; they may account for more than half of the serious crimes committed in the United States (Hare, 1993).

It is important to distinguish antisocial *behavior* from antisocial *personalities*. Most antisocial behavior (as defined by crime statistics on homicide, rape, robbery, assault, burglary, and auto theft) is carried out by young men whose criminal activities peak in late adolescence and drop off sharply by their late 20s. Their behavior seems to be influenced by their age, situation, and peer group, and it does not necessarily reflect a personality disorder. But a smaller number of men begin displaying antisocial behavior in early childhood, are drawn to criminal environments, and end up with confirmed antisocial personalities (Henry et al., 1996). In a review of longitudinal research, Terrie Moffitt (1993) found that the behavior of such individuals might include "biting and hitting at age 4, shoplifting and truancy at age 10, selling drugs and stealing cars at age 16, robbery and rape at age 22, and fraud and child abuse at age 30 . . . [Such] persons lie at home, steal from shops, cheat at school, fight in bars, and embezzle at work."

Some people with antisocial personality disorder can be very "sociable," charming everyone around them, but they have no emotional connection to others or guilt about their wrongdoing. Their inability to feel emotional arousal—empathy, guilt, fear of punishment, anxiety under stress—suggests some abnormality in the central nervous system. Antisocial individuals do not respond to punishments that would affect other people, such as threat of physical harm or loss of approval (Hare, 1965, 1993). This fact may explain why antisocial persons fail to learn that their actions will have unpleasant consequences. Normally when a person is anticipating danger, pain, or shock, the electrical conductance of the skin changes—a classically conditioned response that indicates anxiety or fear. But in several experiments, people with antisocial personality disorder were slow to develop such responses. As you can see in Figure 15.2, it is as if they aren't able to feel the anxiety necessary for avoidance learning.

One theory, based on animal and human studies, maintains that people who are antisocial, hyperactive, addicted, or impulsive have a common inherited disorder (Luengo et al., 1994; Newman, Widom, & Nathan, 1985). These conditions all involve

antisocial personality disorder
A disorder (sometimes called psychopathy or sociopathy) characterized by antisocial behavior such as lying, stealing, manipulating others, and sometimes violence; a lack of social emotions (guilt, shame, and empathy); and impulsivity.

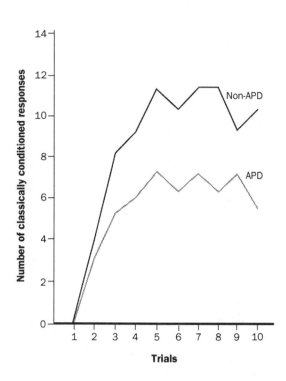

Figure 15.2
The Antisocial Personality

In several experiments, people with antisocial personality disorder (APD) were slow to develop classically conditioned responses to anticipated danger, pain, or shock—responses that indicate normal anxiety (Hare, 1965). This deficit may be related to the ability of people with APD to behave in destructive ways without remorse or regard for the consequences (Hare, 1993).

problems in *behavioral inhibition*—the ability to control responses to frustration or to inhibit a pleasurable action that may have unpleasant repercussions. The biological children of parents with antisocial personality disorder, substance-abuse problems, or impulsivity disorders are at greater than normal risk of developing these disorders themselves, even when they are reared by others (Nigg & Goldsmith, 1994).

Many children who become violent and antisocial have suffered neurological impairments, a result not of genetics but of physical battering and subsequent brain injury (Milner & McCanne, 1991; Moffitt, 1993). Consider the chilling results of a study that compared two groups of delinquents: violent boys who had been arrested for repeated incidents of vicious assault, rape, or murder; and boys whose violence was limited to fistfights. Nearly all of the extremely violent boys (98.6 percent) had at least one neurological abnormality, and many had more than one, compared with 66.7 percent of the less violent boys. More than three-fourths of the violent boys had suffered head injuries as children, had had serious medical problems, or had been beaten savagely by their parents, compared with "only" one-third of the others (Lewis, 1981).

Other research supports a *vulnerability–stress model*, which holds that brain damage can interact with social deprivation and other experiences to produce individuals who are impulsively violent. A study of 4,269 boys, followed from birth to age 18, found that many of those who became violent offenders had had a combination of two risk factors: birth complications (with resulting damage to the prefrontal cortex, as noted in Chapter 4) and early maternal rejection. Their mothers hadn't wanted the pregnancy, and the babies were put in public institutional care for at least four months during their first year. Although only 4.4 percent of the boys had both risk factors, they accounted for 18 percent of all violent crimes committed by the sample as a whole (Raine, Brennan, & Mednick, 1994).

Clearly, cultures and environments can make antisocial behavior more likely or less so (Moffitt, 1993; Patterson, 1994; Persons, 1986). Some societies and subcultures cultivate the qualities of selfishness, professional ruthlessness, and emotional hardheartedness. In contrast, small, close-knit cultures that depend on each member's co-operation and consideration for others would find selfishness and emotional coldness intolerable.

It seems, then, that several routes lead to the development of antisocial personality disorder: Having a genetic disposition toward impulsivity, addiction, or hyperactivity, which leads to rule breaking and crime; being neglected or rejected by parents; having brain damage as a result of birth complications or physical abuse in childhood; and living in a culture or environment that rewards and fosters antisocial traits. These multiple origins may explain why the incidence of antisocial personality disorder varies within and across societies and history.

Quick Quiz

Can you diagnose each of the following disorders?

1. Ann can barely get out of bed in the morning. She feels that life is hopeless and despairs of ever feeling good about herself.
2. Brad lacks guilt, empathy, and moral standards.
3. Connie constantly feels a sense of impending doom; for many weeks, her heart has been beating rapidly and she can't relax.
4. Damon is totally absorbed in his own feelings and wishes.
5. Edna believes that everyone is out to get her and no one can be trusted.

Answers:

1. major depression   2. antisocial personality disorder   3. generalized anxiety disorder   4. narcissistic personality disorder   5. paranoid personality disorder

DISSOCIATIVE DISORDERS

Stress or shock can make any of us feel temporarily dissociated—that is, cut off from ourselves, feeling strange, dazed, or "unreal." In **dissociative disorders,** consciousness, behavior, and identity are split or altered. Unlike normal, short-lived states of dissociation, these symptoms are extremely intense, last a long time, and appear to be out of the individual's control. Like posttraumatic stress disorder, dissociative disorders are often responses to shocking events. But in the former case, people can't get the trauma out of their minds and waking thoughts. In the latter, people apparently escape the trauma by putting it out of their minds, erasing it from memory (Cardeña et al., 1994).

AMNESIA AND FUGUE

On a Hawaiian beach in the spring of 1996, a man was found lying face down, fading in and out of consciousness and complaining of a thumping headache. "His pockets were empty," wrote a reporter from *The New York Times* (July 18, 1996), "and so was his memory." Taken to a local hospital, where tests showed signs of brain swelling but no external bruises or cuts, the man said his name was William Charles D'Souza, that the year was 1988, and that he lived in Wantagh, New York. He was wrong on all counts. After three months of investigation, an enterprising detective learned that D'Souza's real name was Philip Charles Cutajar, that he was from Massapequa, New York, and that he had been living in Maryland and planning a trip to Brazil. But even after calls from his mother and brother, Cutajar wasn't really sure

dissociative disorders Conditions in which consciousness or identity is split or altered.

he recognized them, wasn't really sure who he was, and had no recollection of how he ended up in Hawaii.

Amnesia, according to the DSM-IV, is an inability to remember important personal information, usually of a traumatic or stressful nature, that cannot be explained by ordinary forgetfulness. Amnesia can result from organic conditions, such as head injury, as was probably the case with Cutajar. When no organic causes are apparent, and when the person forgets only selective information that is threatening to the self, the amnesia is considered *dissociative*. In one case of dissociative amnesia, a young man appeared at a hospital complaining that he did not know who he was. After a few days, he awoke in great distress, eventually remembering that he had been in an automobile accident in which a pedestrian was killed. The shock of the experience and his fear that he might have been responsible set off the amnesia.

Dissociative fugue states are even more fascinating. A person in a fugue state not only forgets his or her identity but also gives up customary habits and wanders far from home—as also might have happened to Cutajar. The person may take on a new identity, remarry, get a new job, and live contentedly until he or she suddenly "wakes up"—puzzled and often with no memory of the fugue experiences. The fugue state may last anywhere from a few days to many years. James McDonnell, Jr., left his family in New York in 1971 and wandered to New Jersey, where he took a new name and a new job. Fifteen years later, he "woke up" and made his way back to his wife—who (apparently) greeted him with open arms.

As you might imagine, it is often difficult to determine when people in fugue states have a true disorder and when they are faking. This problem is also apparent in the curious disorder of multiple personality.

DISSOCIATIVE IDENTITY DISORDER ("MULTIPLE PERSONALITY")

The DSM-IV has replaced the familiar term "multiple personality disorder" (MPD) with **dissociative identity disorder** to describe the appearance, within one person, of two or more distinct identities. (In our discussion, however, we will retain the more commonly used term.) In this disorder, each identity appears to have its own memories, preferences, handwriting, and even medical problems. In a case study of one person with four identities, for example, the researcher concluded that it was "as if four different people had been tested" (Larmore, Ludwig, & Cain, 1977).

Cases of multiple personality are extremely dramatic: Those portrayed in the films *The Three Faces of Eve* and *Sybil* fascinated audiences for years, and so do the legal cases that make the news. A woman charges a man with rape, claiming that only one of her personalities consented to having sex with him while another objected; a man commits murder and claims his "other personality"

amnesia (dissociative) When no organic causes are present, a dissociative disorder involving partial or complete loss of memory for threatening information or traumatic experiences.

dissociative identity disorder A controversial dissociative disorder marked by the appearance within one person of two or more distinct personalities, each with its own name and traits; also called *multiple personality disorder.*

In the 1950s the book and film The Three Faces of Eve, *based on a reported case of multiple personality, spawned dozens of imitators, such as Lizzie. Stories about MPD then faded from the public eye, and so did individuals who claimed to have the disorder. In the 1980s, MPD returned in the form of several highly publicized books and case studies, and since then thousands of cases have been reported. Controversy exists about whether this increase is due to better diagnosis, or to unwitting therapist influence and sensational stories in the media.*

did it. Among mental-health professionals, however, two competing and totally incompatible views of MPD currently exist. Some think it is a real disorder, common but often underdiagnosed. Others are skeptical: They think that most cases are generated by clinicians, in unwitting collusion with vulnerable and suggestible clients, and that if it exists at all it is extremely rare.

Those in the MPD-is-real camp believe the disorder originates in childhood, as a means of coping with unspeakable, continuing traumas, such as torture (Gleaves, 1996; Kluft, 1993; Ross, 1995). In this view, the trauma produces a mental "splitting"; one personality emerges to handle everyday experiences and another emerges to cope with the bad ones. MPD patients are frequently described as having lived for years with several personalities of which they were unaware, until hypnosis and other techniques in therapy revealed them. Clinicians who endorse MPD argue that diagnoses can be made more accurately now because the physiological changes that occur within each personality cannot be faked.

Those who are skeptical about MPD, however, have shown that most of the research used to support the diagnosis is seriously flawed (Merskey, 1995; Piper, 1997). A review of the claims that MPD patients have different physiological patterns associated with each personality concluded that most of the studies are anecdotal, have many methodological problems, and have failed to be replicated (Brown, 1994). Most important, research in this area has been marred by that familiar research mistake, the missing control group. When one research team corrected this flaw by comparing the EEG activity of two MPD patients with that of a normal person who merely role-played different personalities, they found EEG differences between "personalities" to be *greater* in the normal person (Coons, Milstein, & Marley, 1982). Other studies comparing MPD patients with control subjects who were merely role-playing have not found any reliable differences (Miller & Triggiano, 1992). Because normal people can create EEG changes by changing their moods, energy levels, and concentration, brain-wave activity cannot be used to verify the existence of MPD.

ASK QUESTIONS; EXAMINE THE EVIDENCE

A man charged with murder claims that one of his "other personalities" committed the crime. You are on the jury, and you know that psychologists disagree about the validity of his defense. What questions would you want to ask about this man's claim, and what evidence would help you reach a decision about it?

Clinicians and researchers who are doubtful about this diagnosis also point out that cases of MPD seem to turn up only in people who go to therapists who believe in it and are looking for it (McHugh, 1993a; Merskey, 1992, 1995; Piper, 1997; Spanos, 1996). Critics fear that clinicians who are convinced of the widespread existence of MPD may actually be creating the disorder in their clients through the power of suggestion. For example, here is the way one psychologist questioned the Hillside Strangler, Kenneth Bianchi, a man who killed more than a dozen young women:

> I've talked a bit to Ken, but I think that perhaps there might be another part of Ken that I haven't talked to, another part that maybe feels somewhat differently from the part that I've talked to. . . . And I would like that other part to come to talk to me. . . . Part, would you please come to communicate with me? (Quoted in Holmes, 1994)

Notice that the psychologist repeatedly asked Bianchi to produce another "part" of himself and even addressed the "part" directly. Before long, Bianchi was maintaining that the murders were really committed by another personality called Steve Walker. Did the psychologist in this case *permit* another personality to reveal itself, or did he actively *create* such a personality by planting the suggestion that one existed?

Proponents of the view that MPD is real and widespread often seem unaware of the difference. One of the best-known advocates of the MPD diagnosis, Richard Kluft

(1987), maintains that efforts designed to determine the presence of MPD—that is, to get the person to reveal a dissociated personality—may require "between $2\frac{1}{2}$ and 4 hours of continuous interviewing. Interviewees must be prevented from taking breaks to regain composure, averting their faces to avoid self-revelation, etc. In one recent case of singular difficulty, the first sign of dissociation was noted in the 6th hour, and a definitive spontaneous switching of personalities occurred in the 8th hour." After eight hours of "continuous interviewing" without a single break, how many of us *wouldn't* do what the interviewer wanted?

An alternative, *sociocognitive explanation* of multiple personality disorder is that it is an extreme form of the ability we all have to present different aspects of our personalities to others (Merskey, 1995; Spanos, 1996). In this view, the diagnosis of multiple personality disorder provides a way for some troubled people to understand and legitimize their problems—or to account for embarrassing, regretted, or even criminal behavior that they commit ("My other personality did it"). In turn, therapists who believe in MPD reward such patients by paying attention to their symptoms and "personalities," thus further influencing the patients to reorganize their memories and make them consistent with the diagnosis (Ofshe & Watters, 1994). Canadian psychiatrist Harold Merskey (1992) reviewed several famous cases of MPD, including those of Eve and Sybil, and was unable to find a single case in which a patient developed MPD without being influenced by the therapist's suggestions or reports about the disorder in books and the media. Sybil's psychiatrist, Cornelia Wilbur, first diagnosed Sybil as being schizophrenic, but later encouraged her to produce multiple personalities and report memories of sexual abuse in childhood (reports that were never corroborated). Some investigators think that this change of diagnosis was part of a marketing strategy for the psychiatrist's book (see Nathan, 1994).

Of course, the fact that MPD is a controversial diagnosis with little empirical evidence to support it does not mean that no legitimate cases exist. It does mean that caution is warranted, especially because diagnoses of MPD have implications regarding responsibility for criminal acts. In the case of the Hillside Strangler, a determined and skeptical prosecutor discovered that Bianchi had read numerous psychology textbooks on multiple personality and had modeled "Steve" on a student he knew! When another psychologist purposely misled Bianchi by telling him that "real" multiple personalities come in packages of at least three, Bianchi suddenly produced a third personality. Bianchi was convicted of murder and sentenced to life in prison. But Paul Miskamen, who battered his wife to death, convinced psychiatrists and a jury that the man who killed his wife was a separate personality named Jack Kelly. Judged insane, Miskamen was committed to a mental hospital and released after 14 months. (For further discussion of the relationship between mental illness and legal responsibility for one's crimes, see "Puzzles of Psychology.")

DRUG ABUSE AND ADDICTION

Perhaps no topic in this chapter better illustrates the problem of finding the shade of the spectrum in which normal blurs into abnormal than that of drug abuse and addiction. Most people use drugs—legal, illegal, or prescription—in moderation, for short-lived effects, but some people overuse them. The consequences of drug abuse for society are costly: loss of productive work, high rates of violence and crime, and family disruption. And the consequences for individuals and their families are tragic: unhappiness, illness, and the increased likelihood of early death from accident or disease.

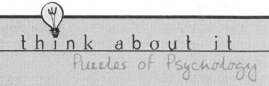

Puzzles of Psychology

When Does a Mental Disorder Cause Diminished Responsibility?

No one disputes the fact that Lyle and Erik Menendez shot their parents to death in a barrage of gunfire, as their parents sat watching television and eating ice cream. After the initial volley, Lyle reloaded his gun and shot their mother several more times because, he later told his therapist, "She was trying to sneak away." At first the brothers maintained their innocence, while spending extravagant amounts of their $14 million inheritance; then, faced with incontrovertible evidence, they confessed. Many months later they explained why they had committed this crime: They were victims of sexual molestation by their father and believed they were in imminent danger of being killed by him. Their first trial ended in hung juries for both defendants. At the second trial, they were convicted of murder and sentenced to life in prison without parole.

Were the Menendez brothers responsible for murdering their parents? "No," say some people, "not if they were abused and humiliated by their parents; no wonder they eventually broke down and lost control. Society must be sympathetic to children who are treated brutally." "Yes," say others; "because that sex-abuse excuse seems awfully unlikely, and everything about their actions was premeditated. And even if they were abused, so are plenty of people who don't commit murder. These young men had all the resources of wealth and class to have simply left home."

The Menendez case raises some fascinating questions for law and psychology. What mental conditions and disorders warrant a defense of diminished responsibility or exoneration of one's actions? What is the proper penalty for someone who temporarily or habitually cannot control his or her actions: treatment or prison? If someone is sentenced to spend time in a mental institution, how can we know when he or she is "cured"? How do we know whether someone is "insane" or just faking?

Insanity is a legal term, not a psychological one. In 1834, a Scot named Daniel M'Naghten tried to assassinate the prime minister of England, killing the prime minister's secretary by mistake. M'Naghten was acquitted of murder on the grounds that he had a "mental defect" that prevented him from understanding what he was doing at the time of the act. The "M'Naghten rule" meant that people could be acquitted "by reason of insanity" and sentenced not to prison, but to mental institutions (or set free). In the United States, the 1954 Durham decision recognized this principle by specifying that "An accused is not criminally responsible if his unlawful act was the product of a mental disease or defect."

Today, because of sensational cases in the news, the public has the impression that hordes of crazed and violent criminals are "getting off" by reason of insanity. Public outrage has caused some states to abolish the insanity defense altogether or to permit only a defense of "insane but guilty." Actually, public perceptions are not accurate. Surveys indicate that the public thinks the insanity defense is raised in 37 percent of all felony cases; in fact, it is raised in only 0.9 percent. The public believes that 44 percent of all those who claim this defense are acquitted; the actual rate is 26 percent. The public believes that only about half of those acquitted actually spend time in mental hospitals; in fact, about 81 percent do (Silver, Cirincione, & Steadman, 1994). And it is getting tougher to claim an insanity defense at all. The defense must show "clear and convincing evidence" that the defendant had a severe, abnormal mental condition and not just a personality defect.

Nevertheless, many defense attorneys, aided by the testimony of psychiatrists and psychologists, keep trying to expand the legal grounds for diminished responsibility, searching for "the mental disease or defect" that might mitigate the sentence a guilty person receives. Because of the differing views within psychology and psychiatry—and because of the subjective nature of many diagnoses—many trials end up as a battle of the experts, and the jury must decide which side to believe. Some psychologists think that the Menendez brothers were suffering from a form of posttraumatic stress disorder resulting from years of abuse. Others think that if the brothers have any mental disorder at all, their cold-bloodedness indicates psychopathy—antisocial personality disorder. How can a jury decide between such competing views when the experts can't?

In a sizzling indictment of the ability of psychologists to determine legal insanity or to predict the future behavior of individuals, psychologists David Faust and Jay Ziskin (who is also a lawyer) reviewed hundreds of studies (Faust & Ziskin, 1988). They learned that clinicians were wrong more often than they were right. In one study, for example, military recruits who were kept in the service, despite psychiatrists' recommendations that they be discharged for "severe psychiatric liabilities," turned out to be as successful and well adjusted as the control group. Overall, clinicians were not very good at detecting efforts to fake insanity, and they were dismal at predicting future violence.

Most legal and mental-health professionals believe that in a humane society, people who are mentally incompetent, delusional, or disturbed should not be held entirely responsible for their actions. But where do we draw the line of responsibility? Should being physically beaten or sexually abused, having experiences with racism, or living in a violent subculture be treated as legitimate reasons for taking violent revenge? What should the treatment or punishment for such individuals be? And if psychologists cannot agree on the answers, how should juries do so? Think about it.

Every drug—including aspirin, cough medicine, and coffee—can be dangerous and even lethal if taken in excess. As we saw in Chapter 5, with many drugs, light or moderate use has different medical and psychological consequences than heavy or excessive use. The problem lies in defining "excess." The DSM-IV definition of *substance abuse* is "a maladaptive pattern of substance use leading to clinically significant impairment or distress." Symptoms of such impairment include the failure to fulfill role obligations at work, home, or school (the person cannot hold a job, care for children, or complete schoolwork because of excessive drug use); use of the drug in hazardous situations (such as driving a car or operating machinery); recurrent arrests for drug use; and persistent conflicts with others about use of the drug or as a result of using the drug.

Why are some people able to use drugs moderately, while others abuse them? In this section, focusing on the example of alcoholism, we will consider the two dominant approaches to addiction and drug abuse—the biological model and the learning model—and conclude with an effort to integrate the contributions of both.

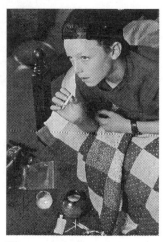

When and why does drug use become abuse?

THE BIOLOGICAL MODEL

In 1960, a book was published that profoundly changed the way most people thought about alcoholics. In *The Disease Concept of Alcoholism*, E. M. Jellinek argued that alcoholism is a disease over which an individual has no control and from which he or she never recovers. Drunkenness is not an inevitable property of alcohol, he said, but a characteristic of some people who have an inbred vulnerability to liquor; for them, complete abstinence is the only solution. The disease theory of alcoholism was tremendously important because it transformed the moral condemnation of the addict as a bad and sinful person into concern for someone who is sick. Today the *biological model* of addiction is widely accepted by researchers and the public, and many people continue to regard alcoholism as a disease. The biological model holds that addiction, whether to alcohol or any other drug, is due primarily to a person's biochemistry, metabolism, or genetic predisposition.

In the biological view, how people respond to drugs begins with their own physiological responses to it. Just as some individuals and ethnic groups cannot physically tolerate the lactose in milk, some individuals and ethnic groups have a low tolerance for alcohol. Women generally will get drunker than men on the same amount of alcohol because women are smaller, on average, and their bodies metabolize alcohol differently (Fuchs et al., 1995). Many Asians have a genetically determined adverse reaction to even small amounts of alcohol, which can cause severe headaches and diarrhea (Cloninger, 1990).

But why are some people in every group more likely than others to become alcoholic? Because having biological relatives who are alcoholic contributes to a person's risk of becoming alcoholic, proponents of the biological model believe that alcoholism involves an inherited predisposition (Cloninger, 1990; Schuckit & Smith, 1996). Researchers are trying to identify the key genes or biological anomalies that might be involved in alcoholism, or at least in some kinds of alcoholism (Blum, 1991; Kendler et al., 1992; Polich, Pollock, & Bloom, 1994). *Type I alcoholism* begins in adulthood, and it is not associated with genetic factors. But *Type II alcoholism*, which begins in adolescence and is linked to impulsivity, antisocial behavior, and violent criminality, does seem to have a hereditary component (Bohman et al., 1987; McGue, Pickens, & Svikis, 1992). Type II alcoholics also have a lowered activity of the enzyme MAOB (monoamine oxidase-B) in their blood cells, compared with nonalcoholics. Low levels of MAOB are not a direct cause of addiction, but they may reflect an underlying physiological deficiency leading to severe alcoholism and other psychiatric problems (Devor et al., 1994).

Genes may also affect a person's *level of response* to alcohol, which is an independent risk factor in becoming alcoholic. In a ten-year longitudinal study of 450 young men (half had alcoholic fathers and half did not), the men who at age 20 had a low response to alcohol—meaning they needed to drink more than most people to feel any effect—were at increased risk of becoming alcoholic within the decade. This was true regardless of their current drinking habits or family history (Schuckit & Smith, 1996).

As with so many other disorders, however, it has been difficult to track down specific genes that might contribute to addiction. Several studies have found that a certain gene, which affects the function of key dopamine receptors on brain cells, is more likely to be present in the DNA of alcoholics than in that of nonalcoholics (Noble et al., 1991). Dopamine helps regulate pleasure-seeking actions, so researchers suspect that this gene might explain why alcoholics drink. However, other studies, using different measurements, have found no difference between alcoholics and controls in the presence of this gene (Baron, 1993; Bolos et al., 1990; Gelernter et al., 1991). Similarly, some researchers, comparing alcoholism rates among identical and fraternal twins, conclude that genetic factors play a part in alcoholism in women (Kendler et al., 1992); but other studies find evidence of genetic factors only in men (McGue, Pickens, & Svikis, 1992).

At present, then, we cannot conclude that a single gene causes alcoholism (or any other addiction) in any direct way. It is possible that several genes in combination may affect the response to alcohol, the compulsive use of alcohol (or other mood-altering drugs), or the progression of alcohol-related diseases such as cirrhosis of the liver. It is possible that genes contribute to temperament or personality traits that predispose some people to become alcoholics. And it is possible that genes affect how the liver metabolizes alcohol. But it is also possible that genes have little to do with alcoholism, and that alcoholism results, basically, from alcohol! Heavy drinking alters brain function, reduces the level of painkilling endorphins, produces nerve damage, shrinks the cerebral cortex, and wrecks the liver. In the view of some researchers, these changes then create biological dependence, an inability to metabolize alcohol, and psychological problems.

THE LEARNING MODEL

The biological model, popular though it is, has been challenged by another approach, which holds that we cannot understand addiction and drug abuse without also taking learning and cultural factors into account. Its proponents note that biological theories of addiction cannot adequately account for the often rapid rise and fall in addiction rates within a country, or for the fact that people can become "addicted" to activities, exercise, television, or the Internet as well as to drugs; what "disease" are they catching?

CONSIDER OTHER EXPLANATIONS

Addiction is often considered a biological problem or a disease, but people can become addicted to jogging, love, work, and the Internet. What "disease" are they catching? What other explanations of addiction are possible?

According to the *learning model,* addiction to any drug is neither a sin nor a disease but "a central activity of the individual's way of life" (Fingarette, 1988). Proponents of this model marshal four arguments in support:

1. *Addiction patterns vary according to cultural practices and the social environment.* In colonial America, the average person actually drank two to three times the amount of liquor that is consumed today, yet alcoholism was

not the serious social problem it is now. Drinking was a universally accepted social activity. Families drank and ate together. Alcohol was believed to produce pleasant feelings and relaxation. The Puritan minister Cotton Mather even called liquor "the good creature of God." If a person committed a crime or became violent while drunk, the colonials did not conclude that liquor was to blame. Rather, they assumed that the person's own immoral tendencies led to drunkenness *and* crime (Critchlow, 1986).

Between 1790 and 1830, when the American frontier was expanding, drinking came to symbolize masculine independence, high-spiritedness, and toughness. The saloon became the place for drinking away from home, and alcoholism rates shot up. Why? The reason, according to the learning model, is that when people do not learn how to drink moderately, they are more likely to drink irresponsibly and in binges (unless they are committed to a cultural or religious rule that forbids all psychoactive drugs).

In fact, alcoholism is much more likely to occur in societies that forbid children to drink but condone drunkenness in adults (as in Ireland) than in societies that teach children how to drink responsibly but condemn adult drunkenness (as in Italy, Greece, France, and colonial America). In cultures with low rates of alcoholism, adults demonstrate correct drinking habits to their children, gradually introducing them to alcohol in safe family settings. These lessons are maintained by adult customs. Alcohol is not used as a rite of passage into adulthood, nor is it associated with masculinity and power (Peele & Brodsky, 1991; Vaillant, 1983). Drinking is considered neither a virtue nor a sin. Abstainers are not sneered at, and drunkenness is not considered charming, comical, or manly; it's considered stupid or obnoxious.

Substance abuse and addiction problems increase not only when people fail to learn how to take drugs in a moderate cultural context, but also when they move from their own culture of origin into another that has different drinking rules (Westermeyer, 1995). For example, in most Latino cultures, such as those of Mexico and Puerto Rico, drinking and drunkenness are considered male activities. Thus Latina women tend to drink little, if at all, and they have few drinking problems—until they move into an Anglo environment, when their rates of alcoholism rise (Canino, 1994).

Some cultures of drinking or other drug abuse are much smaller than a nationality or ethnic group. Colleges and companies create their own subcultures, which may forbid drinking entirely, permit moderate drinking, or encourage drunken

In cultures in which people drink moderately with meals and children learn the rules of social drinking from their families, alcoholism rates are much lower than in cultures in which drinking occurs mainly in bars, in binges, or in privacy.

binges. In a survey of 140 American colleges, rates of heavy and binge drinking ranged from a low of only 1 percent of all students at some colleges to a high of 70 percent at others (Wechsler et al., 1994). In the United States, binge drinking among college students is strongly associated with living in a fraternity or a sorority (Baer, Kivlahan, & Marlatt, 1995).

2. *Policies of total abstinence tend to increase rates of addiction rather than reduce them.* Further compelling evidence for a learning explanation of drug abuse comes from the history of Prohibition in America. The temperance movement of the early twentieth century argued that drinking inevitably led to drunkenness, and drunkenness to crime. The solution it proposed, and won for the Prohibition years (1920 to 1933), was national abstinence. Temperance advocates were not trying to do a scientific study, but they created the perfect conditions for one. As the learning model would predict, Prohibition actually increased rates of alcoholism: Because people were denied the opportunity to learn to drink moderately, they drank excessively when given the chance. Men who were teenagers at the time of Prohibition were far and away more likely to become serious problem drinkers in adulthood than were older men, who had learned how to drink alcohol before it became illegal (McCord, 1989). Similarly, the Inuit of British Columbia were forbidden from drinking alcohol until 1951, when they were permitted to drink only in licensed bars. As a result, the Inuit would drink as much as they could while in a bar. It was a policy virtually guaranteed to create drunkenness.

3. *Not all addicts go through withdrawal symptoms when they stop taking the drug.* During the Vietnam War, nearly 30 percent of American soldiers were taking heroin in doses far stronger than those available on the streets of U.S. cities. These men believed themselves to be addicted. Experts predicted a drug-withdrawal disaster among the returning veterans; it never materialized. Over 90 percent of the men simply gave up the drug, without withdrawal pain, when they came home to new circumstances (Robins, Davis, & Goodwin, 1974). Likewise, the majority of people who are addicted to cigarettes, tranquilizers, or painkillers are also able to stop taking these drugs, without outside help and without withdrawal symptoms (Prochaska, Norcross, & DiClemente, 1994).

Many people go through phases of heavy drinking, yet cut back to social drinking levels once their environments change—again, without withdrawal symptoms. (As we will see, though, there is much dispute about whether true alcoholics can do this.) In a 40-year study, many of the men in the sample went through a period of severe problem drinking but eventually healed themselves. Their drinking was not progressive, permanently incapacitating, or a downward spiral to skid row (Vaillant, 1983).

4. *Addiction does not depend on the drug alone but also on the reason the person is taking it.* Addicts use drugs to escape from the real world, but, as we saw in Chapter 5, people living with chronic pain use some of the same drugs, including opiates, in order to function in the real world; they don't become addicted (Portenoy, 1994). In a study of 100 hospital patients who had been given strong doses of narcotics for postoperative pain, 99 had no withdrawal symptoms upon leaving the hospital (Zinberg, 1974). And of 10,000 burn patients who received narcotics as part of their hospital care, not one became an addict (Perry & Heidrich, 1982).

Although we often think of drug abuse as the cause of psychological problems, having psychological problems is more often the cause of drug abuse. In a surprising study that followed a large sample of children from preschool through age 18, adolescents who had experimented moderately with alcohol and marijuana were the *best* adjusted. Those who had never experimented with any drug were the most anxious, emotionally constricted, and lacking in social skills. And those teenagers who abused drugs were the most maladjusted, alienated, impulsive, and emotionally distressed (Shedler & Block, 1990). Because this study followed these young people over time, the researchers were able to show that drug abuse was largely a *result*, not a *cause*, of psychological maladjustment and other difficulties. The best-adjusted students were able to use drugs moderately *because* they were well adjusted.

To understand why people abuse drugs, therefore, the learning model focuses on the reasons that people take a drug. For example, most people drink simply to be sociable or to conform to the group they are with, but many people drink in order to regulate their emotions. Some drink to reduce negative feelings when they are anxious, depressed, or tense ("coping" drinkers); others to increase positive feelings when they are tired, bored, or stressed ("enhancement" drinkers). Coping drinkers have significantly more drinking problems than enhancement drinkers do (Cooper et al., 1995). Drinking thus has psychologically distinct functions; to understand why some people abuse alcohol, in this view, you would need to know what function drinking serves for them. The same principle applies to other forms of substance abuse.

DEBATING THEORIES OF ADDICTION

The biological and learning models both contribute to our understanding of drug abuse and addiction. Yet among most researchers and public-health professionals these views are quite polarized, as you can see in this summary of the two approaches (adapted from Peele & Brodsky, 1991):

The Biological Model	The Learning Model
Addiction is genetic, biological.	Addiction is a way of coping.
Once an addict, always an addict.	A person can grow beyond the need for alcohol or other drugs.
An addict must abstain from the drug forever.	Most problem drinkers can learn to drink in moderation.
A person is either addicted or not.	The degree of addiction will vary, depending on the situation.
The solution is medical treatment and membership in groups that reinforce one's permanent identity as a recovering addict.	The solution involves learning new coping skills and changing one's environment.
An addict needs the same treatment and group support forever.	Treatment lasts only until the person no longer abuses the drug.

As this table suggests, what we have here is a case of either–or thinking on a national scale, and the reason has to do with the serious, real-world consequences of each model for the treatment of alcoholics and other addicts. The argument is most heated in the debate over controlled drinking—whether it is possible for former alcoholics to drink moderately without showing signs of dependence and intoxication and without causing harm to themselves or others.

To those who hold the biological or disease model, there is no such thing as a "former" alcoholic and controlled drinking is impossible; once an addict has even a single drink, he or she cannot stop. Daniel Flavin, medical and scientific director of the National Council on Alcoholism and Drug Dependence, observes that "In general, it's not a good idea under any circumstances to encourage an alcoholic to moderate [his or her drinking], or the heavy drinker whose natural history would be to go on to alcoholism. How do you tease those people out?" (quoted in Foderaro, 1995). He and others believe that problem drinkers who learn to cut back to social-drinking levels were never true alcoholics in the first place.

To those who adopt a learning model, however, controlled drinking is possible; once a person no longer needs to become drunk, he or she can learn to drink socially and in moderation (Marlatt, 1996). Across North America, alternatives to the total-abstinence program of Alcoholics Anonymous have emerged, such as Rational Recovery, Moderation Management, and DrinkWise. As Frederick Rotgers, director of research at the Center of Alcohol Studies at Rutgers University, says: "Unfortunately, in this country, for many, many years even to talk about people with a drinking problem simply cutting down has been anathema. . . . It is heresy. Among pragmatic people who are reading the scientific literature, it's no longer heresy" (quoted in Foderaro, 1995).

How can we assess these two positions critically? Can we locate a common ground between them? Because alcoholism and problem drinking occur for many and varied reasons, neither model offers the only solution. Many alcoholics, perhaps most, cannot learn to drink moderately, especially if they have had drinking problems for many years (Vaillant, 1995). On the other hand, although Alcoholics Anonymous has unquestionably saved lives, it doesn't work for everyone. According to its own surveys, one-third to one-half of those who join AA drop out, and many of those dropouts benefit from programs that teach people how to drink moderately and keep their drinking under control (Marlatt, 1996; Peele & Brodsky, 1991; Rosenberg, 1993).

According to meta-analyses, the factors that predict whether an addict or problem drinker will be able to learn to control excessive drinking are these: previous severity of dependence on the drug; social stability (not having a criminal record, having a stable work history, being married); and beliefs about the necessity of maintaining abstinence (Rosenberg, 1993). Alcoholics who believe that one drink will set them off—those who accept the alcoholics' creed, "first drink, then drunk"—are in fact more likely to behave that way, compared with those who believe that controlled

---

GET INVOLVED

If you drink, why? Check all of the motives that apply to you:

_____ *to relax*

_____ *to be sociable*

_____ *to escape from worries, stress*

_____ *to handle feelings of depression*

_____ *to enhance a good meal*

_____ *to get drunk and lose control*

_____ *to conform to peer pressure*

_____ *to rebel against authority*

_____ *to relieve boredom*

_____ *other (specify)*

Do your reasons for drinking promote abuse or responsible use? How do you respond physically to alcohol? What have you learned about drinking from your family, your friends, and cultural messages? What do your answers tell you about your own vulnerability to addiction?

drinking is possible. Ironically, then, the course that alcoholism takes may reflect, in part, a person's belief in the disease model or the learning model.

Taken together, this evidence suggests that drug abuse and addiction reflect an interaction of physiology and psychology, person and culture. They occur when an individual who is emotionally and physically vulnerable to abusing drugs finds a culture and environment that support such abuse. More specifically, drug addiction and abuse are likely to occur when:

- People have a genetic or physiological vulnerability to the drug.
- People believe the drug is stronger than they are—that is, they believe they are addicted and will always be.
- People learn (or laws or customs encourage them) to take a drug in binges rather than in moderation.
- People learn that drugs can be used to justify behavior that would not otherwise be socially tolerated.
- People come to rely on a drug as a way of coping with problems, relieving pain, avoiding stress, or providing a sense of power and self-esteem.
- "Everyone" in a person's peer group drinks heavily or uses other drugs excessively.
- Moderate use is neither taught nor encouraged.

Researchers who hold a biological model of addiction hope to discover a medical solution to drug abuse, such as a nonaddictive drug that will break an addict's craving. But researchers who hold a learning model think that this effort is probably doomed. If someone is desperate to escape from reality, they say, he or she will find a way to do it. They believe that the search for a perfect drug that has no addictive qualities is futile; instead, we should look at the human qualities that make a drug seem perfect.

Quick Quiz

If you are addicted to passing exams, try these questions:

1. What seems to be the most reasonable conclusion about the role of genes in alcoholism? (a) Without a key gene, a person cannot become alcoholic; (b) the presence of a key gene or genes will almost always cause a person to become alcoholic; (c) genes may work in combination to increase a person's vulnerability to some kinds of alcoholism.

2. Which cultural practice is associated with *low* rates of alcoholism? (a) drinking in family or group settings, (b) infrequent but binge drinking, (c) drinking as a rite of passage, (d) regarding alcohol as a sinful drink

 3. For a century, people have been searching for a drug that can be used recreationally but is not addictive. Heroin, cocaine, barbiturates, methadone, and tranquilizers were all, at first, thought to be nonaddictive. But in each case some people became addicted, and abuse of the drug became a social problem. Based on what you've read, what are some possible reasons for the failure to find a mood-altering but non-addictive drug?

Answers:

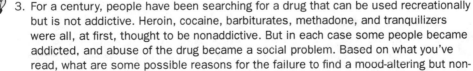

1. c 2. a 3. Perhaps some people are biologically vulnerable to any mind-altering drug. Perhaps the psychological need for addiction exists in the individual and not in the chemical properties of the drug. Perhaps the chemistry of the drug is less important than the cultural practices that encourage drug abuse among some groups. If that is so, we will never find a recreational drug that has no addictive properties for some people.

SCHIZOPHRENIA

To be schizophrenic is best summed up in a repeating dream that I have had since childhood. In this dream I am lying on a beautiful sunlit beach but my body is in pieces. This fact causes me no concern until I realize that the tide is coming in and that I am unable to gather the parts of my dismembered body together to run away. The tide gets closer and just when I am on the point of drowning I wake up screaming in panic. This to me is what schizophrenia feels like; being fragmented in one's personality and constantly afraid that the tide of illness will completely cover me. (Quoted in Rollin, 1980)

In 1911, Swiss psychiatrist Eugen Bleuler coined the term **schizophrenia** to describe cases in which the personality loses its unity: words are split from meaning, actions from motives, perceptions from reality. Schizophrenia is not the same as "split" or "multiple personality." As the quotation illustrates, schizophrenia refers to a fragmented condition, not the coexistence of several different personalities. It is an example of a **psychosis,** a mental condition that involves distorted perceptions of reality and an inability to function in most aspects of life.

THE NATURE OF THE "SCHIZOPHRENIAS"

If depression is the common cold of psychological disorder, said psychiatrist Donald Klein (1980), schizophrenia is its cancer: a baffling and complex problem. Schizophrenia produces *active or positive symptoms* that involve an exaggeration or distortion of normal thinking processes and behavior, and more subtle *negative symptoms* that involve the loss of former traits and abilities. The most common active symptoms include the following:

1. *Bizarre delusions,* such as the belief that dogs are anthropologists from another planet, disguised as pets to infiltrate human families. Some people with schizophrenia have paranoid delusions, taking innocent events—a stranger's cough, a helicopter overhead—as evidence that the world is plotting against them. Some have "delusions of identity," believing that they are Moses, Jesus, Joan of Arc, or some other famous person.

2. *Hallucinations* that usually take the form of voices and consist of garbled, odd words; a running conversation in the head; or two or more voices conversing with each other. Unlike the hallucinations that might occur in a normal person on a drug high, schizophrenic hallucinations feel intensely real and believable to the sufferer (Bentall, 1990). Most are voices, but some are tactile (feeling insects crawling over the body) or visual (seeing Elizabeth Taylor in the mirror).

3. *Disorganized, incoherent speech* consisting of an illogical jumble of ideas and symbols, linked by meaningless rhyming words or by remote associations called *word salads.* A patient of Bleuler's wrote, "Olive oil is an Arabian liquor-sauce which the Afghans, Moors and Moslems use in ostrich farming. The Indian plantain tree is the whiskey of the Parsees and Arabs. Barley, rice and sugar cane called artichoke, grow remarkably well in India. The Brahmins live as castes in Baluchistan. The Circassians occupy Manchuria and China. China is the Eldorado of the Pawnees" (Bleuler, 1911/1950). The story goes that the great novelist James Joyce once asked Carl Jung to explain the difference between Joyce's own stream-of-consciousness writing and the odd associations of his schizophrenic daughter. Jung supposedly replied, "You dive—she falls" (Wender & Klein, 1981).

schizophrenia A psychotic disorder or group of disorders marked by positive symptoms (e.g., delusions, hallucinations, disorganized and incoherent speech, and inappropriate behavior) and negative symptoms (e.g., emotional flatness and loss of motivation).

psychosis An extreme mental disturbance involving distorted perceptions and irrational behavior; it may have psychological or organic causes. (Plural: *psychoses.*)

4. *Grossly disorganized and inappropriate behavior* that may range from childlike silliness to unpredictable and violent agitation. The person may wear three overcoats and gloves on a hot day, start collecting garbage, or hoard scraps of food. Some people with schizophrenia completely withdraw into a private world, sitting for hours without moving, a condition called *catatonic stupor.* In *Autobiography of a Schizophrenic Girl,* Marguerite Sechehaye wrote, "A wall of brass separates me from everybody and everything. In the midst of desolation, in indescribable distress, in absolute solitude, I am terrifyingly alone."

Negative symptoms may appear months before these active ones and often persist when the active symptoms are in remission. Negative symptoms include loss of motivation; poverty of speech (making only brief, empty replies in conversation, because of diminished thought rather than an unwillingness to speak); and, most notably, *emotional flatness*—unresponsive facial expressions, poor eye contact, and diminished emotionality (see Figure 15.3). One man set fire to his house and then sat down calmly to watch TV.

Figure 15.3
Emotions and Schizophrenia

When people with schizophrenia are asked to draw pictures, their drawings are often distorted, lack color, include words, and reveal flat emotion. One patient was asked to copy a picture of flowers from a magazine (left). The initial result is shown bottom left. The drawing on bottom right shows how much the patient improved after several months of treatment.

Some people recover from schizophrenia and others learn to manage its symptoms, the way diabetics learn to live with their disease. Joseph Rogers overcame the symptoms of schizophrenia and became director of the National Mental Health Consumers' Association.

Cases of schizophrenia vary in the severity and duration of symptoms. In some individuals, the symptoms appear abruptly and eventually disappear with the passage of time, with or without treatment. In others, the onset is more gradual and insidious. Friends and family report a slow change in personality. The person may stop working or bathing, become isolated and withdrawn, and start behaving in peculiar ways.

As for prognosis, again schizophrenia is unpredictable. Psychiatrists often speak of the "rule of thirds": Of all people diagnosed and hospitalized with schizophrenia, one-third will recover completely, one-third will improve significantly, and one-third will not get well. The more breakdowns and relapses the individual has had, the poorer the chances for complete recovery (Eaton et al., 1992a, 1992b). Yet many people suffering from this illness learn to live with it, are able to work and have warm family relationships, and eventually outgrow their symptoms (Eaton et al., 1992b; Harding, Zubin, & Strauss, 1992).

The mystery of schizophrenia is that we could go on listing symptoms and variations all day and not finish. Some people with schizophrenia are almost completely impaired in all spheres; others do extremely well in certain areas. Some have normal moments of lucidity in otherwise withdrawn lives. One adolescent crouched in a rigid catatonic posture in front of a television for the month of October; later, he was able to report on all the highlights of the World Series he had seen. A middle-aged man, hospitalized for 20 years, believing he was a prophet of God and that monsters were coming out of the walls, was able to interrupt his ranting to play a good game of chess (Wender & Klein, 1981). People with brain damage usually cannot interrupt their madness to watch the World Series or play chess. How can those with schizophrenia do so?

THEORIES OF SCHIZOPHRENIA

As you might imagine, any disorder that has so many variations and symptoms will pose many problems for diagnosis and explanation. One psychologist concluded that the concept of schizophrenia is "almost hopelessly in tatters" (Carson, 1989), and others think we should drop the label entirely (Sarbin, 1992). The idea that schizophrenia is a single, stable, diagnostic disorder, critics maintain, is simply a convenient myth.

Of course, these critics recognize that some people do behave in bizarre ways and that *something* is wrong with them. In their view, however, "schizophrenia" is a lot of different somethings, and its name is a grab-bag term for rule-breaking actions that must be understood by the cultural context in which they occur. Robert Carson (1989) noted that it is impossible to define a "delusion" without reference to a culture's norms. In every society, he observed, perfectly sane individuals hold patently "false or absurd beliefs" with conviction and zeal. Why do we think a person has schizophrenia if he believes he is the Prophet Ezekiel now, but not if he believes he was the Prophet Ezekiel in a past life?

Other psychologists (and the compilers of the DSM) reply to these criticisms by arguing that in cultures around the world, the same core signs of schizophrenia appear: hallucinations, delusions that are far more disturbed than mere "false beliefs," inappropriate behavior, and disorders of thought. That is why almost everyone studying this disorder believes that schizophrenia is a brain disease of some sort (Heinrichs, 1993; Torrey et al., 1994). "If schizophrenia is a myth," said Seymour Kety (1974) many years ago, "it is a myth with a strong genetic component."

Using brain-imaging techniques, longitudinal studies, and dissections of brains, researchers are unraveling the mysteries of this troubling and fascinating disorder. They are searching for genetic factors, for abnormalities in the brain and in prenatal development, and for the interaction between biological vulnerabilities and a person's life experiences.

   1. *Brain abnormalities.* Some individuals with schizophrenia (but not all of them) have decreased brain weight, a decrease in the volume of the temporal lobe or limbic regions, reduced numbers of neurons in specific layers of the prefrontal cortex, or enlargement of the *ventricles*, the spaces in the brain filled with cerebrospinal fluid; these may all be signs of cerebral damage (Andreasen et al., 1994; Heinrichs, 1993; Raz & Raz, 1990). (See Figure 15.4.) Many people who have schizophrenic symptoms have abnormal eye movements, which some researchers regard as a biological marker of the disease (Clementz & Sweeney, 1990). Men with schizophrenia are more likely than controls to have abnormalities in the thalamus, the traffic-control center for incoming sensations (Andreasen et al., 1994). This finding might explain why the brains of some people with schizophrenia are overly sensitive to everyday stimuli, causing them to retreat into an inner world.

   2. *Genetic predispositions.* Children have a greater risk of schizophrenia if an identical twin develops the disorder, if one parent has the disorder, and especially if both parents are schizophrenic—even if the child is reared apart from the affected relative (Gottesman, 1991, 1994). In the general population, the risk of developing schizophrenia is 1–2 percent, but children with one schizophrenic parent have a lifetime risk of 12 percent; and for children with two schizophrenic parents, the risk jumps to 35–46 percent (Goldstein, 1987).

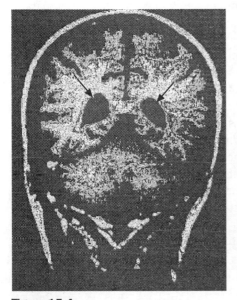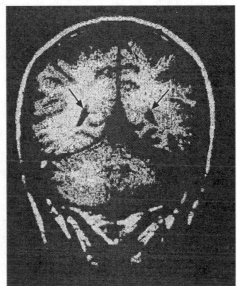

Figure 15.4
Schizophrenia and the Brain

MRI scans show that a person with schizophrenia (left) is more likely than a healthy person (right) to have enlarged ventricles, or spaces, in the brain (see arrows) (Andreasen et al., 1994).

Just as with alcoholism and bipolar disorder, however, it has been hard to track down specific genes or determine the extent of their influence (Holzman & Matthysse, 1990). Great excitement arose when a research team found a link between schizophrenic symptoms and abnormalities on chromosome 5; disappointment followed when other research failed to confirm it (Kennedy et al., 1988). One problem with genetic-origin theories is that even among identical twins, when one twin develops schizophrenia, the chances that the other will do so range from 28 percent to 40 percent—not even half of them (Torrey et al., 1994). Moreover, nearly 90 percent of all persons with schizophrenia do *not* have a schizophrenic parent, and nearly 90 percent of all children with one such parent do not develop the disorder.

3. *Prenatal abnormalities.* In recent years the evidence has mounted that damage to the fetal brain increases the likelihood of schizophrenia (and some other mental disorders). The damage may occur because of severe malnutrition. Babies conceived during times of famine have twice the schizophrenia rate as babies conceived when their mothers ate normal diets during pregnancy (Susser et al., 1996). Or the problem may be a mismatch between the mother's antibodies and the infant's, such as Rh incompatibilities (Hollister, Laing, & Mednick, 1996).

Another culprit in the origins of schizophrenia may be, remarkably, an infectious virus during prenatal development (Torrey, 1988; Torrey et al., 1994). In fact, a longitudinal study that began decades ago found a significant association between exposure to influenza virus during the second trimester of gestation and adult schizophrenia 20 to 30 years later (Mednick, Huttunen, & Machón, 1994). The virus theory accounts for many odd aspects of schizophrenia. It explains why schizophrenic symptoms may not emerge until a person reaches adolescence or young adulthood: Viruses can attack specific areas of the brain, leaving other areas untouched, yet remain latent for many years before causing symptoms to appear. It explains why the births of schizophrenic children show seasonal fluctuations; viruses too are seasonal. And it explains why sometimes only one twin of a genetically identical pair later becomes schizophrenic: Only one was affected prenatally by a virus.

The second trimester of prenatal development is critical because the brain is forming crucial connections during this time. Neurologist H. Stefan Bracha reasoned that if a viral infection or other prenatal trauma (such as lack of oxygen) affected the fetal brain and led to the subsequent development of schizophrenia, its effects should appear elsewhere in the body as well. Bracha's team conducted an ingenious study of 24 pairs of identical twins in which only one twin suffered from schizophrenia. They discovered that the twins who had schizophrenia, unlike their healthy counterparts, were significantly more likely to have abnormalities in their hands, such as fewer ridges in their fingerprints (Bracha et al., 1991). Of course, hand abnormalities do not cause schizophrenia! But hands are formed during the second trimester, so the same environmental accident might have affected the development of both the brain and the hands.

Other evidence also points to the role of abnormalities in fetal brain development. In the second trimester of fetal development, cells migrate to the cortex. If this migration is disrupted, by a virus or a faulty genetic mechanism, cells end up in the wrong place or have faulty connections. This seems to be precisely the problem in many schizophrenics, whose brains are more likely to contain neurons in the prefrontal cortex that are "out of place" (Akbarian et al., 1996; Bunney, Potkin, & Bunney, 1995). By studying the medical records of children who eventually became schizophrenic, and, cleverly, by scrutinizing the home movies their parents took of these children as infants and toddlers, researchers have been able to identify a lifelong pattern of delayed maturation in such individuals. For example, at 6 months, about one-third of all babies are two weeks or more late in sitting up; but of those who later develop schizophrenia, two-thirds are late (Weinberger, 1995).

4. *The vulnerability–stress model.* Although the evidence for brain abnormalities in schizophrenia is compelling, many researchers believe that the onset and course of this disorder—as in the cases of depression, antisocial personality disorder, and addiction—are best explained by an interactive theory (Gottesman, 1991). In this view, genes or brain damage alone will not inevitably produce schizophrenia, and a vulnerable person who lives in a good environment may never show full-fledged signs of it.

For many years, the Copenhagen High-Risk Project has followed 207 children at high risk for schizophrenia (because of having a schizophrenic parent) and a control group of 104 low-risk children. The project has identified factors that, *in combination,* increase the likelihood of schizophrenia: the existence of schizophrenia in the family; physical trauma during childbirth that might damage the brain; exposure to the flu virus or other prenatal trauma during the second trimester of gestation; unstable, stressful environments in childhood and adolescence; and having emotionally disturbed parents (Mednick, Parnas, & Schulsinger, 1987; Olin & Mednick, 1996).

Some researchers hope that a common source of all the schizophrenias may yet be discovered. They note that rheumatic fever can appear as a disease of the nervous system, of the heart, of the joints, or of the skin. It seemed to be four diseases until bacteriologists identified the common source. But other investigators believe that the "schizophrenias" include several unrelated disorders with different causes and that no single culprit is likely to be found. "The likelihood that researchers are studying different illnesses without being able to specify these differences," concluded researcher Walter Heinrichs (1993), ". . . is the major obstacle to scientific progress."

We have come to the end of a long walk along the spectrum of mental disorders. The writer William Styron, who recovered from severe and debilitating depression, used the beginning of Dante's beautiful classic poem, *The Divine Comedy,* to convey his experience of mental illness:

> *In the middle of the journey of our life*
> *I found myself in a dark wood.*
> *For I had lost the right path.*

"For those who have dwelt in depression's dark wood," wrote Styron, "and known its inexplicable agony, the return from the abyss is not unlike the ascent of the poet, trudging upward and upward out of hell's black depths and at last emerging into what he saw as 'the shining world.'" Dante wrote,

> *And so we came forth, and once again beheld the stars.*

Taking Psychology with You

When a Friend Is Suicidal

Suicide is a scary subject, surrounded by mystery and myth. It can be frightening to those who find themselves fantasizing about it, and it is devastating to the family, friends, and acquaintances of those who go through with it. In the United States and Canada, most people who commit suicide are over the age of 45, but suicide rates are rapidly increasing among young people. Between 1960 and 1988, the suicide rate among adolescents rose by more than 200 percent, increasing especially among white males (Garland & Zigler, 1994).

People who attempt suicide have different motives. Some believe they have no reason to live; some feel like failures in a world where they think everyone else is happy and successful; some want revenge against those who they think have made them suffer. In the African-American community, where suicide attempts have been rising, risk factors include parental drug abuse, family losses and low levels of family cohesion, exposure to violence, and being a teenage mother (Summerville, Kaslow, & Doepke, 1996). All suicidal people share the belief that life is unendurable. This belief may be rational in the case of people who are terminally ill and in pain, but more often it reflects the distorted thinking of someone suffering from depression. Often, the suicidal person doesn't really want to die; rather, he or she wants to escape intolerable emotions and despair (Baumeister, 1990).

Friends and family members can help prevent a suicide by recognizing the danger signs.

• *Don't assume you can identify a "suicidal type."* Most adolescents who try to commit suicide are isolated and lonely. Many are children of divorced or alcoholic parents. Some have problems in school and feel like failures. But others who are vulnerable to suicide attempts are college students who are perfectionistic and self-critical. The former may feel like ending their lives because they can foresee no future. The latter may feel suicidal because they do not like the futures they foresee for themselves.

• *Take all suicide threats seriously.* Many people fail to take action when a friend talks about committing suicide. Some believe the friend's intention but think they can't do anything about it. "He'll just do it at another place, another time," they think. In fact, most suicides occur during an acute crisis; once the person gets through the crisis, the desire to die fades. One researcher tracked down 515 people who had attempted suicide by jumping off the Golden Gate Bridge many years earlier. After those attempts, fewer than 5 percent had actually committed suicide in the subsequent decades (Seiden, 1978).

Some people believe that if a friend is talking about suicide, he or she won't really do it. This belief is also false. Few people commit suicide without signaling their intentions. Most are ambivalent: "I want to kill myself, but I don't want to be dead—at least not forever." Most suicidal people want relief from the terrible pain of feeling that nobody cares, that life is not worth living. Getting these thoughts and fears out in the open is an important first step.

• *Know the danger signs.* A depressed person may be at risk of trying to commit suicide if he or she has tried to commit suicide before; has become withdrawn, apathetic, and isolated, or has a history of depression; reveals specific plans for carrying out the suicide or begins to give away cherished possessions; expresses no concern about the usual deterrents to suicide, such as consideration for one's family, adherence to religious rules, or the fact that suicide is irreversible; and has access to a lethal method, such as a gun (Garland & Zigler, 1994).

• *Take constructive action.* If you believe a friend is in danger of suicide, do not be afraid to ask, "Are you thinking of suicide?" This question does not "put the idea" in anyone's mind. If your friend is contemplating the action, he or she will probably be relieved to talk about it, and you will know that it is time to get help. Let your friend talk without argument or disapproval. Don't try to talk your friend out of it by debating whether suicide is right or wrong, and don't put on phony cheerfulness. If your friend's words or actions scare you, say so. By listening nonjudgmentally, you are showing that you care. By allowing your friend to unburden his or her grief, you help the person get through the immediate crisis.

Most of all, don't leave your friend alone. If necessary, get the person to a counselor, health professional, or emergency room of a hospital; or call a local suicide hot line. Don't worry about doing the wrong thing. In an emergency, the worst thing you can do is nothing at all.

SUMMARY

DEFINING DISORDER

1) "Mental disorder" is not necessarily the same as behavior that is statistically abnormal. *Mental disorder* has been defined as a violation of cultural standards; as maladaptive or destructive behavior; as emotional distress; and as "insanity," the legal term for incompetence to stand trial.

DILEMMAS OF DIAGNOSIS

2) Diagnosing psychological disorders is a complicated process. Clinicians typically use *projective tests* and also *objective tests or inventories* such as the *MMPI.* Reliability and validity are better with objective tests than with projective ones. *The Diagnostic and Statistical Manual of Mental Disorders* (DSM) tries to provide objective criteria for the diagnosis of mental disorder. But some critics argue that the manual fosters overdiagnosis and creates self-fulfilling prophecies; inflates normal problems in living into disorders; can be misused to absolve people of responsibility for their actions; and implies that diagnosis is scientific when really it is a subjective process. Because of human bias and judgment, reliability in diagnosing most mental disorders is low. Supporters of the DSM reply that when the DSM criteria are used correctly, reliability in diagnosis improves; and that although some diagnoses are subjective and culture-specific, certain mental disorders (such as depression and delusion) occur in all societies.

ANXIETY DISORDERS

3) *Generalized anxiety disorder* is a condition of continuous anxiety, with signs of nervousness, worry, and physiological arousal. Other anxiety disorders include *posttraumatic stress disorder* and *acute stress disorder* (anxiety symptoms that may follow traumatic or stressful experiences), *phobias, panic attack, agoraphobia,* and *obsessive–compulsive disorder.*

MOOD DISORDERS

4) *Mood disorders* include major depression, dysthymia, and bipolar disorder. Symptoms of *major depression* include distorted thinking patterns, low self-esteem, physical ailments such as fatigue and loss of appetite, and prolonged grief and despair. *Dysthymia* is chronic depressed mood. In *bipolar disorder,* depression alternates with mania or euphoria. Women are more likely than men to be treated for depression, but it is not clear whether the sex difference is real or is a result of differences in expressing emotions and willingness to seek help.

5) *Biological* explanations of depression emphasize a depletion of neurotransmitters in the brain and the role of specific genes in mood disorders. *Social* explanations consider the conditions of people's lives that might generate depression (and cause gender differences), such as work and family life, motherhood, and sexual abuse. *Attachment* or *interpersonal theories* argue that depression results from broken or conflicted relationships. *Cognitive* explanations emphasize having a pessimistic explanatory style, distorted thoughts, and habits of brooding or rumination that cause depressive symptoms to last. *Vulnerability–stress models* look at how specific interactions between individual characteristics (biological, cognitive, or personality traits) and environmental stress can produce depression.

PERSONALITY DISORDERS

6) *Personality disorders* are characterized by rigid, self-destructive traits that cause distress or an inability to get along with others. They include *paranoid, narcissistic,* and *antisocial* personality disorders. A person with *antisocial personality disorder* (sometimes also called a psychopath or sociopath) shows extreme forms of antisocial behavior; lacks guilt, shame, and empathy; and is impulsive and lacks self-control. The disorder may involve a neurological defect that is genetic or caused by brain or central nervous-system damage at birth or during childhood; parental rejection and abuse; and living in environments that reward some antisocial traits and behaviors.

DISSOCIATIVE DISORDERS

7) *Dissociative disorders* involve a split in consciousness or identity. They include *amnesia, fugue* states, and *dissociative identity disorder* (*multiple personality disorder*, or MPD), in which two or more distinct personalities and identities appear within one person. Considerable controversy surrounds the validity and nature of MPD. Some clinicians think it is a common but often undiagnosed disorder, originating in childhood trauma; others hold a *sociocognitive* explanation, arguing that most cases of MPD are manufactured in unwitting collusion between therapists who believe in the disorder and suggestible patients who find it a congenial explanation for their problems.

DRUG ABUSE AND ADDICTION

8) The effects of drugs depend on whether they are used moderately or are abused. Signs of *substance abuse* include impaired ability to work or get along with others, use of the drug in hazardous situations, recurrent arrests for drug use, and conflicts with others caused by drug use. According to the *biological or disease model* of addiction, some people have a biological vulnerability to addictions such as alcoholism. The vulnerability may result from a genetic factor or from years of heavy drinking or other drug use. Advocates of the *learning model* of addiction point out that addiction patterns vary according to culture, learning, and accepted practice; that many people can stop taking a drug, even a narcotic, with no withdrawal symptoms; that drug abuse depends on the reasons people take a drug; and that drug abuse increases when people are not taught moderate use. Addiction and abuse appear to reflect an interaction of individual vulnerability (because of genetics, physiology, or psychological need) and a person's culture, learning history, and situation.

SCHIZOPHRENIA

9) *Schizophrenia* is a psychotic disorder involving *positive* or *active symptoms*—delusions, hallucinations, disorganized speech (*word salads*), and grossly inappropriate behavior—and *negative symptoms*—loss of motivation, poverty of speech, and emotional flatness. The "schizophrenias" vary in severity, duration, and prognosis. Research on their causes is focusing on brain abnormalities; genetic predispositions; abnormalities of prenatal development, resulting from viral infection or other trauma during the second trimester; and, in the *vulnerability–stress model*, interactions between such factors and a person's environment during childhood or young adulthood.

KEY TERMS

insanity 8

mental disorder 8

objective tests (inventories) 9

Minnesota Multiphasic Personality Inventory (MMPI) 9

Diagnostic and Statistical Manual of Mental Disorders (DSM) 10

generalized anxiety disorder 15

posttraumatic stress disorder (PTSD) 15

acute stress disorder 15

phobia 15

social phobia 16

agoraphobia 16

panic attack 16

Testing Your Understanding—Unit I

Psychology, **Chapter 15: Psychological Disorders**

Pages 6–14
CHECKING YOUR COMPREHENSION

Choose the best answer for each of the following questions.

1. According to the text, the MMPI has been criticized because it
   a. includes validity scales.
   b. identifies emotional disorders.
   c. is culturally biased.
   d. asks questions about how a person feels.

2. Which of the following statements most accurately describes the author's attitude toward the DSM-IV?
   a. It is a useful prescriptive tool.
   b. It is a powerful tool with definite limitations.
   c. It provides reliable and objective diagnostic information.
   d. It is relatively free of cultural bias and political prejudices.

3. The chapter describes a study in which therapists judged nontraditional men as being more disturbed than traditional men. This study illustrates the point that therapists
   a. are often unaware of their own subjectivity and biases.
   b. tend to absolve clients of responsibility for their actions.
   c. usually assume everyday difficulties are the same as mental disorders.
   d. know that most people who work at home become depressed.

Identify the following statements as true or false.

4. The term "insanity" has been categorized in the DSM-IV.

5. Most psychological problems are easily defined because of their dramatic symptoms.

6. Asking yourself "Am I normal?" is an abnormal response to difficulties.

Answer the following questions.

7. Identify five factors which the DSM uses to classify disorders.

8. List four criteria currently used to define mental disorders.

9. Describe two types of diagnostic tools used to assess mental disorders.

Define each term as it is used in the chapter.

10. validity

11. reliability

12. mental disorder

13. abnormal behavior

14. maladaptive

Discussion and Critical Thinking Questions

1. Why might insurance companies be opposed to adding new diagnoses to the DSM? Why might medical doctors want additional diagnoses?

2. One of the latest controversies in mental health diagnoses is "road rage," the irrepressible aggression of drivers. Should this disorder be included in the next edition of the DSM?

3. In the section "Diagnosis: Art or Science?" the author analyzes five concerns about the scientific basis of diagnosis and the DSM. Regarding the fostering of overdiagnosis, what kind of data or research is there to lend validity to this concern?

4. There are records of women in the nineteenth century being placed into mental institutions for dressing in "mannish" clothes, hunting, and being sexually aggressive with their husbands. What criteria seem to be the basis for their admission to an institution? What do these records suggest about the nineteenth century?

Pages 14–29
CHECKING YOUR COMPREHENSION

Choose the best answer for each of the following questions.

1. Which of the following factors would be classified as a precipitating factor for chronic anxiety?
   a. You are working in a comfortably-paced job.
   b. You were visiting New York City when the World Trade Center was bombed.
   c. Both of your parents and your paternal grandfather have been diagnosed with depression.
   d. Your boss constantly criticizes your job performance.

2. Some mental health professionals are skeptical about multiple personality disorder (MPD) diagnoses because
   a. most of the research used to support the diagnosis is flawed.
   b. cases of MPD seem to appear only in people who go to therapists who believe in it and are looking for it.
   c. brain-wave activity cannot be used to verify the existence of MPD.
   d. all of the above.

3. The primary purpose of Figure 15.1 is to
   a. show how depression causes an increase in glucose.
   b. track the metabolism of norepinephrine.
   c. illustrate the biological component of depression.
   d. demonstrate the effect of insufficient serotonin.

Identify the following statements as true or false.

4. Anxiety seems to have an inherited component.

5. Manic episodes do not usually occur without alternating depressive episodes.

6. Narcissistic personality disorder is characterized by a pervasive, unfounded suspiciousness and mistrust of other people.

7. Dissociative fugues typically occur following a head injury.

Answer the following questions.

8. List the five theories of depression.

9. Describe the two primary biological and environmental sources of anti-social personality disorder.

10. Describe three symptoms of obsessive-compulsive disorder.

Match the terms with the most accurate description.

11. Posttrraumatic stress disorder   a. inability to remember information

12. Bi-polar disorder   b. depression alternating with mania

13. Agorophobia   c. unfounded mistrust of others

14. Amnesia   d. fear of being alone in a public place

15. Paranoid personality disorder   e. anxiety following a shock

Discussion and Critical Thinking Questions

1. The chapter describes how one personality disorder has been called various names over the years, beginning in the 1830s with "moral insanity," to "psychopathic personality" in 1900, then "sociopath," and now, "antisocial personality disorder." What do the terms suggest about the times in which they were used?

2. What is the relationship between multiple personality disorder and legal responsibility for actions? Should people judged legally insane be forced to stand trial?

3. Discuss the relationship between gender and environmental causes of antisocial personality disorder.

Pages 29–44
CHECKING YOUR COMPREHENSION

Choose the best answer for each of the following questions.

1. Which of the following supports the biological theory of alcoholism?
   a. onset in adulthood
   b. low levels of monoamine oxidase-B (MAOB) in the blood
   c. both a and b
   d. neither a nor b

2. The vulnerability-stress theory has been applied to all of the following except
   a. schizophrenia.
   b. addiction.
   c. suicide.
   d. anti-social personality disorder.

3. According to the passage "When a Friend is Suicidal," friends and family members can help prevent a suicide by
   a. taking all threats of suicide seriously.
   b. knowing specific danger signs.
   c. listening nonjudgmentally to the suicidal person.
   d. all of the above.

Identify the following statements as true or false.

4. Researchers have recently isolated the gene directly responsible for alcoholism.

5. Schizophrenics are able to participate in complex mental activities.

6. Schizophrenia and multiple personality disorder are synonymous.

Answer the following questions.

7. Identify three cultural practices associated with high rates of alcoholism.

8. Identify four active symptoms of schizophrenia.

9. Identify four danger signs for suicide.

10. Define the following terms as they are used in the chapter: psychosis, word salad, catatonia.

Discussion and Critical Thinking Questions

1. In a study of college students and their behavior with alcohol, the same group of students was invited to two different parties on subsequent days. Although the students were actually served non-alcoholic beer at both parties, at one party they were told that they were receiving alcoholic beer and at the other they were told they were being served non-alcoholic beer. Videotapes of the parties indicated that students at the "alcoholic" beer party were acting noticeably different. What attitudes are reflected in the study?

2. How would you develop a common ground of the two theories of addiction?

3. If schizophrenia has a prenatal/developmental component, what are the ethical dilemmas for prenatal care?

4. A friend confides to you that he is thinking about suicide and begs you not to tell anyone. What should you do?

Chapter Review

End of Chapter Analysis

1. Identify two mental disorders which researchers believe have biological components.

2. Identify five types of reading aids used in the chapter.

Group Projects

1. Incorporating biological, learned, and stress factors, develop a mental health policy for dealing with employee or student behaviors at your workplace or college.

2. The editor of the chapter would like to add another table, box, or extended example. What kind of information would be useful to add to the chapter?

Journal Ideas

1. Develop a five-stage continuum of specific behaviors for any one mental disorder. Place yourself on the continuum at the present time. Have you ever been in a different place on the continuum? If not, what do you think it would be like?

2. What is one thing you spend a lot of time doing? How do your actions exhibit signs of addiction?

UNIT II

From

John D. Daniels
Lee H. Radebaugh

International Business

Eighth Edition

Chapter 2:
The Cultural Environments
Facing Business

Chapter 2

The Cultural Environments Facing Business

*To change customs is
a difficult thing.*
—Lebanese Proverb

Objectives

- To demonstrate problems and methods of examining cultural environments

- To explain the major causes of cultural difference and change

- To examine major customs that differentiate business practices among countries

- To present guidelines for companies that operate internationally

Case
Parris-Rogers
International (PRI)[1]

In June 1996, a car bomb in Saudi Arabia killed nineteen American servicemen. The victims were among approximately 9000 U.S. troops remaining in Saudi Arabia, Kuwait, Bahrain, and the United Arab Emirates since the end of the 1991 Persian Gulf War to liberate Kuwait from Iraq. Although no group claimed responsibility for the blast, most analysts reasoned that cultural conflict was an underlying cause. Traditionalists wanted to rid the area of Western influences, such as music, entertainment, and dress, that they considered immoral. At the same time, a Western-educated middle class was questioning many of the traditional rules. The cultural conflict and accommodation is illustrated by the rules imposed by the U.S. army on female troops during the war. They were not permitted to jog, drive, or show their legs outside the military base. In deference to U.S. sensitivities, Saudi Arabia suspended beheadings in central squares during the Gulf crisis.

A few years earlier, Parris-Rogers International (PRI), a British publishing house, sold its floundering Bahraini operations. This branch had been set up to edit the first telephone and business directories for five Arab states on or near the Arabian peninsula, plus the seven autonomous divisions making up the United Arab Emirates (the region is shown in Map 2.1). Although the U.S. Army had protocol officers to advise it on accepted behavior, PRI had no such guidance. Further, although the Saudis were willing to make some accommodations to assure the defense of their country, PRI's directories were less

Map 2.1
The Scope of PRI's
Business Contract

PRI's contract included Bahrain, Kuwait, Oman, Qatar, Saudi Arabia, and the United Arab Emirates (Abu Dhabi, Ajman, Dubai, Fuzaira, Ras al-Khaimah, Sharjah, and Umm al-Qaiwain).

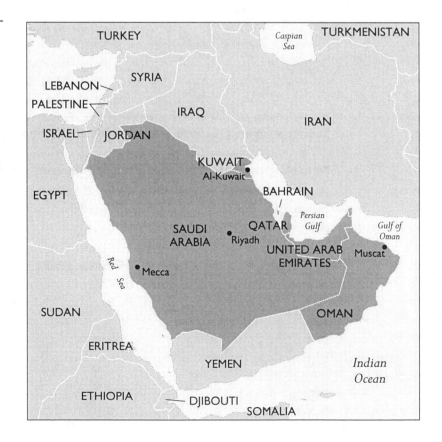

important to the twelve Arab states. The ensuing lack of understanding between the Arab states and PRI and PRI's failure to adapt to a different culture contributed directly to the company's failure.

Most Middle Eastern oil-producing countries have an acute shortage of local personnel, so many foreign workers have been hired. They now make up a large portion of the population in those countries. In the United Arab Emirates in 1995, for example, 70 percent of the population was foreign, mainly from India and Pakistan. In Saudi Arabia, about 40 percent was foreign. Thus when PRI could not find sufficient qualified people locally, it filled four key positions through advertisements in London newspapers. Angela Clarke, an Englishwoman, was hired as editor and researcher, and three young Englishmen were hired as salesmen. The four new hires left immediately for Bahrain. None had visited the Middle East before; all expected to carry out business as usual.

The salesmen, hired on a commission basis, expected that by moving aggressively they could make the same number of calls as they normally could in the United Kingdom. They were used to working about eight hours a day, to having the undivided attention of potential clients, and to restricting most conversation to the specifics of the business transaction.

The salesmen found instead an entirely different situation. There was less time to sell, first, because the Muslims were required to pray five times a day and, second, because the workday was reduced even further during the sacred ninth month of the Muslim year, Ramadan, when there is fasting from sunrise to sunset. The Muslim year is based on a lunar rather than a solar calendar; thus Ramadan may begin in different solar months, such as in January for 1997, or December 1997 for 1998. Moreover, the start of Ramadan is based on the sighting of a new moon; thus longitudinal, latitudinal, and weather conditions usually cause the start to vary by a day or two among countries and cannot be determined in advance. The salesmen also felt that the Arabs placed little importance on appointments. Appointments seldom began at the scheduled time. When the salesmen finally got in to see Arab businessmen, they were often expected to go to a café where the Arabs would engage in what seemed to them to be idle chitchat. Whether in a café or in the office, drinking coffee or tea seemed to take precedence over business matters. The Arabs also frequently diverted their attention to friends who joined them at the café or in the office.

Angela Clarke, too, encountered considerable resistance as she sought to do her job. And, since she was paid a salary instead of a commission, PRI had to bear all of the expense resulting from her work being thwarted in unexpected ways. PRI had based its budgets for preparing the directories on its English experience. In Bahrain, however, preparing such books turned out to be more time-consuming and costly. For example, in the traditional Middle Eastern city, there are no street names or building numbers. Thus, before getting to the expected directory work, Clarke had to take a census of Bahraini establishments, identifying the location of each with such prepositions as "below," "above," or "in front of" some meaningful landmark.

Clarke encountered other problems because she was a single woman. She was in charge of the research in all twelve states and had planned to hire freelance assistants in most of them. But her advertisements to hire such assistants were answered by personal harassment and obscene telephone calls. In addition, Saudi authorities denied her entry to Saudi Arabia, while her visa for Oman took six weeks to process *each time she went there.* These experiences were particularly frustrating for her because both Saudi Arabia and Oman sometimes eased the entry of a single woman when her business was of high local priority and/or when she would be serving as a housemaid or nanny where her only contact would be with women and children. In the states she could enter, Clarke sometimes was required to stay only in hotels that government officials had approved for foreign women, and even there, she was prohibited from eating in the dining room unless accompanied by the hotel manager.

PRI's salesmen never adjusted to working in the new environment. Instead of pushing PRI to review its commission scheme, they tried to change the way the Arab businessmen dealt with them. For example, after a few months they refused to join their potential clients for refreshments and began showing their irritation at "irrelevant" conversations, delays, and interruptions from outsiders. The Arab businessmen responded negatively. In fact, PRI received so many complaints from them that the salesmen had to be replaced. By then, however, irrevocable damage had been done to PRI's sales.

Clarke fared better, thanks to her compromises with Arab customs. She began wearing a wedding ring and registering at hotels as a married woman. When traveling, she ate meals in her room, conducted meetings in conference rooms, and had all incoming calls screened by the hotel operators. To avoid arrest by decency patrols, she wore long-sleeved blouses and below-the-knee skirts in plain blue or beige. Still, in spite of her compromises, her inability to enter Saudi Arabia caused PRI to send in her place a salesman, who was not trained to do the research.

The rapidly growing number of foreigners in the Middle East has created adjustment problems for both the foreigners and the local societies. In many cases, foreigners are expected to conform; in others, they are allowed to pursue their own customs in isolation from the local populace. For example, according to traditional Islamic standards, most Western television programming is immoral. However, in some places foreigners are permitted to acquire unscramblers to view Western programs; local people may not. At the same time, although satellite dishes are technically illegal in Saudi Arabia, these "devils' dishes"—a term used by hard-line Islamic fundamentalists—are seen on rooftops everywhere. Nevertheless, the BBC axed its Arabic Television Service in 1996 because of disagreements over program content. This led a BBC executive to remark, "Looking at the partners involved, the Saudis and the BBC, who would have thought two such different cultures could comfortably coexist?"

The Saudi government also has had second thoughts about some of its culture's double standards. For example, at one time, male and female hotel guests were allowed to swim in the same pools in Saudi Arabia. This permission was rescinded, however, because Saudis frequent the hotels. It was feared they might be corrupted by viewing "decadent" behavior. Also, when Angela Clarke and the salesmen first arrived in Bahrain, there were prohibitions on the sale of pork products, including imported canned foods. This prohibition was later modified, but grocers had to stock pork products in separate rooms in which only non-Muslims could work or shop.

These dual and changing standards for foreigners and citizens hamper foreign efforts to adapt. This situation has been further complicated because the Middle East is going through a period of substantial, but uneven, economic and social transformation. As contact increases between Arabs and Westerners, cultural borrowing and meshing of certain aspects of traditional and modern behavior will increase. These changes are apt to come slowly, perhaps more so than many think.

Introduction

The PRI case illustrates how behavioral differences give rise to different business practices in various parts of the world. Understanding the cultures of groups of people is useful because business employs, sells to, buys from, is regulated by, and is owned by people. An international company must consider these differences in order to predict and control its relationships and operations. Further, it should realize that its accustomed way of doing business may not be the only or best way. When doing business abroad, a company first should determine whether a usual business practice in a foreign country differs from its home-country experience or from what its management ideally would like to see exist. If the practice differs, international management then must decide what, if any, adjustments are necessary to operate efficiently in the foreign country. When individuals come in contact with groups whose cultures differ from their own—abroad or within their own countries—they must decide if and how they can cope.

Some differences, such as those regarding acceptable attire, are discerned easily; others may be more difficult to perceive. For example, people in all cultures have culturally ingrained responses to given situations. They expect that people from other cultures will respond the same ways as people in their own culture do and that people in similar stations or positions will assume similar duties and privileges. All of these expectations may be disproved in practice. In the PRI case, the British salesmen budgeted their time and so regarded drinking coffee and chatting about nonbusiness activities in a café as "doing nothing," especially if there was "work to be done." The Arab businessmen, on the other hand, had no compulsion to finish at a given time, viewed time spent in a café as "doing something," and considered "small talk" a necessary prerequisite for evaluating whether they could interact satisfactorily with potential business partners. The Englishmen, because of their belief that "you shouldn't mix business and pleasure," became nervous when friends of the Arab businessmen intruded. In contrast, the Arabs felt "people are more important than business" and saw nothing private about business transactions.

After a company successfully identifies the differences in the foreign country in which it intends to do business, must it alter its customary or preferred practices in order to be successful there? There is no easy answer. Although the PRI case illustrates the folly of not adjusting, international companies nevertheless sometimes have been very successful in introducing new products, technologies, and operating procedures to foreign countries. At times, these introductions have not run counter to deep-seated attitudes. At others, the host society is willing to accept unwanted change as a trade-off for other advantages. In addition, in some cases the local society is willing to accept behavior from foreigners that it would not accept from its own citizens. For example, Western female managers in Hong Kong have expressed that they are seen by local people primarily as foreigners, not as women; thus, they are not subject to the same operating barriers that local females face as managers.[2] Members of the host society may even feel they are being stereotyped in an uncomplimentary way when foreigners adjust too much.[3] For example, Angela Clarke might have been even less effective for PRI if she had worn the traditional Arab woman's dress with veil.

The Nation as a Definition of a Society

There is no universally satisfactory definition of a society, but in international business the concept of the nation provides a workable one, since basic similarity among people is both a cause and an effect of national boundaries. The laws governing business operations apply primarily along national lines. Within the bounds of a nation are people who share essential attributes perpetuated through rites and symbols of nationhood—flags, parades, rallies—and a subjective common perception of and maintenance of their history, through the preservation of national sites, documents, monuments, and museums. These shared attributes do not mean that everyone in a country is alike. Neither do they suggest that each country is unique in all respects; in fact, nations may include various subcultures, ethnic groups, races, and classes. However, the nation is legitimized by being the mediator of the different interests.[4] Failure to serve adequately in this mediating role may cause dissolution of the nation, as occurred recently in the former Soviet Union and the former Yugoslavia and almost in Canada through a Quebec separatist movement. In the mid-1990s there was ethnic unrest in the form of violence or strong separatist movements in about a third of nations; thus the boundaries of countries as we know them are far from secure.[5] Nevertheless, each country possesses certain characteristic physical, demographic, and behavioral norms that constitute its national identity and that may affect a company's methods of conducting business in that country.

In using the nation as a point of reference, remember that some countries have much greater internal variation than do others. Geographical and economic barriers in some countries can inhibit people's movements from one region to another, thus limiting their personal interactions. Decentralized laws and government programs may increase regional separation, and linguistic, religious, and ethnic differences within a country usually preclude the fusing of the population into a homogeneous state. For example, for all the reasons just given, India is much more diverse than Denmark.

Of course, nationality is not the only basis on which to group people. Everyone belongs to various other groups—for example, those based on profession, age, religion, and place of residence. Many similarities exist that in some ways can link

The nation is a useful definition of society because
- **Similarity among people is a cause and an effect of national boundaries**
- **Laws apply primarily along national lines**

Country-by-country analysis has limitations because
- **Not everyone in a country is alike**
- **Variations within some countries are great**
- **Similarities link groups from different countries**

groups from different countries more closely than groups within a country. For instance, regardless of the country examined, people in urban areas differ in certain attitudes from people in rural areas, and managers have different work-related attitudes than production workers do.[6] When you compare countries, therefore, you must be careful to examine relevant groups.

There are thousands of possible relationships between human variables and business functions—too many to discuss exhaustively in one chapter.[7] However, keep in mind that different attitudes and values affect how any business function may be conducted, such as what and how products will be accepted, how they are best produced, and how the operation should be organized, financed, managed, and controlled. This chapter first concentrates on just a few of the variables that have been found to influence business practices substantially. It then highlights alternative approaches for determining and dealing with differences in foreign countries as well as the changes that may occur in international companies as they come in contact with new human environments.

The Concept of Culture

Businesspeople agree that cultural differences exist but disagree on what they are.

Culture consists of specific learned norms based on attitudes, values, and beliefs, all of which exist in every society. Visitors remark on differences; experts write about them; and people managing affairs across countries find that they affect operating results.[8] Great controversy surrounds these differences because there is an acknowledged problem with measuring variances.[9] Culture cannot easily be isolated from such factors as economic and political conditions and institutions. For example, an opinion survey may reflect a short-term response to temporary economic conditions rather than basic values and beliefs that will have longer-term effects on managing business. Further, some national differences in specific work behavior that have generally been attributed to culture may be due to other factors, such as climatic differences.[10]

Despite these problems, considerable evidence indicates that some aspects of culture differ significantly across national borders and have a substantial impact on how business is normally conducted in different countries. Some evidence is derived by anthropologists or so-called country experts who rely on qualitative techniques, such as interviews and observations, used to uncover people's ideas, attitudes, and relationships to other people in the society. They then interpret processes and events and describe national character. Other evidence is derived by researchers who compare the opinions of carefully paired samples of people in more than one country. For example, questionnaires may be used to determine attitudes toward specific business practices, such as an advertising message or shared decision making in the workplace.[11]

Cultural value systems are set early in life and are difficult to change, but change may come through
- Choice or imposition
- Contact with other cultures

Causes of Cultural Difference and Change

Culture is transmitted by various patterns, such as from parent to child, from teacher to pupil, from social leader to follower, and from one age peer to another. Studies among diverse societies indicate that the parent-to-child route is especially important in the transmission of religious and political affiliations.[12] Developmental psychologists believe that by age 10 most children have their basic value systems firmly in place, after which changes are difficult to make. These basic values include such concepts as evil versus good, dirty versus clean, ugly versus beautiful, unnatural versus natural, abnormal versus normal, paradoxical versus logical, and irrational versus rational.[13] The relative inflexibility of values helps explain the deeply rooted opinions of an American female soldier and Saudi female doctor during the Persian Gulf War. The soldier said, "I'm thankful I'm not a Saudi woman. I just don't know how they do it." The doctor said, "It is so strange, I am glad not to be an American woman. Women are not made for violence and guns."[14]

However, because of multiple influences, individual and societal values and customs may evolve over time. Change may come about through choice or imposition.[15] Change by choice may take place as a by-product of social and economic change or because of new contacts that present reasonable alternatives. For example, the choice of rural people in many places to accept factory jobs changed their previous customs by requiring them to work regular hours and to forgo social activities with their families during work hours. A person's choice to embrace a different religion requires acceptance of a new set of values and beliefs. Change by imposition, sometimes called *cultural imperialism,* has occurred, for example, when colonial powers introduced their legal systems abroad by prohibiting established practices and defining them as being criminal.[16] The process of introducing some, but not all, elements of an outside culture often is referred to as *creolization, indigenization,* or *cultural diffusion.*

Isolation tends to stabilize a culture, whereas contact tends to create cultural borrowing. In addition to national boundaries and geographical obstacles, language is a major factor that affects cultural stability. Map 2.2 shows the world's major language groups. When people from different areas speak the same language, culture is transmitted from one area to another much more easily. Thus more cultural similarity exists among English-speaking countries or among Spanish-speaking ones than between English-speaking and Spanish-speaking countries. This is due partially to heritage and partially to the ease of communicating. Map 2.2 does not include the hundreds of languages that are spoken in limited areas. When people speak only one of those languages, they tend to adhere to their culture because meaningful contact with others is difficult. For example, in Guatemala, the official language is Spanish; however, there are twenty-two ethnic groups, three main ethnic languages, and derivations of those three. These groups have cultures that are much the same as those of their ancestors hundreds of years ago. The Guatemalan Nobel Peace Prize winner Rigoberta Menchú is from the Quiché group. She recounted that parents in that group do not permit their children to go to school, because all public schools

Map 2.2
Major Languages of the World

Hundreds of languages are spoken globally, but a few dominate. This map shows the eleven major ones. Note that English, French, or Spanish is the primary language in over half of the world's countries. Some other languages, such as Mandarin and Hindi, are prevalent in only one country but are important because of the number of native speakers.

Source: From *The Economist World Atlas and Almanac,* The Economist Books/Henry Holt & Co., Inc., pp. 116–117. Reprinted with permission. The number of native speakers is taken from *The World Almanac and Book of Facts, 1995,* Funk & Wagnalls, p. 598.

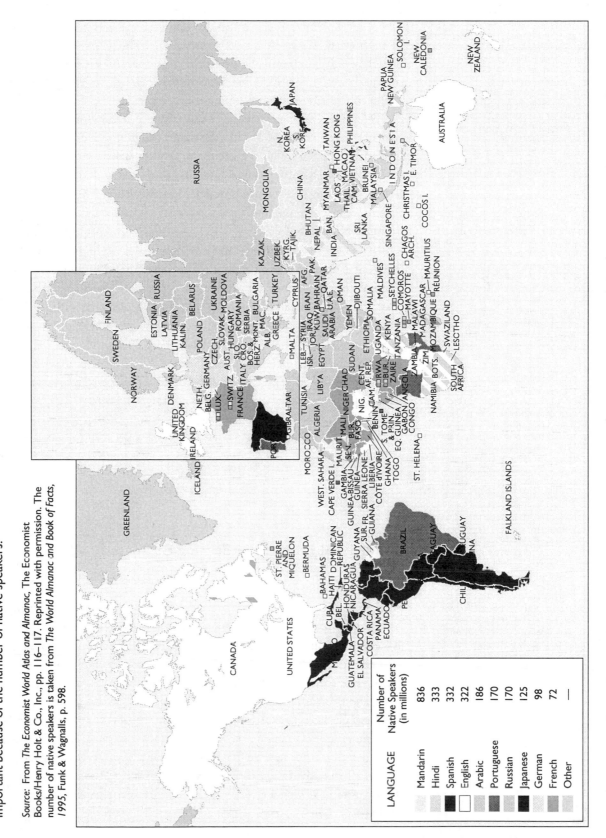

LANGUAGE	Number of Native Speakers (in millions)
Mandarin	836
Hindi	333
Spanish	332
English	322
Arabic	186
Portuguese	170
Russian	170
Japanese	125
German	98
French	72
Other	—

use Spanish; by learning Spanish, the children will lose their values and customs. She broke out of this linguistic isolation when she learned Spanish as an adult in order to fight governmental policies.[17] Her position has been to promote the multi-cultural diversity within Guatemala rather than have ethnic groups either embrace a different culture or form separate countries.[18]

Religion is a strong shaper of values. Map 2.3 shows the distribution of the world's major religions. Within the major religions—Buddhism, Christianity, Hinduism, Islam, and Judaism—are many factions whose specific beliefs may affect business. For example, some Christian groups forgo alcohol, but others do not. Differences among nations that practice the same religion also can affect business. For example, Friday is normally not a workday in predominantly Muslim countries because it is a day of worship; however, Tunisia adheres to the Christian work calendar in order to be more productive in business dealings with Europe.[19] When a religion is dominant in an area, it is apt to have great influence on laws and governmental policies. It also is apt to limit acceptance of products or business practices that are considered unorthodox (recall the Bahraini prohibition of pork in the PRI case). Consequently, foreign companies may have to alter their usual business practices. For example, because of criticism from fervent Hindus, McDonald's agreed not to serve beef in its restaurants in India.[20] In countries in which rival religions vie for political control, the resulting strife can cause so much unrest that business is disrupted. In recent years, violence among religious groups has erupted in India, Lebanon, Northern Ireland, and the former Yugoslavia.

The following discussion provides a framework for understanding how cultural differences affect business.

Behavioral Practices Affecting Business

Group Affiliations

Group affiliations can be
- Ascribed or acquired
- A reflection of resources and position

The populations of all countries are commonly subdivided into groups, and individuals belong to more than one group. Affiliations determined by birth—known as **ascribed group memberships**—include those based on gender, family, age, caste, and ethnic, racial, or national origin. Affiliations not determined by birth are called **acquired group memberships** and include those based on religion, political affiliation, and professional and other associations. A person's affiliations often reflect that person's class or status in a country's social-stratification system. And every society uses group membership for social stratification, such as by valuing members of managerial groups more highly than members of production groups. Social stratification affects such business functions as marketing. For example, companies choose to use people in their advertisements who are from groups admired by their target audience.

Map 2.3
Major Religions of the World

Almost all areas have people of various religious beliefs, but the culture of a region is most influenced by the dominant religion. Note that some countries have different dominant religions in different areas and that religions' areas of dominance transcend national boundaries.

Source: Mapping © Bartholomews, 1990. Extract taken from Plate 5 of *The Times Comprehensive Atlas of the World*, 8th Edition. Reprinted with permission of HarperCollins. MM-0397-300. Numbers are taken from *The World Almanac and Book of Facts*, 1995, Funk & Wagnells, p. 731.

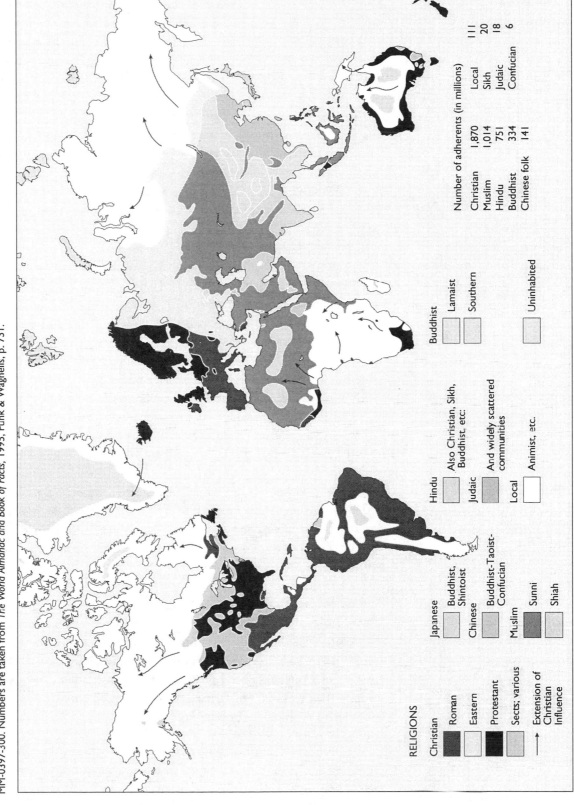

RELIGIONS

Christian
- Roman
- Eastern
- Protestant
- Sects; various

→ Extension of Christian Influence

Japanese
- Buddhist, Shintoist

Chinese
- Buddhist-Taoist-Confucian

Muslim
- Sunni
- Shiah

Hindu
- Also Christian, Sikh, Buddhist; etc.

Judaic

Local
- And widely scattered communities
- Animist, etc.

Buddhist
- Lamaist
- Southern

Uninhabited

Number of adherents (in millions)

Christian	1,870	Local	111
Muslim	1,014	Sikh	20
Hindu	751	Judaic	18
Buddhist	334	Confucian	6
Chinese folk	141		

Competence is rewarded
highly in some societies.

Role of competence   In some societies, such as that of the United States, a person's acceptability for jobs and promotions is based primarily on competence. Thus the workplace is characterized more by competition than by cooperation. This does not mean, of course, that U.S. society has no discrimination against people on the basis of group affiliation. However, the belief that competence should prevail is valued highly enough in the United States that legislative and judicial actions have aimed at preventing discrimination on the basis of sex, race, age, and religion. This value is far from universal. In many cultures, competence is of secondary importance, and the belief that it is right to place some other criterion ahead of competence is just as strong in those cultures as the belief in competence is in the United States. Whatever factor is given primary importance—whether seniority, as in Japan (where the workplace is characterized more by cooperation than by competition), or some other quality—will largely influence a person's eligibility for certain positions and compensation.[21]

Egalitarian societies place
less importance on ascribed
group memberships.

The more egalitarian, or open, a society is, the less difference ascribed group membership makes for access to rewards; however, in less open societies, legal proscriptions sometimes enforce distinctions on the basis of ascribed group memberships. In other cases, group memberships prevent large numbers of people from getting the preparation that would equally qualify them. For example, in countries with poor public education systems, elite groups send their children to private schools but other children receive inferior schooling.

Local attitudes may force
hiring according to local
norms or opinions.

Even when individuals qualify for certain positions and there are no legal barriers to hiring them, social obstacles may make companies wary of employing them. Other workers, customers, local stockholders, or governmental officials may oppose certain groups, making it even more difficult for their members to succeed.

Country-by-country
attitudes vary toward
• Male and female roles
• Respect for age
• Family ties

Importance of different group memberships   Although there are countless ways of defining group memberships, three of the most significant are in terms of gender, age, and family. An international comparison reveals the wide differences in attitudes concerning these memberships and how important they are to business considerations.

Gender-based groups   There are strong country-specific differences in attitudes toward males and females. The Chinese and Indians show an extreme degree of male preference. Because of governmental and economic restrictions on family size and the desire to have a son to carry on the family name, the practices of aborting female fetuses and killing female babies are widespread despite governmental opposition to the practices.[22] In Afghanistan, the 1996 takeover by religious fundamentalists led to prohibitions of women to attend school and to work. They were also required to be shrouded from head to toe.[23]

Recall that in the PRI case the female editor could not get permission to enter Saudi Arabia, a country that exhibits an extreme degree of behavioral rigidity related to gender. Schools are separate, as is most social life, such as wedding parties and zoo outings. Women are legally prohibited from driving cars and socially restricted from riding in a taxi without a male relative. Only about 10 percent of women work outside the home, and those who do remain separate from men. Most jobs for women are in professions that entail little or no contact with males, such as teaching or providing medical treatment to other women. When women do work in integrated organizations, the Saudis place partitions between them and male employees.

Even among countries in which women constitute a large portion of the working population, vast differences exist in the types of jobs regarded as "male" or "female." For example, in the United States, more than 40 percent of administrative and managerial positions are filled by women; in Japan, that figure is less than 10 percent.[24]

Culturally mandated male and female behaviors may carry over to other aspects of the work situation. For example, Molex, a U.S. manufacturing company in Japan, invited its Japanese workers and their spouses to a company dinner one evening. Neither wives nor female employees appeared. To comply with Japanese standards, the company now has a "family day," which the women feel comfortable attending.[25]

Age-based groups Attitudes toward age involve some curious variations. Many cultures assume that age and wisdom are correlated. These cultures usually have a seniority-based system of advancement. In the United States, retirement at age 60 or 65 was mandatory in most companies until the 1980s, and relative youthfulness has been a professional advantage. However, this esteem for youthfulness has not carried over into the U.S. political realm, where representatives must be at least 25, senators 30, and the president 35—none of which carries a mandatory retirement age.

Barriers to employment based on age or gender are changing substantially in many parts of the world. Thus statistical and attitudinal studies that are even a few years old may be unreliable. One change has involved the growing numbers of women and men in the United States employed in occupations previously dominated by the other gender. For example, recently the proportion of male secretaries, telephone operators, and nurses has risen substantially, as has the proportion of female architects, bartenders, and bus drivers. Further, the proportion of the workforce made up by women has been increasing throughout most of the world; however, the increase is largely in part-time employment, where women dominate.[26]

Family-based groups In some societies, the family constitutes the most important group membership. An individual's acceptance in society is largely based on the family's social status or respectability rather than on the individual's achievement. Because family ties are so strong, there also may be a compulsion to cooperate closely within the family unit while distrusting links involving others. In societies where there is low trust outside the family, such as in China and southern Italy, family-run companies are more successful than large business organizations, where people are from many different families. The difficulty of sustaining large-scale companies retards these countries' economic development.[27]

Importance of Work

In industrial countries, most people work more than they would need to simply to satisfy basic needs.

People work for a number of reasons. Many, especially in industrial societies, could satisfy their basic needs for food, clothing, and shelter by working fewer hours than they do. What motivates them to work more? The reasons for working and the relative importance of work among human activities may largely be explained by the interrelationship of the cultural and economic environments of the particular country. The differences in motivation help to explain management styles, product demand, and levels of economic development.

The motives for working are different in different places.

Protestant ethic   Max Weber, a German sociologist, observed near the beginning of the twentieth century that the predominantly Protestant countries were the most economically developed. Weber attributed this fact to the attitude toward work held by most of those countries, an attitude he labeled the *Protestant ethic*. According to Weber, the Protestant ethic was an outgrowth of the Reformation, when work was viewed as a means of salvation. Adhering to this belief, people preferred to transform productivity gains into additional output rather than into additional leisure.[28]

Although Weber's conclusions on the relationship between work and Protestantism were simplistic, there is evidence that some societies have more leisure than others. For example, on average, the Japanese take less leisure than do people in any other industrial country. But in a survey of over 1,200 companies in more than 60 countries covering about 26,000 employees, the Japanese were the least satisfied with both their jobs and employers. (The Swiss were the most satisfied.) Thus it is unclear why the Japanese take so little leisure. In the United States, another country where incomes probably allow for considerably more leisure time than most people use, there is still much disdain, on the one hand, for the millionaire socialite who contributes nothing to society and, on the other hand, for the person who lives on welfare. People who are forced to give up work, such as retirees, complain strongly of their inability to do anything "useful." This view contrasts with those that predominate in some other societies. In much of Europe, the highest place in the social structure is held by the aristocracy, which historically has been associated with leisure. Therefore, upward mobility is associated with more leisure activities, but only those that are broadening, such as trips, reading, or sports endeavors, and not household-related activities, such as gardening and taking care of children.[30] In rural India, living a simple life with minimum material achievements still is considered a desirable end in itself.

Attitudes toward work may change as economic gains are achieved.

Today, personal economic achievement is considered commendable not only in industrial countries but also in most rapidly developing ones. Some observers note that many economies, in contrast, are characterized by limited economic needs that are an outgrowth of the culture. If incomes start to rise, workers in these economies tend to reduce their efforts, and thus personal income remains unchanged. This cultural trait has been noted as an essential difference that underpins national self-identity in many lower-income countries. Rather than rejecting the labels of "traditional" for themselves and "progressive" for the higher-income nations, leaders of these countries have stressed the need for a superior culture—one that combines material comforts with spirituality.[31] Other observers, however, have argued that limited economic needs may be a very short-lived phenomenon because expectations rise slowly as a result of past economic achievement. Most of us believe we would be happy with just "a little bit more," until we have that "little bit more," which then turns out to be not quite enough.

Belief in success and reward   One factor that influences a person's attitude toward working is the perceived likelihood of success and reward. The concepts of success and reward are closely related. Generally people have little enthusiasm for efforts that seem too easy or too difficult, that is, where the probability of either success or failure seems almost certain. For instance, few of us would be eager to run a foot race against either a snail or a racehorse because the outcome in either case is too certain. Our highest enthusiasm occurs when the uncertainty is high—in this example, probably when racing another human of roughly equal ability. The reward for successfully completing an effort, such as winning a race, may be high or low as well. People usually will work harder at any task when the reward for success is high compared with the reward for failure.

> People are more eager to work if
> * Rewards for success are high
> * There is some uncertainty of success

The same tasks performed in different countries will have different probabilities of success and different rewards associated with success and failure. In cultures where the probability of failure is almost certain *and* the perceived rewards of success are low, there is a tendency to view work as necessary but ungratifying. This attitude may exist in harsh climates, in very poor areas, or in subcultures that are the objects of discrimination. At the other extreme, in areas such as Scandinavia, where the tax structures and public policies redistribute income from higher earners to low earners, there also is less enthusiasm for work. In this case, the probability of success is high and rewards tend to be high, but the rewards are similar regardless of how hard one works. The greatest enthusiasm for work exists when high uncertainty of success is combined with the likelihood of a very positive reward for success and little or no reward for failure.[32]

> The work ethic is related to habit.

Work as a habit   Another factor in the trade-off between work and leisure is that the pursuit of leisure activities may itself have to be learned. After a long period of sustained work, a person may have problems deciding what to do with free time. This insight helps to explain the continued drive for greater achievement seen in some societies in which most people already have considerable material comforts. One study that attempted to determine why some areas of Latin America developed a higher economic level and greater desire for material achievement than others attributed differences to the fact that some Spanish settlers worked themselves rather than using slave or near-slave labor. In such areas as Antioquia in Colombia, the Spanish settlers who labored themselves developed a work ethic and became the industrial leaders of the country.[33] Clearly, when comparing the importance of work from one country to another, the effects of habit cannot be overlooked. An international company thus may find it easier in some societies than in others to motivate its workforce with shorter hours or longer vacation periods.

High-need achievement   The **high-need achiever** is a person who will work very hard to achieve material or career success, sometimes to the detriment of social relationships or spiritual achievements.[34] Three attributes distinguish high-need achievers:

High-need achievers want
- **Personal responsibility**
- **To take calculated risks in order to achieve reasonable goals**
- **Performance feedback**

Lower-need achievers often prefer smooth social relationships.

1. They like situations that involve personal responsibility for finding solutions to problems.
2. They set moderate achievement goals and take calculated risks.
3. They want concrete feedback on performance.

The average manager's interest in material or career success varies substantially among countries. For example, one study compared the attitudes of employees from 50 countries on what was called a *masculinity index*. Employees with a high masculinity score were those who had (among other attributes) more sympathy for the successful achiever than for the unfortunate, preferred to be the best rather than like others, more of a money-and-things orientation than a people orientation, a belief that it is better "to live to work" than "to work to live," and a preference for performance and growth over quality of life and the environment. The masculinity index also included attitudes toward gender roles, with higher scores going for beliefs that roles should be differentiated by gender and that men should dominate. The countries with the highest masculinity scores were Japan, Austria, Venezuela, and Switzerland. Those with the lowest scores were Sweden, Norway, the Netherlands, and Denmark.[35] These attitudinal differences help explain situations in which the local manager reacts in ways that the international management may neither expect nor wish. For instance, a purchasing manager with a high need for smooth social relationships may be much more concerned with developing an amiable and continuing relationship with suppliers than with reducing costs and speeding delivery. Or local managers in some countries may place such organizational goals as employee and social welfare ahead of the foreign company's priorities for growth and efficiency.

Need hierarchy   The **hierarchy of needs** is a well-known motivation theory, which is shown schematically in Fig. 2.1. According to the theory, people try to fulfill lower-order needs sufficiently before moving on to higher ones.[36] People will work to satisfy a need, but once it is fulfilled, it is no longer a motivator. This fulfill-

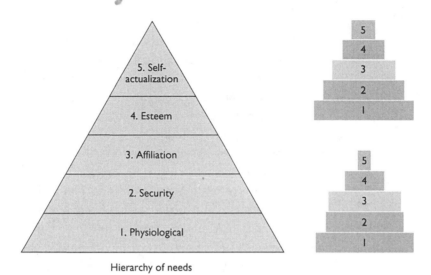

Hierarchy of needs

**Figure 2.1
The Hierarchy of Needs and Need-Hierarchy Comparisons**

The lower hierarchy on the right has a wider affiliation bar (3) and a narrower self-actualization bar (5) than the upper one. People represented by the lower hierarchy require more affiliation needs to be fulfilled before a self-esteem need (4) will be triggered as a motivator. These people would be less motivated by self-actualization than would those represented by the upper hierarchy.

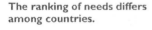
The ranking of needs differs among countries.

ment is not an all-or-nothing situation. However, because lower-order needs are more important than higher-order ones, they must be nearly fulfilled before any higher-order need becomes an effective motivator. For instance, the most basic needs are physiological, including the needs for food, water, and sex. Physiological needs may have to be nearly satisfied (say, 85-percent satisfied), before a security need becomes a powerful motivator. The security need, centering around a safe physical and emotional environment, may have to be nearly satisfied before triggering the influence of the need for affiliation, or social belongingness (acceptance by peers and friends). After the affiliation need is sufficiently satisfied, a person may be motivated by an esteem need, the need to bolster one's self-image through receipt of recognition, attention, and appreciation for one's contributions. The highest-order need is that for self-actualization, which refers to self-fulfillment, or becoming all that it is possible for one to become. The relative fulfillment requirements are shown by the horizontal bars in Fig. 2.1.

The hierarchy of needs theory is helpful for differentiating the reward preferences of employees in different countries. In very poor countries, most workers may be so deprived that a company can motivate them simply by providing enough food and shelter. Elsewhere, other needs have to be addressed to motivate workers. Researchers have noted that people from different countries attach different degrees of importance to various needs and even rank some of the higher-order needs differently. For example, studies have compared employees on *individualism versus collectivism*. Countries with the highest individualism scores are the United States, Australia, the United Kingdom, Canada, and the Netherlands. Attributes of high individualism are low dependence on the organization and a high desire for personal time, freedom, and challenge. Countries with the highest collectivism scores (opposite to individualism) are Guatemala, Ecuador, Panama, Venezuela, and Colombia. Attributes of high collectivism are high dependence on the organization and a high desire for training, physical conditions, and benefits.[37] In those countries with high individualism scores, one should expect that self-actualization will be a workable motivator because employees want challenges; however, in countries with high collectivism scores, one may expect that the provision of a safe physical and emotional environment (security need) will be a workable motivator because employees depend more on the organization.

Importance of Occupation

In every society, certain occupations are perceived to bring greater economic, social, or prestige rewards than others do. This perception to a great extent determines the numbers and qualifications of people who will seek employment in a given occupation. Although overall patterns are universal (for example, professionals are ranked ahead of street cleaners), there are some national differences. For instance, university professors are more influential as opinion leaders in Korea and Japan than in the United States and the United Kingdom.[38] The importance of business as a profession also is predictive of how difficult it may be for an international company to hire qualified managers. If jobs in business are not held in high esteem, a company may have to spend more to attract and train local managers, or it may have to rely more on managers transferred from abroad.

Another international difference involves the desire to work for an organization rather than to be one's own boss. For example, the Belgians and the French, more than most other nationalities, prefer, if possible, to go into business for themselves. Thus Belgium and France have more retail establishments per capita than most other countries do. One reason for this is that owning a small or medium-sized enterprise, rather than earning more income, is a means for Belgian and French people to get out of the working class and to move up socially. Further, psychological studies show that Belgian and French workers place a greater importance on personal independence from the organizations employing them than do workers in many other countries.[39]

Jobs with low prestige usually go to people whose skills are in low demand. In the United States, for example, such occupations as babysitting, delivering newspapers, and carrying groceries traditionally have been largely filled by teenagers, who leave these jobs as they age and gain additional training. In most less-developed countries, these are not transient occupations; rather, they are filled by adults who have very little opportunity to move on to more rewarding positions. (In the United States, there is rising concern that many low-paying menial jobs are becoming more permanent, thus perpetuating income disparities.)

Self-Reliance

Superior-subordinate relationships   In some countries, an autocratic style of management is preferred; in others, a consultative style prevails. Studies on what is known as *power distance* show that in Austria, Israel, New Zealand, and the Scandina-

There are national variations in
- Preference for autocratic versus consultative management
- Degree of trust among people
- Attitudes of self-determination versus fatalism

vian countries, the consultative style is strongly preferred, but in Malaysia, Mexico, Panama, Guatemala, and Venezuela, the autocratic style is favored. Interestingly, those preferring an autocratic style are also willing to accept decision making by a majority of subordinates. What they don't accept is the interaction between superiors and subordinates in decision making. Clearly, it may be easier for organizations to initiate certain types of worker-participation methods in some countries than in others.

Uncertainty avoidance   Studies on what is known as *uncertainty avoidance* show that in Greece, Portugal, Guatemala, Uruguay, El Salvador, and Belgium employees prefer that rules should be set out and that they should not be broken—even if breaking them is in the company's best interest. Further, these employees plan to work for the company a long time. At the opposite end of the spectrum are Singapore, Jamaica, Denmark, Sweden, Hong Kong, the United Kingdom, and Ireland.[40] When uncertainty avoidance is high, superiors may need to be more precise and assured in the directions they give to subordinates.

Trust   Surveys that measure trust among countries by having respondents evaluate such statements as "Most people can be trusted" and "You can't be too careful in dealing with people" indicate substantial national differences. For example, 61.2 percent of Norwegians think that most people are trustworthy, but only 6.7 percent of Brazilians feel that way. Where trust is high, there tends to be a lower cost of doing business because managers do not have to spend time trying to write contracts foreseeing every possible contingency and then monitoring every action for compliance. Instead, they can spend their efforts on investing and innovating.[41]

Degree of fatalism   If people believe strongly in self-determination, they may be willing to work hard to achieve goals and take responsibility for performance. A belief in fatalism, on the other hand, may prevent people from accepting a basic cause-effect relationship. In this regard, religious differences play a part: Conservative or fundamentalist Christian, Buddhist, Hindu, and Muslim societies tend to view occurrences as "the will of God." For example, Muslim mosques in the United States now generally rely on computer-generated programs to decide ahead of time when the new moon will be in the right place for Ramadan to begin; however, in conservative countries such as Saudi Arabia the view is, "How can you say six months before that it [the moon] will appear that day? You're not the one that controls the universe."[42] In a fatalistic atmosphere, people plan less for contingencies; for example, they may be reluctant to buy insurance. Studies have shown national differences in degree of fatalism even among managers in economically developed societies.[43]

Individual versus group   Japan has a much more collectivist culture than the United States does, one that values submergence of individual concerns to those of a group. For Japanese, the dominant group loyalty is to the work group."[44] For example, a U.S. scientist was invited to work in a Japanese laboratory; however, he was treated as an outsider until he realized he had to demonstrate his willingness to subordinate his personal interests to those of the group. He did so by mopping the lab floor for several weeks, after which he was invited to join the experiment.[45]

Although China and Mexico are also characterized as collectivist cultures, they differ from Japan in that the collectivism is based on kinship that does not carry over to the workplace.[46] Further, the concept of family in China and Mexico includes not only a nuclear family (a husband, wife, and minor children), but also a vertically extended family (several generations) and/or a horizontally extended one (aunts, uncles, and cousins). This difference affects business in several ways. First, material rewards from an individual's work may be less motivating because these rewards are divided among more people. Second, geographical mobility is reduced because relocation means other members of a family also have to find new jobs. Even where extended families do not live together, mobility may be reduced because people prefer to remain near relatives. Third, purchasing decisions may be more complicated because of the interrelated roles of family members. Fourth, security and social needs may be met more extensively at home than in the workplace.

Communications

All languages are complex and reflective of environment.

A common language within countries is a unifying force.

Language   Linguists have found that all societies have complex languages that reflect the environment in which their people live. Because of varying environments, translating one language directly into another can be difficult. For example, people living in the temperate zone of the Northern Hemisphere customarily use the word *summer* to refer to the months of June, July, and August. People in tropical zones may use that term to denote the dry season, which occurs at different times in different countries. Some concepts simply do not translate. For instance, in Spanish there is no word to refer to everyone who works in a business organization. Instead, there is one word, *empleados,* that refers to white-collar workers, and another, *obreros,* that refers to laborers. This distinction reflects the substantial class difference between the groups. Further, common language usage is constantly evolving. Microsoft purchased a thesaurus code for its Spanish version of Word 6.0, but many synonyms turned out to be too derogatory to be currently acceptable. The company corrected the software after newspapers and radio reports denounced the program.[47]

English, French, and Spanish have such widespread acceptance (they are spoken prevalently in forty-four, twenty-seven, and twenty countries, respectively) that native speakers of these languages generally are not very motivated to learn others. Commerce and other cross-border associations can be conducted easily with other nations that share the same language. When a second language is studied, it usually is chosen because of its usefulness in dealing with other countries. English and

French traditionally have been chosen because of commercial links developed during colonial periods. But English is gaining in relative importance as countries, such as Vietnam, are switching to English studies. Further, more young people in Europe are learning English than in the past.[48] In countries that do not share a common language with other countries (for example, Finland and Greece), there is a much greater need for citizens to study other languages in order to function internationally.

English, especially American English, words are being added to languages worldwide, partly because of U.S. technology that develops new products and services for which new words must be coined. When a new product or service enters another language area, it may take on an Anglicized name. For example, Russians call tight denim pants *dzhinsi* (pronounced "jeansy"); the French call a self-service restaurant *le self;* and Lithuanians go to the theater to see *moving pikceris*.[49] An estimated 20,000 English words have entered the Japanese language. However, some countries, such as Finland, have largely developed their own new words rather than using Anglicized versions.

Translating one language into another does not always work as intended. The following are examples of signs in English observed in hotels around the world:

France: "Please leave your values at the desk."
Mexico (to assure guests about the safety of drinking water): "The manager has personally passed all the water served here."
Japan: "You are invited to take advantage of the chambermaid."
Norway: "Ladies are requested not to have children in the bar."
Switzerland: "Because of the impropriety of entertaining guests of the opposite sex in the bedroom, it is suggested that the lobby be used for this purpose."
Greece (at check-in line): "We will execute customers in strict rotation."

Even within the same language there often are differences in usage or meaning. *Corn, maize,* and *graduate studies* in the United Kingdom correspond to *wheat, corn,* and *undergraduate studies,* respectively, in the United States. These are among the approximately 4000 words used differently in these two countries. Although the wrong choice of words usually is just a source of brief embarrassment, a poor translation may have tragic consequences. For example, inaccurate translations have been blamed for structural collapses and airplane crashes.[50] In contracts, correspondence, negotiations, advertisements, and conversations, words must be chosen carefully.

Silent language includes such things as color associations, sense of appropriate distance, time and status cues, and body language.

Silent language Of course, formal language is not our only means of communicating. We all exchange messages by a host of nonverbal cues that form a *silent language*.[51] Colors, for example, conjure up meanings that are based on cultural experience. In most Western countries, black is associated with death; white has the same connotation in parts of Asia and purple in Latin America. For products to be successful, their colors and their advertisements must match the consumers' frame of reference.

Another aspect of silent language is the distance between people during conversations. People's sense of appropriate distance is learned and differs among societies. In the United States, for example, the customary distance for a business discussion is five to eight feet; for personal business, it is eighteen inches to three feet.[52] When the distance is closer or farther than is customary, people tend to feel very uneasy. For example, a U.S. manager conducting business discussions in Latin America may be constantly moving backward to avoid the closer conversational distance to which the Latin American official is accustomed. Consequently, at the end of the discussion, each party may inexplicably distrust the other.

Perception of time, which influences punctuality, is another unspoken cue that may differ across cultures and create confusion. In the United States, participants usually arrive early for a business appointment. For a dinner at someone's home, guests arrive on time or a few minutes late, and for a cocktail party, they may arrive a bit later. In another country, the concept of punctuality may be radically different. For example, a U.S. businessperson in Latin America may consider it discourteous if a Latin American manager does not keep to the appointed time. Latin Americans may find it equally discourteous if a U.S. businessperson arrives for dinner at the exact time given in the invitation.

Cues concerning a person's relative position may be particularly difficult to perceive. A U.S. businessperson, who tends to place a greater reliance on objects as prestige cues, may underestimate the importance of a foreign counterpart who does not have a large private office with a wood desk and carpeting. A foreigner may react similarly if U.S. counterparts open their own entry doors and mix their own drinks.

Body language or *kinesics* (the way in which people walk, touch, and move their bodies) also differs among countries. Few gestures are universal in meaning. For example, the "yes" of a Greek, Turk, or Bulgarian is indicated by a sideways movement of the head that resembles the negative headshake used in the United States and elsewhere in Europe. In some cases, one gesture may have several meanings: The joining of the index finger and thumb to form an O means "okay" in the United States, money in Japan, and "I will kill you" in Tunisia.[53]

Cues—especially those concerning time and status—are perceived selectively and differ among societies.

Perception and processing   We perceive cues selectively. We may identify what things are by means of any of our senses (sight, smell, touch, sound, or taste) and in various ways within each sense. For example, through vision we can sense color, depth, and shape. The cues people use to perceive things differ among societies. The reason for this is partly physiological; for example, genetic differences in eye pigmentation enable some groups to differentiate colors more finely than others can. It also is partly cultural; for example, a relative richness of vocabulary can allow people to notice and express very subtle differences in color.[54] Differences in vocabulary reflect cultural differences. For example, Arabic has more than 6000 different words for camels, their body parts, and the equipment associated with them.[55]

Regardless of societal differences, once people perceive cues, they process them. Information processing is universal in that all societies categorize, plan, and quantify. In terms of categorization, people bring objects together according to their major shared function: A piece of furniture to sit on is called a chair in English, whether it is large or small, wood or plastic, upholstered or not. The languages of all societies express the future and conditional situations; thus all societies plan. All societies have numbering systems as well. But the specific ways in which societies go about grouping things, dealing with the future, and counting differ substantially.[56] For example, in U.S. telephone directories, the entries are organized by last (family) names; in Iceland, they are organized by first (given) names. Icelandic last names are derived from the father's first name: Jon, the son of Thor, is Jon Thorsson, and his sister's last name is Thorsdottir (daughter of Thor).[57]

National norms differ in preference for
- Focused versus broad information
- Sequential versus simultaneous handling of situations
- Handling principals versus small issues first

Obtaining and evaluating information   In spite of vast differences within countries, some, such as those in northern Europe, are categorized as being **low-context cultures**—that is, most people consider relevant only information that they receive firsthand and that bears very directly on the decision they need to make. They also spend little time on "small talk" in business situations. However, other countries, such as in southern Europe, are **high-context cultures**—that is, most people consider that peripheral and hearsay information are necessary for decision making because they bear on the context of the situation. Northern Europeans are also called **monochronic,** which means that most prefer to deal with situations sequentially (especially those involving other people), such as finishing with one customer before dealing with another. On the other hand, **polychronic** southern Europeans are more comfortable in dealing simultaneously with all the situations facing them. For example, they feel uncomfortable when not dealing immediately with all customers who need to be served.[58]

There are also national norms that govern the degree to which people will try to determine principles before they try to resolve small issues, or vice versa. In other words, people will tend toward either **idealism** or **pragmatism.** From a business standpoint, the differences manifest themselves in a number of ways. The idealist sees the pragmatist as being too interested in trivial details, whereas the pragmatist considers the idealist to be too theoretical. In a society of pragmatists, labor tends to focus on very specific issues, such as a pay increase of a dollar per hour. In a society of idealists, labor tends to make less precise demands and to depend instead on mass action, such as general strikes or support of a particular political party, to publicize its principles.[59]

Reconciliation of International Differences

Cultural Awareness

Where cultural differences exist, businesspeople must decide whether and to what extent they should adapt home-country practices to the foreign environment. But before making that decision, managers must be aware of what the differences are. As discussed earlier in this chapter, there is much disagreement about such differences. Thus building cultural awareness is not an easy task, and no foolproof method exists for doing so.

In any situation, some people are prone to say the right thing at the right time and others to offend unintentionally. Most people are more aware of differences in things they have learned consciously, such as table manners, than of differences in things they have learned subconsciously, such as methods of problem solving. Nevertheless, there is general agreement that awareness and sensitivity can be improved and that training about other cultures will enhance the likelihood of success in operating within those cultures, a subject discussed in detail in Chapter 21. This chapter has presented a framework of some of the human cultural factors that require special business adjustments on a country-to-country basis. By paying special attention to these factors, businesspeople can start building cultural awareness.

Reading about and discussing other countries and researching how people regard a specific culture can be very instructive. The opinions presented must be measured carefully. Very often they represent unwarranted stereotypes, an accurate assessment of only a subsegment of the particular country, or a situation that has since undergone change. By getting varied viewpoints, businesspeople can better judge assessments of different cultures. In a given society, managers can also observe the behavior of those people who are well accepted or those with whom they would like to be associated in order to become aware of and learn to emulate acceptable behavior. Samsung, Korea's largest company, is experimenting with a cultural awareness program that involves sending 400 junior employees abroad for a year. In the United States, for example, they don't work; rather, they idle at malls, watch people, and try to develop international tastes. The company is convinced this program will pay off in more astute judgments about what customers want.[60]

There are so many behavioral rules that businesspeople cannot expect to memorize all of them for every country in which business relations might be attempted. Wide variations exist even in form of address; for example, it may be difficult to know whether to use a given name or surname, which of several surnames to use, and whether a wife takes the husband's name.[61] Fortunately, there are up-to-date guidebooks that have been compiled for particular geographical areas, based on the experiences of many successful international managers.[62] A manager also may consult with knowledgeable people at home and abroad, from governmental offices or in the private sector.

A person who moves to a foreign country or who returns home after an extended stay abroad frequently encounters **culture shock.** "This is a generalized trauma one experiences in a new and different culture because of having to learn and cope with a vast array of new cultural cues and expectations, while discovering that your old ones probably do not fit or work."[63] People working in a very different culture may pass through stages. First, like tourists, they are elated with "quaint" differences. Later, they may feel frustrated, depressed, and confused—the culture shock phase—and their usefulness in a foreign assignment may be greatly impaired. Fortunately for most people, culture shock begins to ebb after a month or two as optimism and satisfaction improve.[64] Interestingly, some people also encounter culture shock when they return to their home countries—a situation known as **reverse culture shock**—because they have learned to accept what they have encountered abroad.

Grouping Countries

Some countries are relatively similar to one another, usually because they share many attributes that help mold their cultures, such as language, religion, geographical location, ethnicity, and level of economic development. In Map 2.4, countries are grouped by attitudes and values based on data obtained from a large number of cross-cultural studies. A company should expect fewer differences when moving within a cluster (a Peruvian company doing business in Colombia) than when moving from one cluster to another (a Peruvian company doing business in Thailand).[65] Such relationships must be used with caution, however. They deal only with overall similarities and differences among countries, and managers may easily be misled when considering specific business practices to use abroad. In fact, there is some tendency to expect that seemingly similar countries are more alike than they really are; thus a company may be lulled into a complacency that overlooks subtleties that are important for performance. For example, in the PRI case the company expected the twelve Middle Eastern Arab countries to be more similar than they turned out to be—and the PRI experience only touches the "tip of the iceberg" as far as national differences are concerned.[66]

Cultural Needs in the Internationalization Process

Not all companies need to have the same degree of cultural awareness. Nor must a particular company have a consistent degree of awareness during the course of its operations. As we discussed in Chapter 1 companies usually increase foreign operations over time. They may expand their knowledge of cultural factors in tandem with their expansion of foreign operations. In other words, they may increase their cultural knowledge as they move from limited to multiple foreign functions, from one to many foreign locations, from similar to dissimilar foreign environments, and from external to internal handling of their international operations. Thus, for example, a small company that is new to international business may have to gain only a minimal level of cultural awareness, but a highly involved company needs a high level.

Map 2.4
A Synthesis of Country Clusters

Not all countries have been studied extensively in terms of attitudinal variables that may have different effects on the efficient conduct of business. However, it has been noted that, of the countries that have been studied, some can be grouped together as having similar attitudes and values.

Source: Groupings taken from Simcha Ronen and Oded Shenkar, "Clustering Countries on Attitudinal Dimensions: A Review and Synthesis," *Academy of Management Review,* Vol. 10, No. 3, 1985, p. 449.

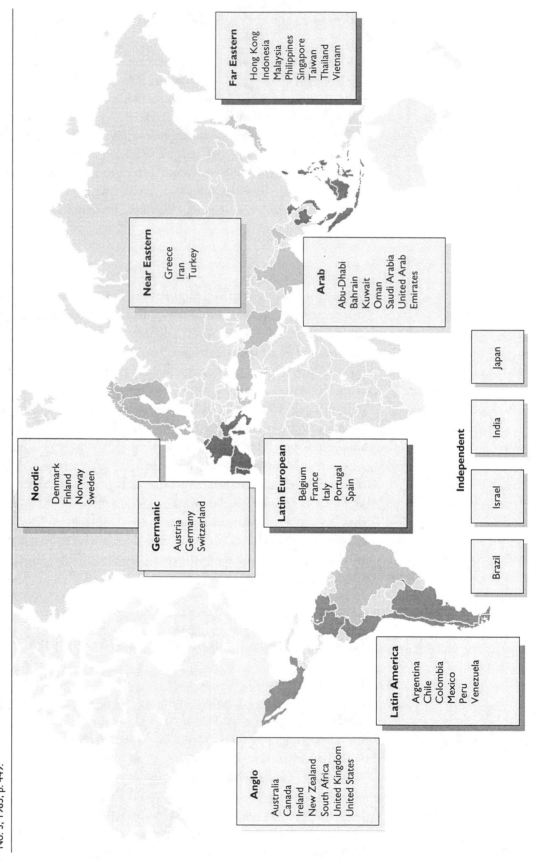

Far Eastern
Hong Kong
Indonesia
Malaysia
Philippines
Singapore
Taiwan
Thailand
Vietnam

Near Eastern
Greece
Iran
Turkey

Arab
Abu-Dhabi
Bahrain
Kuwait
Oman
Saudi Arabia
United Arab
Emirates

Nordic
Denmark
Finland
Norway
Sweden

Germanic
Austria
Germany
Switzerland

Latin European
Belgium
France
Italy
Portugal
Spain

Latin America
Argentina
Chile
Colombia
Mexico
Peru
Venezuela

Anglo
Australia
Canada
Ireland
New Zealand
South Africa
United Kingdom
United States

Independent

Brazil

Israel

India

Japan

When foreign functions are limited, for example, in a purely market-seeking operation, such as exporting from the home country, a company must be aware of cultural factors that may influence the marketing program. Consider advertising, which may be affected by the real and ideal physical norms of the target market, the roles of group membership in terms of status and buying decisions, and the perception of different words and images. A company undertaking a purely resource-seeking foreign activity can ignore the effects of cultural variables on advertising but must consider factors that may influence supply, such as methods of managing a foreign workforce. For multifunctional activities, such as producing *and* selling a product in a foreign country, a company must be concerned with a wider array of cultural relationships.

The more countries in which a company is doing business, the more cultural nuances it must consider. Think of the adjustments a manager from corporate headquarters who visits the company's foreign distributors would undergo. The more countries visited, the more cultural differences would be encountered on the trip and the more predeparture training time would be needed.

There is a relationship in the similarity between countries and the relative need for cultural awareness. For example, a U.S. firm starting a new business in Australia will find cultural differences that may be important enough to create operating problems; however, the number and intensity of these differences are apt to be less than if it were starting a new business in Japan.

A company may handle foreign operations on its own or contract with another company to handle them. The risk of making operating mistakes because of misunderstanding may effectively be reduced if foreign operations are turned over to another company at home or abroad that is experienced in the foreign country. If the operations are contracted to a company abroad, then some cultural awareness is necessary because of nuances that may influence the relationship between the two companies, such as the means of negotiating an agreement or the ordering of objectives for the operation. As a company takes on activities that had previously been contracted to another company, it will need to know much more about the cultures where it is doing business.

Polycentrism

Polycentrists are overwhelmed by national differences and risk not introducing workable changes.

In organizations characterized by **polycentrism,** control is decentralized so that "our manager in Rio" is free to conduct business in what he thinks is "the Brazilian way." When the concept is taken to extremes, a polycentric individual or organization is "overwhelmed by the differences, real and imaginary, great and small, between its many operating environments."[67] Since most discussions of international business focus on uniquenesses encountered abroad and the attendant problems that companies have experienced, it is understandable that many managers develop a polycentric view. Polycentrism may be, however, an overly cautious response. In reality, it is uncertain how much companies adjust when operating abroad and whether their practices abroad are any more prone to failure than those at home.

A company that is too polycentric may shy away from certain countries or may avoid transferring home-country practices or resources that may, in fact, work well abroad. For example, American Express assembled its worldwide personnel managers for an exchange of views. The complaints from the overseas managers centered on certain corporate directives that they claimed did not fit "their" countries. The impression was created that foreign operations were so unique that each overseas office should develop its own procedures. Further talks, however, revealed that the complaints really focused on only one particular personnel evaluation form. If the company had delegated procedural control, as these overseas managers were suggesting, it would have risked not introducing abroad some of its other standard forms and procedures that would work reasonably well. Furthermore, it would have risked duplicating efforts, which might have been more costly than trying to administer the ill-suited form. The additional discussions also generated for the first time comments from personnel managers in U.S. offices who had received the same corporate instructions. They indicated that they had had just as many problems with the form as their foreign counterparts had. Thus the problem, originally attributed to environmental differences, was seen to be universal.

To compete effectively with local companies, an international company usually must perform some functions in a distinct way. Polycentrism, however, may lead to such extensive delegation or such extensive imitation of proven host-country practices that innovative superiority is lost. Furthermore, control may be diminished as managers within each country foster local rather than worldwide objectives.

Ethnocentrism

Ethnocentrism is the belief that one's own group is superior to others. The term is used in international business to describe a company or individual so imbued with the belief that what worked at home should work abroad that environmental differences are ignored. Ethnocentrism can be categorized into three types:

Ethnocentrists overlook national differences and
- **Ignore important factors**
- **Believe home-country objectives should prevail**
- **Think change is easily introduced**

1. Important factors are overlooked because management has become so accustomed to certain cause-effect relationships in the home country that differences abroad are ignored. To combat this type of ethnocentrism, managers can refer to checklists of human variables in order to assure themselves that all the major factors are at least considered.
2. Management recognizes both the environmental differences and the problems associated with change but is focused on achieving home-country rather than foreign or worldwide objectives. The result may be diminished long-term competitive viability because the company does not perform as well as its competitors and because opposition to its practices develops abroad.
3. Management recognizes differences but assumes that the introduction of change is both necessary and easily achieved. (The problems accompanying

this type of ethnocentrism are discussed in the next subsection, "Geocentrism.")

Geocentrism

International companies often use practices that are hybrids of home and foreign norms.

Between the extremes of polycentrism and ethnocentrism are hybrid business practices that are neither exactly like the international company's home operations nor exactly like those of the typical host-country company. When the host-country environment is substantially different, the international company must decide whether to persuade people in that country to accept something new (in which case, the company would be acting as a change agent) or to make changes in the company itself. **Geocentrism** refers to operations based on an informed knowledge of both home and host country needs, capabilities, and constraints.

The more a change upsets important values, the more resistance it will engender.

Value system   It is much easier to adapt to things that do not challenge our value systems than to things that do. We usually can be flexible about whether we eat the salad before or after the main course, but we would probably think twice before exposing more of our bodies in public or paying bribes to government officials, actions that would require some moral adjustment if we do not do them in our country. For example, Eritreans eat only 175 grams of fish per capita per year (compared with 20 kilos in the United States and 70 kilos in Japan), despite having a long coastline rich in seafood and a recent experience with famine. The Eritrean government and the United Nations World Food Program have faced formidable opposition in trying to persuade Eritrean adults to eat more seafood because their value systems are too set. Many have religious taboos about eating insect-like sea creatures (such as shrimp and crayfish) and fish without scales, and most grew up believing that seafood tasted putrid. But there is little opposition among school children who are being fed seafood that adults find unpalatable. Simply, their value systems and habits are not yet set, so they can be easily influenced.[68] The important lesson here is that the more a change disrupts basic values, the more the people affected will resist it. When changes do not interfere with deep-seated customs, accommodation is much more likely.

The cost of change may exceed the benefit gained.

Cost-benefit of change   Some adjustments to foreign cultures are costly to undertake; others are inexpensive. Some result in greatly improved performance, such as higher productivity or sales; others may improve performance only marginally. A company must consider the expected cost-benefit relationship of any adjustments it makes abroad. For example, Cummins Engine shuts down its plant in Mexico each December 12 so workers may honor the Virgin of Guadalupe. It throws a celebration in the company cafeteria for employees and their families that includes a priest who offers prayers to the Virgin at an altar.[69] The cost is small in relation to the resultant employee commitment to the company.

Resistance to change may be lower if the number of changes is not too great.

Resistance to too much change   When Germany's Gruner + Jahr bought the U.S. magazine *McCall's,* it quickly began to overhaul the format. Gruner + Jahr changed the editor, eliminated long stories and advice columns, increased coverage on celebrities, made the layouts more dense, initiated the use of sidebars and boxes in articles, and refused discounts for big advertisers. But employee turnover began to increase because of low morale, and revenues fell because the new format seemed too different to advertisers.[70] Acceptance by employees and advertisers might have been easier to obtain if Gruner + Jahr had made fewer demands at one time and had phased in other policies more slowly.

People are more willing to implement change when they are involved in the decision to change.

Participation   One way to avoid undue problems that could result from change is to invite the prior participation of stakeholders, such as employees, who might otherwise feel they have no say in their own destinies. By discussing a proposed change with stakeholders in advance, the company may ascertain how strong resistance to the change is, stimulate in the stakeholders a recognition of the need for improvement, and allay their fears of adverse consequences resulting from the change. Managers sometimes think that delegation and participation are unique to highly developed countries, in which people have educational backgrounds that enable them to make substantial contributions. Experience with economic development and population control programs, however, indicates that participation may be extremely important even in countries with a preference for authoritarian leadership. However, participation is limited to the extent that proposed actions do not violate conditions in the prevailing value system and to the extent that participants are not so fatalistic that they believe they can have no control over the results of actions taken.

People are more apt to support change when they expect personal or group rewards.

Reward sharing   Sometimes a proposed change may have no foreseeable benefit for the people whose support is needed to ensure its success. For example, production workers have little incentive to shift to new work practices unless they see some benefits for themselves. A company's solution may be to develop a bonus system for productivity quality.

Managers seeking to introduce change should first convince those who can influence others.

Opinion leaders   By discovering the local channels of influence, an international company may locate opinion leaders who can help speed up the acceptance of change. Opinion leaders may emerge in unexpected places. For example, in rural Ghana, government health workers frequently ask permission from and seek the help of village shamans before inoculating people or spraying huts to fight malaria. Doing this achieves the desired result without destroying important social structures. Characteristics of opinion leaders may vary by country, such as generally being more mature people in India and Korea, but not in Australia.[71]

ow companies and businesspeople should react to cultural practices that run counter to their own values is itself a value judgment. On the one hand, *relativism* affirms that ethical truths are relative to the groups holding them; thus intervention would be unethical. On the other hand, *normativism* holds that there are universal standards of behavior that should be upheld; thus nonintervention would be unethical. Respect for other cultures is itself a Western cultural phenomenon that goes back at least as far as St. Ambrose's fourth-century advice: "When in Rome, do as the Romans do."

Neither international companies nor their employees are expected always to adhere to the norms of a host society. This would seem to remove ethical questions; however, exposure to certain practices may be traumatic to foreigners. For example, many practices that are considered "wrong" in home country cultures are elsewhere either customary or only recently abolished and liable to be reinstated—including slavery, polygamy, concubinage, child marriage, and the burning of widows.[72] Some companies have avoided operating in locales in which such practices occur; others have pressured a host country to change the "wrong" behaviors. For example, complaints from international business leaders induced Papua New Guinea, which depends on foreign investment, to abandon policies of payback killings.[73]

ETHICAL DILEMMAS & SOCIAL RESPONSIBILITIES

Although the preceding examples are extreme and seldom, if ever, encountered by international managers, many other behavioral differences may violate a manager's own ethical code to a lesser degree. It is easier to adjust in these cases, although dilemmas still exist. For example, using gifts and flattery to gain business advantages may seem unethical to some people. But in many countries, particularly in Asia, failure to bring a small gift may not only be considered a breach of etiquette but also be interpreted as indicating a lack of interest in doing business. The difference is due to the fact that most Westerners are conditioned to express gratitude verbally, and most Asians, particularly Chinese, are conditioned to express appreciation tangibly, such as with gifts.[74] Giving gifts to government officials may be particularly perplexing to Westerners. In many places such gifts or payments are customary to obtain governmental services or contracts. Although this practice may be condemned officially, it is so well embedded in local custom and precedent that it has nearly the prescribed enforcement of common law. In Mexico, for example, companies commonly give tips once a month to the mail carrier; otherwise, their mail simply gets lost.[75] The going rate of payment is rather easily ascertained and is usually graduated on the ability to pay. The practice of making payments to government officials is, in effect, a fairly efficient means of taxation in countries that pay civil servants poorly and do not have the means for collecting income taxes. Still, these payments are considered bribes by many MNEs, and the practice frequently is viewed by home-country constituents as so unethical that home-country laws against it are enforced in foreign operations.

In situations such as that of making payments to government officials, companies may incur operational inefficiencies or loss of business if they do not comply with local custom. This brings up the question of whether operational performance should be considered along with potential violation of ethical standards. For example, many people feel it is more acceptable to give payments to government officials when a large, rather than a small, amount of business is at stake and when small, rather than large, payments are expected.

Another thorny ethical question concerns practices by international businesses that do not clash with foreign values directly but that nevertheless may undermine the long-term cultural identity of the host country. Examples of such practices are the use of a company's home-country language and the introduction of products and work methods that effect changes in social relationships. Companies may face unexpected criticism that may affect their performance. For example, Finns have criticized MNEs for introducing non-Finnish architecture[76], Poles delayed McDonald's start-up because of its architecture[77], Greeks are resisting TVX Gold's building of a processing plant near a unique archeological site[78], and France fined Bodyshop for using English in its French stores and a branch of Georgia Tech for using English on the Internet.[79]

The Society for Applied Anthropology, which advises agencies on instituting change in different cultures, has adopted a code of ethics to protect foreign cultures with which such agencies interact. The code considers whether a project or planned change actually will benefit the target population. Because the definition of what constitutes a benefit depends on cultural value systems, implementing this code is a challenge. Further, there may be trade-offs to inducing changes, such as a trade-off between economic gains for the target population and the perpetuation of ways of life that have heretofore given that population great satisfaction. Thus, we often hear of "spiritual poverty in the midst of plenty" as aesthetic, philosophical, and human dimensions of development have been ignored or neglected.[80] Further, the concept of "quality of life" varies substantially among cultures.[81] The result is that an international company may be criticized as being socially irresponsible if it ignores the total spectrum of human needs for each place in which it operates.

Companies often lack complete information to guide them in advance of taking action abroad. There are many anecdotes about companies unwittingly violating a foreign country's values, even when they had sought advice from local managers or consultants. For example, consider the area of human rights. In 1948, before most of today's nations were in existence, the United Nations adopted the Universal Declaration of Human Rights. The Declaration has been criticized for having too Western an orientation, which does not consider distinctive values of specific countries or religions. Some provisions that lack universal acceptance include the right to individual ownership of property, the right to governance through universal secret elections, and the implicit statement that the nuclear family is the fundamental unit of society. In fact, not all countries have explicitly declared their concept of human rights. Without such an explicit delineation, there is uncertainty about the accuracy of descriptions of the human rights sentiments of many countries.[82] Further, any human rights code must enjoy cultural legitimacy for it to work as a normative (universal) system.[83]

Companies should time change to occur when resistance is likely to be lower.

Timing   Many good ideas are never applied effectively because they are ill timed. Change brings uncertainty and insecurity. For example, a labor-saving production method will create resistance because people fear losing their jobs, regardless of what management says will happen to employment. However, less resistance will occur if the labor-saving method is introduced when there is a labor shortage rather than a surplus. Attitudes and needs may change slowly or rapidly, so keeping abreast of these changes helps in determining timing.

International companies
- **Change some things abroad**
- **Change themselves when encountering foreign environments**
- **Learn things abroad that they can apply at home**

Learning abroad   The discussion so far has centered on the interaction between an international company and the host society. This interaction is a two-way street. The company not only affects the relationship but is affected by it. The company may change things abroad or alter its activities to fit the foreign environment; it also may learn things that will be useful in its home country or in other operations. This last point is the essence for undertaking transnational practices, in which the company seeks to capitalize on diverse capabilities among the countries in which it operates. In fact, the management within a given foreign country may serve effectively as the worldwide headquarters for a specific product or function.

The national practices most likely to be scrutinized for possible use in other countries are those found in the countries that are doing best economically.[84] For example, in the nineteenth century, when Britain was the world economic leader, interest focused on the British cultural character. At the turn of the century, such attention was diverted to Germany and the United States. More recently, it has shifted toward Japan and the newly industrialized countries of Asia. Whether a company is importing or exporting business practices, managers must consider the same factors when questioning whether and how change can be introduced.

Cultures are becoming more similar in some respects but not in others.

COUNTERVAILING

FORCES

Contact across cultures is becoming more widespread than ever. This should lead to a leveling of cultures, which, on the surface, is occurring. People around the world wear similar clothes and listen to the same recording stars. Competitors from all over the world often buy the same production equipment, the use of which imposes more uniform operating methods on workers. This globalization of culture is illustrated by the fact that Japanese tourists may hear a Philippine group sing a U.S. song in a hotel in Thailand.[85]

However, below the surface people continue to hold fast to their national differences.[86] In other words, although some tangibles have become more universal, the ways in which people cooperate, attempt to solve problems, and are motivated have tended to remain the same. Religious differences are as strong as ever. And language differences continue to bolster separate ethnic identities. These differences fragment the globe into regions and stymie global standardization of products and operating methods.

One factor that inhibits the leveling of cultures is nationalism. Without perceived cultural differences, people would not see themselves so apart from other nationalities; thus cultural identities are used to mobilize national identity and separateness. This is done by regulating and encouraging the so-called national culture.

Language is regulated in many ways, such as by designating an official language, preventing bilingual education, or requiring "Made in _____" labels printed in the language of the importing country. A religion may be designated a country's official one or made a requisite to holding certain governmental posts or to voting.

Those things that are part of the essential national heritage are perpetuated by marketing them to visitors at home and abroad, as the image of Britain is used in promotions to foreign tourists. They also may be off-limits to foreign ownership. For example, the French government has prevented foreign acquisition of vineyards for reasons based on heritage. Canada prevents foreign ownership in culturally sensitive industries. And, although the game of baseball has spread in popularity from the United States to Japan, when a Japanese group bought the Seattle Mariners team, there was an uproar in the United States—not on economic or national security grounds but on the basis of heritage. Maintaining a national identity may extend beyond heritage. For example, most countries have a national airline that is government subsidized so that there is a national identity associated with the flag painted on the aircraft.

As long as nations seek to perpetuate themselves through the promotion of separate cultural or national identities, companies will be constrained in their global competitive moves.

LOOKING TO THE FUTURE

International companies are likely to continue to face diverse cultural trends in different parts of the world and for different parts of their operations. In some areas, diversity will decrease as small cultural groups are absorbed into more dominant national ones. For example, in recent years such absorption has led to the extinction of many regional languages. Such extinction is sometimes expedited by governmental assimilation programs and by bans on religious groups or the use of anything except the official language.[87] At the same time, there is evidence of more powerful subcultures *within* countries because of the influx of people from other countries, the global rise in religious fundamentalism, and the growing belief of ethnic groups that they should be independent.

All of these factors might lead to future problems in defining culture along national lines. Subcultures may transcend borders, and the distinct subcultures within a country may have less in common with each other than they do with subcultures in other countries. Examples of transnational subcultures are the Inuits in Arctic lands and the Kurds of the Middle East. Simultaneously, cultural similarity will continue to be used to mobilize a sense of national identity, for example, religious separatism in Iran or the independence movement among the Québeçois in Canada and among the Tamils in Sri Lanka. Such activities may retard or even prevent the homogenization of cultures.[88]

An interesting potential scenario is that cultural competition—the promotion of ideas, attitudes, norms, and values—among nations will become more important.[89] With the termination of the Cold War, cultural competition may become a more important means to bring about economic growth as nations try to harness their distinctive human resource capabilities as a means of outperforming other countries.

Three scenarios for future international cultures:
- Smaller cultures will be absorbed by national and global ones.
- Subcultures will transcend national boundaries.
- Cultural similarity will be used to mobilize a sense of national identity.

WEB CONNECTION

Check out our home page for links to the Web of Culture (an index of links dealing with cultural issues such as cuisine, gestures, holidays, languages, religions, and so on) and the Multicultural Pavilion (another index of links to resources on multicultural issues, located at the University of Virginia).

Summary

- International companies must evaluate their business practices to ensure that national norms in behavioral characteristics are taken into account.

- A given country may encompass very distinct societies. People also may have more in common with similar groups in foreign countries than with different groups in their own country.

- Culture includes norms of behavior based on learned attitudes, values, and beliefs. Businesspeople agree that there are cross-country differences in these but disagree as to what the differences are.

- Cultural change may take place as a result of choice or imposition; however, isolation from other groups tends to stabilize cultures.

- Group affiliations based on gender, family, age, caste, religion, political preference, professional associations, and ethnic, racial, or national origin often affect a person's degree of access to economic resources, prestige, social relations, and power. An individual's affiliations may determine his or her qualifications and availability for given jobs.

- Some people work far more than is necessary to satisfy their basic needs for food, clothing, and shelter. The relative importance of work is determined largely by the interrelationship of the cultural and economic environments. People are motivated to work for various reasons, including the Protestant ethic, the belief that work will bring success and reward, habit, the need for achievement, and the fulfillment of higher-order needs.

- Different occupations bring different economic, social, and prestige rewards in different countries. People gravitate to jobs for which they perceive they will receive high rewards. The many differences among societies result in varied attitudes toward working for business organizations.

- National groups differ as to whether they prefer an autocratic or a consultative working relationship, in the degree to which individuals trust others, in attitudes toward self-determination and fate, and in the importance placed on group memberships, especially family-based ones.

- People communicate through both formal language and silent language based on culturally determined cues. Information processing is greatly affected by cultural background. The failure to perceive subtle distinctions can result in misunderstandings in international dealings.

- Companies can build awareness about other cultures. The amount of effort needed to do this depends on the similarity between countries and the type of business operation undertaken.

- People working in a foreign environment should be sensitive to the dangers of either excessive polycentrism or excessive ethnocentrism. Instead they should try to become geocentric.

- In deciding whether to try to bring change to home or host country operations or to develop new practices to fit conditions, an international company should consider several factors, including how important the change is to each party, the cost and benefit to the company of each alternative, the possibility of participation in decision making, the need to share the rewards of change, the use of opinion leaders, and the timing of change.

- There usually is more interest in studying and possibly adopting business practices from countries that are showing the greatest economic success. Cultural factors may determine whether the practices can work successfully in another society.

- Although increased contact among people is evoking more widespread cultural similarity among nations, people nevertheless tend to hold on to their basic values. These values are bolstered by efforts to protect cultural separateness and national identity.

Chapter Notes

1. Most data were taken from an interview with Angela Clarke, a protagonist in the case. Additional background information came from Samira Harfoush, "Non-Traditional Training for Women in the Arab World," *Bridge,* Winter 1980, pp. 6–7; "British Premier Visits Saudi Arabia," *New York Times,* April 20, 1981, p. A2; Karen Elliott House, "Modern Arabia," *Wall Street Journal,* June 4, 1981, p. 1; Geraldine Brooks, "Mixed Blessing," *Wall Street Journal,* September 11, 1990, p. A1; Tony Horwitz, "Thought Police," *Wall Street Journal,* May 2, 1991, p. A1+; Tony Horwitz, "Arabian Backlash," *Wall Street Journal,* January 13, 1993, p. A1; Robin Allen, "Imported Labour May Not Be Cheap for Gulf States," *Financial Times,* October 13, 1995, p.5; Macon Morehouse, "Western Influence Brings Wealth, Strain, to Saudi Society," *The Atlanta Journal,* June 26, 1996, p. 10A; Sandra Mackey, "Perspectives on the Saudi Bombing," *Los Angeles Times,* June 28, 1996, p. B9; Thomas W. Lippman, "Mission to Bolster Saudi Security Also Provokes Rulers' Enemies," *Washington Post,* June 27, 1996, p. A24; Robin Allen, "Oil Price Alert on Saudi State Finances," *Financial Times,* June 26, 1996, p. 4; "The Shockwaves That Unsettle," *Financial Times,* July 26, 1996, p. 16; Mathew Horsman and Edward Waller, "The BBC's Arabian Plight," *The Independent,* April 16, 1996, p. 18; Daniel Pearl, "Moon Over Mecca: It's Tough to Pinpoint Start of Holy Month," *Wall Street Journal,* January 7, 1997, p. A1+.

2. R. I. Westwood and S. M. Leung, "The Female Expatriate Manager Experience," *International Studies of Management and Organization,* Vol. 24, No. 3, 1994, pp. 64–85.

3. June N. P. Francis, "When in Rome? The Effects of Cultural Adaptation on Intercultural Business Negotiations," *Journal of International Business Studies,* Vol. 22, No. 3, 1991, pp. 421–422.

4. Robert J. Foster, "Making National Cultures in the National Ecumene," *Annual Review of Anthropology,* Vol. 20, 1991, pp. 235–260, discusses the concept and ingredients of a national culture.

5. David Binder and Barbara Crossette, "As Ethnic Wars Multiply, U.S. Strives for a Policy," *New York Times,* February 7, 1993, p. A1+; Marcus W. Brauchli and David P. Hamilton, "Tensions in Asia," *Wall Street Journal,* August 18, 1995, p. A6; Bob Davis, "Global Paradox," *Wall Street Journal,* June 20, 1994, p. A1.

6. Marshall H. Segall, *Cross-Cultural Psychology: Human Behavior in Global Perspective* (Monterey, Calif.: Brooks/Cole, 1979), p. 143; and Luis R. Gomez-Mejia, "Effect of Occupation on Task Related, Contextual, and Job Involvement Orientation: A Cross-Cultural Perspective," *Academy of Management Journal,* Vol. 27, No. 4, 1984, pp. 706–720.

7. Richard N. Farmer and Barry M. Richman, *Comparative Management and Economic Progress,* rev. ed. (Bloomington, Ind.: Cedarwood, 1970), pp. 20–21, for example, list 15 behavioral variables relating to each of 36 business functions. George P. Murdock listed 72 cultural variables in "The Common Denominator of Culture," in *The Science of Man in the World Crises,* Ralph Linton, ed. (New York: Columbia University Press, 1945), pp. 123–142.

8. Ian Jamieson, *Capitalism and Culture: A Comparative Analysis of British and American Manufacturing Organizations* (Farnborough, England: Gower Press, 1980), Chapter 1.

9. Nancy J. Adler and Jill de Villafranca, "Epistemological Foundations of a Symposium Process: A Framework for Understanding Culturally Diverse Organizations," *International Studies of Management and Organization,* Winter 1982–1983, pp. 7–22.

10. Evert Van de Vliert and Nico W. Van Ypern, "Why Cross-National Differences in Role Overload? Don't Overlook Ambient Temperature!" *Academy of Management Journal,* Vol. 39, No. 4, 1996, pp. 986–1004.

11. Maureen J. Giovannini and Lynne M. H. Rosansky, *Anthropology and Management Consulting: Forging a New Alliance* (N.P.: National Association for the Practice of Anthropology, Bulletin 9, 1990), pp. 19–27. For discussion breaking techniques into four categories, see P. Christopher Earley, "International and Intercultural Management Research: What's Next?" *Academy of Management Journal,* Vol. 38, No. 2, 1995, pp. 327–340.

12. L. L. Cavalli-Sforza, M. W. Feldman, K. H. Chen, and S. M. Dornbusch, "Theory and Observation in Cultural Transmission," *Science,* Vol. 218, 1982, pp. 19–27.

13. Geert Hofstede, *Cultures and Organizations* (London: McGraw-Hill, 1991), p. 8.

14. James Le Moyne, "Army Women and the Saudis Shock One Another," *New York Times,* September 25, 1990, p. A1.

15. William H. Durham, "Applications of Evolutionary Culture Theory," *Annual Review of Anthropology,* Vol. 21, 1992, pp. 331–355.

16. Sally Engle Merry, "Anthropology, Law, and Transnational Processes," *Annual Review of Anthropology,* Vol. 21, 1992, p. 364.

17. Rigoberta Menchú, *I, Rigoberta Menchú: An Indian Woman in Guatemala* (London: Verso, 1984).

18. Rigoberta Menchú, "Asserting Our Dignity," *Harvard International Review,* Winter 1994-95, pp. 42–44+.

19. Vern Terpstra and Kenneth David, *The Cultural Environment of International Business,* 3rd ed. (Cincinnati: South-Western, 1991), p. 93.

20. "Big Mac vs. Sacred Cows," *Business Week,* March 1, 1993, p. 58.

21. Harry C. Triandis, "Dimensions of Cultural Variation as Parameters of Organizational Theories," *International Studies of Management and Organization,* Winter 1982–1983, pp. 143–144.

22. "China's Gender Imbalance," *Wall Street Journal,* June 7, 1990, p. A12.

23. Barbara Crossette, "Afghans Draw U.N. Warning Over Sex Bias," *New York Times,* October 8, 1996, p. A1.

24. "Comparing Women Around the World," *Wall Street Journal,* July 26, 1995, p. B1.

25. Kenneth Dreyfack, "You Don't Have to Be a Giant to Score Big Overseas," *Business Week,* April 13, 1987, p. 63.

26. Lin Leam Lin, *More and Better Jobs for Women—An Action Guide* (Geneva: International Labor Organization, 1996).

27. Francis Fukuyama, *Trust: The Social Virtues and the Creation of Prosperity* (New York: The Free Press, 1995).

28. Max Weber, "The Protestant Ethic and the Spirit of Capitalism," and Kember Fullerton, "Calvinism and Capitalism," both in *Culture and Management,* Ross A. Webber, ed. (Homewood, Ill.: Richard D. Irwin, 1969), pp. 91–112.

29. Robert Taylor, "Work Culture That Brings No Satisfaction," *Financial Times,* August 25, 1995, p. 8, referring to a study by ISR, International Survey Research.

30. Jean J. Boddewyn, "Fitting Socially in Fortress Europe: Understanding, Reaching, and Impressing Europeans," *Business Horizons,* November–December 1992, pp. 35–43.

31. R. Inden, "Tradition Against Itself," *American Ethnologist,* Vol. 13, No. 4, 1986, pp. 762–775; and P. Chatterjee, *Nationalist Thoughts and the Colonial World: A Derivative Discourse* (London: Zed Books, 1986).

32. Triandis, op. cit., pp. 159–160.

33. Everett E. Hagen, *The Theory of Social Change: How Economic Growth Begins* (Homewood, Ill.: Richard D. Irwin, 1962), p. 378.

34. David C. McClelland, *The Achieving Soci-*

ety (Princeton, N.J.: Van Nostrand, 1961); David C. McClelland, "Business Drives and National Achievement," *Harvard Business Review,* July–August 1962, pp. 92–112; and M. L. Maehr and J. G. Nicholls, "Culture and Achievement Motivations: A Second Look," in *Studies in Cross Cultural Psychology,* Neil Warren, ed. (London: Academic Press, 1980), Vol. 2, Chapter 6.

35. Geert Hofstede, "National Cultures in Four Dimensions," *International Studies of Management and Organization,* Spring-Summer 1983, pp. 46–74.

36. Abraham Maslow, *Motivation and Personality* (New York: Harper, 1954).

37. Hofstede, op. cit., pp. 46–74; and for an earlier comparison among countries, see Mason Haire, Edwin Ghiselli, and Lyman Porter, *Managerial Thinking* (New York: Wiley, 1966), pp. 90–103.

38. Mary Jordan, "Respect Is Dwindling in the Hallowed Halls," *Washington Post,* June 20, 1994, p. A3, citing data collected by the Carnegie Foundation for the Advancement of Teaching in a survey of 20,000 professors in 13 nations and Hong Kong.

39. Hofstede, op. cit., pp. 54–55; Boddewyn, op. cit., p. 36.

40. Hofstede, loc. cit.

41. Stephen Knack, "Low Trust, Slow Growth," *Financial Times,* June 26, 1996, p. 12; and Francis Fukuyama, *Trust: The Social Virtues and the Creation of Prosperity* (London: Hamish Hamilton, 1995).

42. Pearl, loc. cit.

43. L. L. Cummings, D. L. Harnett, and D. J. Stevens, "Risk, Fate, Conciliation and Trust: An International Study of Attitudinal Differences among Executives," *Academy of Management Journal,* September 1971, p. 294, found differences among the United States, Greece, Spain, Central Europe, and Scandinavia.

44. R. M. Kanter, "Transcending Business Boundaries: 12,000 World Managers View Change," *Harvard Business Review,* May–June 1991, pp. 151–164.

45. Book review of Patricia Gercik, *On the Track with the Japanese* (Kodansha, 1992), by James B. Treece, *Business Week,* December 28, 1992, p. 20.

46. John J. Lawrence and Reh-song Yeh, "The Influence of Mexican Culture on the Use of Japanese Manufacturing Techniques in Mexico," *Management International Review,* Vol. 34, No. 1, 1994, pp. 49–66; P. Christopher Earley, "East Meets West Meets Mideast: Further Explorations of Collectivistic and Individualistic Work Groups," *Academy of Management Journal,* Vol. 36, No. 2, 1993, pp. 319–346.

47. Don Clark, "Hey, #@*% Amigo, Can You Translate the Word 'Gaffte'?" *Wall Street Journal,* July 8, 1996, p. B6.

48. Barry Newman, "Global Chatter: The World Speaks English, But Often None Too Well," *Asia Wall Street Journal,* March 23, 1995, p. 1+.

49. Vivian Ducat, "American Spoken Here—and Everywhere," *Travel & Leisure,* Vol. 16, No. 10, October 1986, pp. 168–169; Bill Bryson, *The Mother Tongue: English and How It Got That Way* (New York: Morrow, 1990).

50. Newman, op. cit.; Mark Nicholson, "Language Error 'Was Cause of Indian Air Disaster,'" *Financial Times,* November 14, 1996, p. 1.

51. This term was first used by Edward T. Hall, "The Silent Language in Overseas Business," *Harvard Business Review,* May–June 1960, and included five variables (time, space, things, friendships, and agreements).

52. Ibid.

53. Emmanuelle Ferrieux, "Hidden Messages," *World Press Review,* July 1989, p. 39.

54. For a survey of major research contributions, see Harry C. Triandis, "Reflections on Trends in Cross-Cultural Research," *Journal of Cross-Cultural Psychology,* March 1980, pp. 46–48.

55. Benjamin Lee Whorf, *Language, Thought and Reality* (New York: Wiley, 1956), p. 13.

56. Segall, op. cit., pp. 96–99.

57. Tony Horwitz, "Iceland Pushes Back English Invasion in War of the Words," *Wall Street Journal,* July 25, 1990, p. A8.

58. For an examination of subtle differences within northern Europe, see Malene Djursaa, "North Europe Business Culture: Britain vs. Denmark and Germany," *European Management Journal,* Vol. 12, No. 2, June 1994, pp. 138–146.

59. E. Glenn, *Man and Mankind: Conflict and Communication Between Cultures* (Norwood, N.J.: Ablex, 1981).

60. "Sensitivity Kick," *Wall Street Journal,* December 30, 1992, p. A1.

61. Peter Gosling, "Culture and Commerce: What's in a Name?" *Southeast Asia Business,* No. 6, Summer 1985, pp. 30–38; Frank L. Acuff, "Just Call Me Mr. Ishmael," *Export Today,* July 1995, p. 14.

62. A list of books appears in Katherine Glover, "Do's & Taboos," *Business America,* August 13, 1990, p. 5. See also Roger Axtell, *Do's and Taboos Around the World* (New York: John Wiley, 1992).

63. Philip R. Harris and Robert T. Moran, *Managing Cultural Differences* (Houston: Gulf, 1979), p. 88, quoting Kalervo Oberg.

64. Adrian Furnham and Stephen Bochner, *Culture Shock* (London: Methuen, 1986), p. 234.

65. Ben L. Kedia and Rabi S. Bhagat, "Cultural Constraints on Transfer of Technology Across Nations: Implications for Research in International and Comparative Management," *Academy of Management Review,* Vol. 13, No. 4, October 1988, pp. 559–571.

66. Two recent books that explain differences among these countries are Judith Miller, *God Has Ninety-Nine Names* (New York: Simon & Schuster, 1996); and Bernard Lewis, *The Middle East: 2000 Years of History from the Rise of Christianity to the Present Day* (London: Weidenfeld & Nicolson, 1996).

67. Hans B. Thorelli, "The Multi-National Corporation as a Change Agent," *The Southern Journal of Business,* July 1966, p. 5.

68. Geraldine Brooks, "Eritrea's Leaders Angle for Sea Change in Nation's Diet to Prove Fish Isn't Foul," *Wall Street Journal,* June 2, 1994, p. A10.

69. Marjorie Miller, "A Clash of Corporate Cultures," *Los Angeles Times,* August 15, 1992, p. A1.

70. Patrick M. Reilly, "Pitfalls of Exporting Magazine Formulas," *Wall Street Journal,* July 24, 1995, p. B1+.

71. Roger Marshall and Indriyo Gitosudarmo, "Variation in the Characteristics of Opinion Leaders Across Cultural Borders," *Journal of International Consumer Marketing,* Vol. 8, No. 1, 1995, pp. 5–21.

72. Bernard Lewis, "Western Culture Must Go," *Wall Street Journal,* May 2, 1988, p. 18.

73. Merry, op. cit., pp. 366–367.

74. Boye de Mente, *Chinese Etiquette and Ethics in Business* (Lincolnwood, Ill.: NTC, 1989).

75. William Stockton, "Bribes Are Called a Way of Life in Mexico," *New York Times,* October 25, 1986, p. 3.

76. Pirkko Lammi, "My Vision of Business in Europe," in *Business Ethics in a New Europe,* Jack Mahoney and Elizabeth Vallance, eds. (Dordrecht, the Netherlands: Kluwer Academic, 1992), pp. 11–12.

77. "Golden Arches Raise Eyebrows in Poland," *The State* (Columbia, S.C.), September 10, 1993, p. 5A.

78. Kerin Hope, "Aristotle Provides Inspiration in Fight for Cultural Crock of Gold," *Financial Times,* June 16, 1996, p. 22.

79. Andrew Jack, "French Prepare to Repel English Advance," *Financial Times,* January 7, 1997, p. 2.

80. D. Paul Schafer, "Cultures and Economics," *Futures,* Vol. 26, No. 8, 1994, pp. 830–845.

81. William Kuyken, John Orley, Patricia Hudelson, and Norman Sartorius, "Quality of Life Assessment Across Cultures," *International Journal of Mental Health,* Vol. 23, No. 2, 1994, pp. 5–27

82. Alison Dundes Renteln, "The Concept of Human Rights," *Anthropos,* Vol. 83, 1988, pp. 343–364.

83. Ingrid Mattson, "Law, Culture, and Human Rights: Islamic Perspectives in the Contemporary World," summary of a conference at Yale Law School (November 5–6, 1993) in *The American Journal of*

Islamic Social Sciences, Vol. 11, No. 3, 1994, pp. 446–450.

84. Ian Jamieson, "The Concept of Culture and Its Relevance for an Analysis of Business Enterprise in Different Societies," *International Study of Management and Organization,* Winter 1982, pp. 71–72.

85. Foster, op. cit., p. 236.

86. J. D. Child, "Culture, Contingency and Capitalism in the Cross-National Study of Organizations," in *Research in Organizational Behavior,* L. L. Cummings and B.

M. Staw, eds. (Greenwich, Conn.: JAI, 1981), Vol. III, pp. 303–356; Andre Laurent, "The Cross-Cultural Puzzle of International Human Resource Management," *Human Resource Management,* Vol. 25, No. 1, pp. 91–102.

87. See, for example, "Asians May Ban Islamic Sect," *Wall Street Journal,* August 4, 1994, p. A6; and Simone Veil, "Forging Cultural Unity: Assimilation and Integration in France," *Harvard International Review,* Summer 1994, pp. 30–31.

88. Lourdes Arizpe, "On Cultural and Social Sustainability," *Development,* Vol. 1, 1989, pp. 5–10.

89. J. Ørstrøm Møller, "The Competitiveness of U.S. Industry: A View from the Outside," *Business Horizons,* November–December 1991, pp. 27–34; Richard Tomkins, "US Tops Poll on Cultural Exports," *Financial Times,* December 4, 1996, p. 9.

Testing Your Understanding—Unit II

*International Business, Chapter 2: The Cultural
Environments Facing Business*

Pages 58–66
CHECKING YOUR COMPREHENSION

Identify the following statements as true or false.

1. A local society usually applies the same rules of behavior to citizens and foreigners.

2. Unless a company changes its business practices, it will never be successful in a foreign country.

3. A decentralized government often creates a diverse country.

Choose the best answer for each of the following questions.

4. According to the chapter, which of the following best defines a nation?
   a. people within a geographic region who share a common ethnic or racial background
   b. a governmental entity that accommodates several different ethnicities, classes, and subcultures
   c. people within political boundaries who share a common history, common rituals, and common symbols
   d. a physical or geographical region bound by centralized laws and government institutions

5. In the introduction, the authors indicate that all of the following topics will be discussed in this chapter except
   a. legal issues facing a company as it expands into international markets.
   b. factors influencing international business.
   c. alternative ways of dealing with cultural differences.
   d. changes in a company doing business in an international arena.

6. Which of the following factors would probably create the most flexible culture?
   a. strong religious beliefs
   b. geographical obstacles
   c. extended family structure
   d. a language similar to that in an adjacent country

7. The process of introducing some, but not all, elements of an outside culture is referred to as
   a. creolization
   b. indegenization
   c. cultural diffusion
   d. all of the above

Answer the following questions.

8. Identify four of the major influences on cultural values.

9. Study map 2.2. Identify the major languages in South America.

10. Study map 2.3. Identify the major religions in Africa.

11. Identify two ways researchers learn about different cultures in order to aid businesses.

Define each term as it is used in the chapter.

12. society

13. culture

14. cultural imperialism

Discussion and Critical Thinking Questions

1. Identify three things PRI (the company in Case Study 1) could have done differently to make its experience more profitable.

2. Using the information in the chapter as background, discuss the relationship between culture, economics and politics.

3. Using the information in the chapter as background, what do you think is the long-term effect of cultural imperialism?

Pages 66–79
CHECKING YOUR COMPREHENSION

Identify the following statements as true or false.

1. Although ideas about how hard one needs to work differ among countries, the prestige attached to a business management job is consistently high.

2. According to the chapter, barriers to individuals based on gender may be legal as well as social.

3. In cultures in which trust between most people is low, business costs also tend to be lower.

Choose the best answer for each of the following questions.

4. According to the chapter, all of the following aspects of communication can affect business communications except
   a. distance between people.
   b. hierarchy of needs.
   c. perceptions of time.
   d. translations.

5. According to the chapter, high-need achievers typically
   a. continue to be highly motivated even when feedback is delayed.
   b. have a high collectivism score.
   c. prefer to follow autocratic company policies rather than try innovative personal solutions to problems.
   d. advance in their careers by calculating risks against probability of success in a series of goals.

6. Which of the following statements is true about people/cultures motivated by a sense of collectivism?
   a. Loyalty is always to the work group.
   b. Time away from work is relatively unimportant since work provides for the social needs of the individual.
   c. Personal safety is more important than personal challenges.
   d. The need for self-determination leads them to establish their own businesses.

Answer each of the following questions.

7. List the five major categories of behavior practices that affect business.

8. List the three major group affiliations discussed in the chapter.

9. Identify two reasons why English is gaining importance in the international business world.

10. Explain what is meant by the Protestant work ethic.

Define each term as it is used in the chapter.

11. hierarchy of needs

12. power distance

13. uncertainty avoidance

14. monochronic

15. polychronic

Discussion and Critical Thinking Questions

1. In the chapter, the authors state that "in societies where there is low trust outside the family ... family-run companies are more successful than large business organizations, where people are from many different families. The difficulty of sustaining large-scale companies retards these countries' economic development." In this comment, what value do the authors place on small businesses in the international economy? Do they maintain the same stance toward small businesses throughout the chapter?

2. Using the five major categories of behavior that affect international business, create a "hierarchy of effect." Which of these behaviors is the most basic? Which is a higher-order effect? Why?

3. How would you describe the United States in each of the following categories?
- importance of family
- masculinity index
- importance of occupation
- acquired group membership

4. What is meant by "effects of habit"?

Pages 80–90
CHECKING YOUR COMPREHENSION

Identify the following statements as true or false.

1. A country with high economic advances is more likely to have business practices exported than one with less economic advancement.

2. Reverse culture shock refers to the shock people feel on encountering a foreigner who has recently moved into their country bringing different ideas.

3. A company exporting a product to another country and one manufacturing a product within another country must address the same cultural factors.

Choose the best answer for each of the following questions.

4. Map 2.4 suggests that business ventures between which of the following pairs of countries would have the most difficulties?
   a. Brazil and Spain
   b. United States and South Africa
   c. Greece and Turkey
   d. Belgium and Portugal

5. Which of the following cultural differences would a person most likely be aware of as a potential source of difficulty?
   a. problem-solving techniques
   b. perceptions of time
   c. food preferences
   d. attitudes about privacy

6. It can be inferred from the passage that which of the following changes would meet the most resistance?
   a. gifts to business associates in Mexico
   b. introduction of a new fish product in Japan
   c. an innovation advocated by a long-term employee in Korea
   d. "made in U.S.A." labels in English on goods sold in France

Answer each of the following questions.

7. List the three stages through which people working in different cultures typically pass.

8. List four factors a company must consider in deciding whether to adapt or transplant home operating systems to an international setting.

9. List three types of resistance to a homogenous international culture.

10. List five factors companies should consider in order to make change easier.

Define each term as it is used in the chapter.

11. culture shock

12. reverse culture shock

13. polycentrism

14. ethnocentrism

15. geocentrism

16. relativism

17. normativism

18. nationalism

19. globalization

Discussion and Critical Thinking Questions

1. Why is it advantageous for young executives to spend time in another country?

2. In what ways do the employees of PRI (case example 1) illustrate three types of ethnocentrism?

3. Why will the rise in subcultures affect international business?

4. According to the chapter, the concept of "quality of life" varies substantially among cultures. How do the differing concepts hinder the development of universal standards of behavior, codes of ethics, or declaration of human rights?

CHAPTER REVIEW

End of Chapter Analysis

Choose the best answer for each of the following questions.

1. Which of the following best describes the overall purpose of the chapter?
    a. an exploration of typical changes that occur in a company as it moves from a national to an international area
    b. an analysis of cultural issues that can affect international business and suggestions for dealing with them
    c. a plan for changing customs in a country in which a company is about to do business
    d. predictions on how companies will need to adapt in future negotiations with other cultures

2. Which of the following statements best represents the relation of the box entitled "Ethical Dilemmas and Social Responsibilities" to the rest of the chapter?
    a. The chapter analyzes causes of differences, while the box synthesizes changes to make.
    b. The chapter advances a theoretical argument on reasons for cultural differences, while the box provides specific examples to support the theories.
    c. The box introduces an alternative interpretation on how important cultural differences are.
    d. The chapter focuses on conflicts arising between representations of two different cultures, while the box focuses on conflicts arising within an individual or company that is trying to deal with another culture.

3. Which of the following sentences most clearly reveals the authors' attitude toward doing business in other cultures?
    a. "When in Rome, do as the Romans."
    b. "A company must consider the expected cost-benefit relationship of any adjustments it makes abroad."
    c. "The best international executive was one who retained a belief in the fundamentals of the home point of view while also understanding foreign attitudes."
    d. "International companies have been very successful in introducing new products, technologies, and operating procedures to foreign countries."

Group Project

Several countries are used as examples in the chapter (Japan, Germany, etc.). Choose one of the countries and develop a business profile for that country that you would present to an employee about to move there. Include in your profile the other types of facts or information you need to gather.

Journal Ideas

1. Write a plan for how you could become more culturally aware, exploring three specific suggestions.

2. What three specific areas do you think would be most troublesome for you if you were living in a different culture?

UNIT III

From

H. L. Capron

Computers:
Tools for an Information Age
Brief Edition

Chapter 8:
Security and Privacy:
Computers and the Internet

Harley Bjornson owns his own manufacturing company, a company begun by his father. His father had come to America from Norway and knew something about fishing boats. As a young man, the father invented and received a patent for a winch of particular interest to gill-netters. That invention has been a large part of the success of the company, now run by Harley and his son Erik.

It was Erik who pushed Harley into the computer age, making a case for seven networked personal computers. The two of them, working with a consultant, gave a lot of thought to what business functions could be computerized and who should use the computers for what purpose. They even planned to access the Internet. They gave no thought, however, to security or privacy. They came to regret that oversight in January 1997, the month of the mudslide. That month, as it turned out, was significant in more ways than one.

The mudslide followed two weeks of first snow and then torrential rains. Harley's office building, at the bottom of a hill, was overcome by a mudslide that ruined all the furniture—and the four computers—on the first floor. The server, fortunately, was on the second floor. Harley had no disaster plan in place. Replacing the computers was the least of it; several files that had been scattered among them were lost, and there were no backup copies. The business limped along for several weeks while the files were painstakingly reconstructed.

Harley contracted with computer professionals to help sort out the mess. In the process, a consultant discovered that their network had been invaded by intruders. In particular, a patent application that his son was preparing on a new invention, possibly another breakthrough in winch technology, had been tampered with. Looking further, they also discovered that the records for one employee showed a trail of Internet access to distinctly unbusinesslike sites. Finally, old e-mail records showed that one employee sent hundreds of non-business communications, some of them complaining about the boss. Rather overwhelmed, Harley and Erik sat down for a serious discussion with the computer professionals. They mapped out a disaster plan and employee computer-use policies.

They also built a large retaining wall between the hill and their office building.

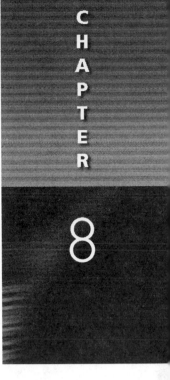

Security and Privacy

Computers and the Internet

► A First Look at Security and Privacy

There was a time when security and privacy issues related to computers were easily managed: simply lock the computer room door. Those centralized days are, of course, long gone. Now, in theory, anyone can hook up to any computer from any location. In light of data communications access, the first issue is security. The vast files of computer-stored information must be kept secure—safe from destruction, accidental damage, theft, even espionage.

A second issue is privacy. Private data—salaries, medical information, Social Security numbers, bank balances, and much more—must be kept from prying eyes. The problems are many and the solutions complex. The advent of the Internet and its escalating expansion has only heightened the existing problems and added new problems of its own.

These issues and more will be addressed in this chapter as we march through security, privacy, and the specific problems associated with the Internet. However, we begin with a fascinating aspect of the security problem: computer crime.

► Computer Crime

It was 5 o'clock in the morning, and 14-year-old Randy Miller was startled to see a man climbing in his bedroom window. "FBI," the man announced, "and that computer is mine." So ended the computer caper in San Diego where 23 teenagers, ages 13 to 17, had used their home computers to invade computer systems as far away as Massachusetts. The teenagers are **hackers**, people who attempt to gain access to computer systems illegally, usually from a personal computer, via a data communications network.

The term *hacker* used to mean a person with significant computer expertise, but the term has taken on the more sinister meaning with the advent of computer miscreants. In this case the hackers did not use the system to steal money or property. But they did create fictitious accounts and destroyed or changed some data files. The FBI's entry through the bedroom window was calculated: The agents figured that, given even a moment's warning, the teenagers were clever enough to alert each other via computer.

This story—except for the name—is true. Hackers ply their craft for a variety of reasons but most often to show off for their peers or to harass people they do not like. A favorite trick, for example, is to turn a rival's telephone into a pay phone, so that when his or her parents try to dial a number an operator would interrupt to say, "Please deposit 35 cents." A hacker may have more sinister motives, such as getting computer services without paying for them or getting information to sell.

You will probably not be surprised to learn that hackers have invaded web sites. These vandals show up with what amounts to a digital spray can, defacing sites with taunting boasts, graffiti, and their own private jokes. Although the victims feel violated, the perpetrators view their activities as mere pranks.

Hackers and Other Miscreants

Hacking has long been thought the domain of teenagers with time on their hands. The pattern is changing, however. A recent government survey showed that the computer systems of over half of the largest U.S. corporations had been invaded, but not by teenagers. Most intruders were competitors stealing proprietary information. For example, suppose a biomedical company discovers just one little research secret in a competitor's computer files; the snooping company may then be the first to market with a drug that the invaded company has been working on for years. Even more astounding, federal investigators told a U.S. Senate hearing that the U.S. Department of Defense computers are attacked more than 200,000 times per year. Most worrisome is the emerging computer attack abilities of other nations, which, in a worst-case scenario, could seriously degrade the military's ability to deploy and sustain military forces.

Hackers ply their craft by surprisingly low-tech means. Using what is called **social engineering**, a tongue-in-cheek term for con artist actions, hackers simply persuade unsuspecting people to give away their passwords over the phone. Recognizing the problem, employers are educating their employees to be alert to such scams.

Getting Practical

KEEPING A SECRET

Employers wish that computer passwords were better-kept secrets. Here are some hints on password use.

■ Do not name your password after your child or car or pet, an important date, or your phone number. Passwords that are easy to remember are also easy to crack.

■ Make passwords as random as possible. Include both letters and numbers. The more characters the better. Embed at least one nonalphabetic character, and consider mixing upper- and lowercase letters. Example: Go*TOP6.

■ Keep your password in your head or in a safe. Astonishingly, an occasional thoughtless user will scribble the password on paper and stick it on

the computer screen where anyone can see it.

■ Change your password often, at least once a month. In some installations, passwords are changed so seldom that they

become known to many people, thus defeating the purpose.

■ Do not fall for hacker phone scams—"social engineering"—to obtain your password. Typical ruses are callers posing as a neophyte employee ("Gosh, I'm so confused, could you talk me through it?"); a system expert ("We're checking a problem in the network that seems to be coming from your workstation. Could you please verify your password?"); a telephone company employee ("There seems to be a problem on your phone line"); or even an angry top manager ("This is outrageous! How do I get into these files anyway?").

Most people are naturally inclined to be helpful. Do not be inappropriately so. Keep in mind that you will be—at the very least—embarrassed if you are the source of information to a hacker who damages your company.

Hackers are only a small fraction of the security problem. The most serious losses are caused by electronic pickpockets who are usually a good deal older and not so harmless. Consider these examples:

- A brokerage clerk sat at his terminal in Denver and, with a few taps of the keys, transformed 1700 shares of his own stock, worth $1.50 per share, to the same number of shares in another company worth ten times that much.
- A Seattle bank employee used her electronic fund transfer code to move certain bank funds to an account held by her boyfriend as a "joke"; both the money and the boyfriend disappeared.
- A keyboard operator in Oakland, California, changed some delivery addresses to divert several thousand dollars' worth of department store goods into the hands of accomplices.
- A ticket clerk at the Arizona Veteran's Memorial Coliseum issued full-price basketball tickets for admission and then used her computer to record the sales as half-price tickets and pocketed the difference.

These stories point out that computer crime is not always the flashy, front-page news about geniuses getting away with millions of dollars. These people are ordinary employees in ordinary businesses—committing computer crimes.

The problems of computer crime have been aggravated in recent years by increased access to computers (Figure 8-1). More employees now have access to computers on their jobs. In fact, computer crime is often just white-collar crime with a new medium: Every time an employee is trained on the computer at work, he or she also gains knowledge that—potentially—could be used to harm the company.

The Changing Face of Computer Crime

Computer crime once fell into a few simple categories, such as theft of software or destruction of data. The dramatically increased access to networks has changed the focus to damage that can be done by unscrupulous people with online access. The most frequently reported computer crimes fall into these categories:

- **Credit card fraud.** Customer numbers are floating all over public and private networks, in varying states of protection. Some are captured and used fraudulently.
- **Data communications fraud.** This category covers a broad spectrum, including piggybacking on someone else's network, the use of an office network for personal purposes, and computer-directed diversion of funds.
- **Unauthorized access to computer files.** This general snooping category covers everything from accessing confidential employee records to the theft of trade secrets and product pricing structure.
- **Unlawful copying of copyrighted software.** Whether the casual sharing of copyrighted software among friends or assembly line copying by organized crime, unlawful copying incurs major losses for software vendors.

Although it is not our purpose to write a how-to book on computer crime, the margin note called *Some "Bad Guy" Tricks* mentions the methods some criminals use.

Disgruntled or militant employee could

- Sabotage equipment or programs
- Hold data or programs hostage

Competitor could

- Sabotage operations
- Engage in espionage
- Steal data or programs
- Photograph records, documentation, or CRT screen displays

Data control worker could

- Insert data
- Delete data
- Bypass controls
- Sell information

Clerk/supervisor could

- Forge or falsify data
- Embezzle funds
- Engage in collusion with people inside or outside the company

System user could

- Sell data to competitors
- Obtain unauthorized information

Operator could

- Copy files
- Destroy files

User requesting reports could

- Sell information to competitors
- Receive unauthorized information

Engineer could

- Install "bugs"
- Sabotage system
- Access security information

Data conversion worker could

- Change codes
- Insert data
- Delete data

Programmer could

- Steal programs or data
- Embezzle via programming
- Bypass controls

Report distribution worker could

- Examine confidential reports
- Keep duplicates of reports

Trash collector could

- Sell reports or duplicates to competitors

Figure 8-1 The perils of increased access. By letting your imagination loose, you can visualize many ways in which people can compromise computer security. Computer-related crime would be far more rampant if all the people in these positions took advantage of their access to computers.

Discovery and Prosecution

Prosecuting the computer criminal is difficult for several reasons. To begin with, discovery is often difficult. Many times the crime simply goes undetected. In addition, crimes that are detected are—an estimated 85 percent of the time—never reported to the authorities. By law, banks have to make a report when their computer systems have been compromised, but other businesses do not. Often they choose not to report such crimes because they are worried about their reputations and credibility in the community.

Most computer crimes are discovered by accident. For example, a bank employee changed a program to add 10¢ to every customer service charge under $10 and $1 to every charge over $10. He then placed this overage into the last account, a bank account he opened himself in the name of Zzwicke. The system worked fairly well, generating several hundred dollars each month, until the bank initiated a new marketing campaign in which it singled out for special honors the very first depositor—and the very last. In another instance some employees of a city welfare department created a fictitious work force, complete with Social Security numbers, and programmed the computer to issue paychecks, which the employees would then intercept and cash. They were discovered when a police officer investigated an illegally parked overdue rental car and found the fraudulent checks inside.

Even if a computer crime is detected, prosecution is by no means assured. There are a number of reasons for this. First, some law enforcement agencies do not fully understand the complexities of computer-related fraud. Second, few attorneys are qualified to handle computer crime cases. Third, judges and juries are not always educated about computers and may not understand the nature of the violation or the seriousness of the crime.

In short, the chances of having a computer crime go undetected are, unfortunately, good. And the chances that, if detected, there will be no ramifications are also good: A computer criminal may not go to jail, may not be found guilty if prosecuted, and may not even be prosecuted.

But this situation is changing. Since Congress passed the **Computer Fraud and Abuse Act** in 1986, there has been a growing awareness of computer crime on the national level. This law is supplemented by state statutes; most states have passed some form of computer crime law. Computer criminals who are successfully prosecuted are subject to fines, jail time, and confiscation of their computer equipment.

▶ Security: Playing It Safe

As you can see from the previous section, the computer industry has been vulnerable in the matter of security. **Security** is a system of safeguards designed to protect a computer system and data from deliberate or accidental damage or access by unauthorized persons. That means safeguarding the system against such threats as natural disasters, fire, accidents, vandalism, theft or destruction of data, industrial espionage, and hackers (Figure 8-2).

Identification and Access: Who Goes There?

How does a computer system detect whether you are the person who should be allowed access to it? Various means have been devised to give

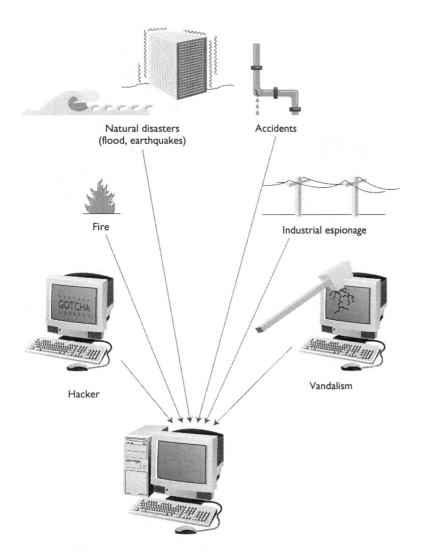

access to authorized people without compromising the system. These means fall into four broad categories: what you have, what you know, what you do, and what you are.

- **What you have.** You may have a key, badge, token, or plastic card to give you physical access to the computer room or to a locked-up terminal or personal computer. A card with a magnetized strip, for example, can give you access to your bank account via a remote cash machine. Taking this a step further, some employees begin each business day by donning an **active badge**, a clip-on identification card with an embedded computer chip. The badge signals its wearer's location—legal or otherwise—by sending out infrared signals, which are read by sensors sprinkled around the building.
- **What you know.** Standard what-you-know items are a password or an identification number for your bank cash machine. Cipher locks on doors require that you know the correct combination of numbers.
- **What you do.** In their daily lives people often sign documents as a way of proving who they are. Though a signature is difficult to copy, forgery is not impossible. Today, software can verify both scanned and online signatures.
- **What you are.** Now it gets interesting. Some security systems use **biometrics,** the science of measuring individual body characteristics.

(a)

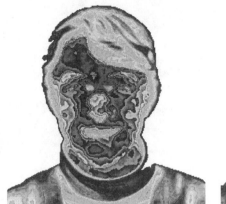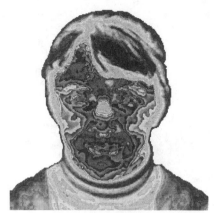

(b)

Figure 8-3 Identification. (a) The eye can be a means of personal identification. A user first keys a unique identification code number. The security system then matches the person's unique retina pattern to the individual's computer-stored retina pattern for conclusive identification of authorized users. (b) A person's entire face is used for identification in some security systems. Identification is based on a unique pattern of heat radiating from an individual's facial blood vessels.

Fingerprinting may seem to be old news, but not when you simply insert your finger into an identification machine. Some systems use the characteristics of the entire hand. Another approach is identification by voice recognition. Even newer is the concept of identification by the retina of the eye, which has a pattern that is harder to duplicate than a voiceprint (Figure 8-3a), or by the entire face, which draws its uniqueness from heat radiating from blood vessels (Figure 8-3b).

Some systems use a combination of the preceding four categories. For example, access to an automated teller machine requires both something you have—a plastic card—and something you know—a personal identification number (PIN).

When Disaster Strikes: What Do You Have to Lose?

In New York a power outage shut down computer operations and effectively halted business, air traffic, and transportation throughout the United States. In Italy armed terrorists singled out corporate and state computer centers as targets for attack and, during a ten-month period, bombed ten such centers throughout the country. In California a poem, a pansy, a bag of cookies, and a message, "Please have a cookie and a nice day," were left at the Vandenberg Air Force Base computer installation—along with five demolished mainframe computers. Computer installations of any kind can be struck by natural or man-made disasters that can lead to security violations. What kinds of problems might this cause an organization?

Your first thoughts might be of the hardware, the computer and its related equipment. But loss of hardware is not a major problem in itself; the loss will be covered by insurance, and hardware can be replaced. The true problem with hardware loss is the diminished processing ability that exists while managers find a substitute facility and return the installation to its former state. The ability to continue processing data is critical. Some information industries, such as banking, could literally go out of business in a matter of days if their computer operations were suspended. Loss of software should not be a problem if the organization has heeded industry warnings—and used common sense—to make backup copies of program files.

A more important problem is the loss of data. Imagine trying to reassemble lost or destroyed files of customer records, accounts receivable, or design data for a new airplane. The costs would be staggering. Software and data security will be presented in more detail later in this chapter. First, however, consider an overview of disaster recovery, the steps to restoring processing ability.

Disaster Recovery Plan

A **disaster recovery plan** is a method of restoring computer processing operations and data files if operations are halted or files are damaged by major destruction. There are various approaches. Some organizations revert temporarily to manual services, but life without the computer can be difficult indeed. Others arrange to buy time at a service bureau, but this is inconvenient for companies in remote or rural areas. If a single act, such as a fire, destroys your computing facility, it is possible that a mutual aid pact will help you get back on your feet. In such a plan two or more companies agree to lend each other computing power if one of them has a problem. This would be of little help, however, if there were a regional disaster and many companies needed assistance.

Banks and other organizations with survival dependence on computers sometimes form a **consortium**, a joint venture to support a complete computer facility. Such a facility is completely available and routinely tested but used only in the event of a disaster. Among these facilities, a **hot site** is a fully equipped computer center, with hardware, environmental controls, security, and communications facilities. A **cold site** is an environmentally suitable empty shell in which a company can install its own computer system.

The use of such a facility or any type of recovery at all depends on advance planning—specifically, the disaster recovery plan. The idea of such a plan is that everything except the hardware has been stored in a safe place somewhere else. The storage location should be several miles away, so it will not be affected by local physical forces, such as a hurricane. Typical items stored at the backup site are program and data files, program listings, program and operating systems documentation, hardware inventory lists, output forms, and a copy of the disaster plan manual.

The disaster recovery plan should include a list of priorities identifying the programs that must be up and running first, plans for notifying employees of changes in locations and procedures, a list of needed equipment and where it can be obtained, a list of alternative computing facilities, and procedures for handling input and output data in a different environment.

Computer installations actually perform emergency drills. At some unexpected moment a notice is given that "disaster has struck," and the computer professionals must run the critical systems at some other site.

Software Security

Software security has been an industry concern for years. Initially, there were many questions: Who owns custom-made software? Is the owner the person who wrote the program or the company for which the author wrote the program? What is to prevent a programmer from taking copies of programs from one job to another? The answer to these questions are well established. If the author of the software—the programmer—is in the employ of the organization, the software belongs to the organization, not the programmer. The programmer may not take the software along to

LEAVING CANADA

STOP AND REPORT TO U.S. CUSTOMS

They Know My Voice at the Border

If you have ever crossed the border between the United States and Canada, you may have waited in a long line of cars. But if you happened to pass through at night, you were probably processed quickly. Both of these statements apply, however, only at major border crossings, which are open 24 hours a day.

If you want to pass through an obscure open-only-sometimes crossing, you may have to make a run for it at closing time. This is especially hard on the locals who must cross often. If you miss the border opening times at Scobey, Montana, for example, you face a 120-mile detour to the nearest crossing. But help is now in place. It is computer help, of course: an electronic border crossing.

After applying to the local Immigration and Naturalization office, an approved user receives an ID card, is assigned a four-digit number, and records a brief voice phrase. To get across an unattended border, a user need only punch in the number and then speak the prerecorded words, and—presto—the gate opens.

the next job. If the programmer is a consultant, however, the ownership of the software produced should be spelled out specifically in the contract—otherwise, the parties enter extremely murky legal waters. According to a U.S. Supreme Court decision, software can be copyrighted.

Data Security

We have discussed the security of hardware and software. Now consider the security of data, which is one of an organization's most important assets. Here too there must be planning for security. Usually, this is done by security officers who are part of top management.

What steps can be taken to prevent theft or alteration of data? There are several data-protection techniques; these will not individually (or even collectively) guarantee security, but they make a good start.

Secured Waste   Discarded printouts, printer ribbons, and the like can be sources of information to unauthorized persons. This kind of waste can be made secure by the use of shredders or locked trash barrels.

Internal Controls   Internal controls are controls that are planned as part of the computer system. One example is a transaction log. This is a file of all accesses or attempted accesses to certain data.

Auditor Checks   Most companies have auditors go over the financial books. In the course of their duties, auditors frequently review computer programs and data. From a data security standpoint, auditors might also check to see who has accessed data during periods when that data is not usually used. Today auditors can use off-the-shelf audit software, programs that assess the validity and accuracy of the system's operations and output.

Applicant Screening   The weakest link in any computer security system is the people in it. At the very least, employers should verify the facts that job applicants list on their résumés to help weed out dishonest applicants before they are hired.

Passwords   A password is a secret word or number, or a combination of the two, that must be typed on the keyboard to gain access to a computer system. Cracking passwords is the most prevalent method of illicit entry to computer systems.

Built-in Software Protection   Software can be built into operating systems in ways that restrict access to the computer system. One form of software protection system matches a user number against a number assigned to the data being accessed. If a person does not get access, it is recorded that he or she tried to tap into some area to which that person was not authorized. Another form of software protection is a user profile: Information is stored about each user, including the files to which the user has legitimate access. The profile also includes each person's job function, budget number, skills, areas of knowledge, access privileges, supervisor, and loss-causing potential. These profiles are available for checking by managers if there is any problem.

Worms and Viruses: Uninvited Guests

Worms and *viruses* are rather unpleasant terms that have entered the jargon of the computer industry to describe some of the insidious ways that computer systems can be invaded.

A **worm** is a program that transfers itself from computer to computer over a network and plants itself as a separate file on the target computer's disks. One newsworthy worm, originated by Robert Morris when he was a student at Cornell University, traveled the length and breadth of the land through an electronic mail network, shutting down thousands of computers. The worm was injected into the network and multiplied uncontrollably, clogging the memories of infected computers until they could no longer function.

A virus, as its name suggests, is contagious. That is, a **virus**, a set of illicit instructions, passes itself on to other programs or documents with which it comes in contact. In its most basic form, a virus is the digital equivalent of vandalism. It can change or delete files, display words or obscene messages, or produce bizarre screen effects. In its most vindictive form, a virus can slowly sabotage a computer system and remain undetected for months, contaminating data or, in the case of the famous Michelangelo virus, wiping out your entire hard drive. A virus may be dealt with by means of a **vaccine**, or **antivirus**, a computer program that stops the spread of and often eradicates the virus. However, a **retrovirus** has the ability to fight back and may even delete antivirus software.

Viruses seem to show up when least expected. In one instance a call came to a company's information center at about 5:00 p.m. The caller's computer was making a strange noise. With the exception of an occasional beep, computers performing routine business chores do not usually make noises. Soon employees were calling from all over the company, all with "noisy" computers. One caller said that it might be a tune coming from the computer's small internal speaker. Finally, one caller recognized a tinny rendition of "Yankee Doodle," confirmation that an old virus had struck once again. The Yankee Doodle virus, once attached to a system, is scheduled to go off at 5:00 p.m. every eight days. Viruses, once considered merely a nuisance, are costing American business over $2 billion a year. Unfortunately, viruses are easily transmitted.

You may wonder who produces viruses. At one point, the mischief makers were merely teenagers with too much time on their hands. Now, virus makers are older and actually trade notes and tips on the Internet. They do what they do, psychologists say, mostly to impress their friends. Experts have estimated that there are hundreds of virus writers worldwide. However, although there are thousands of known viruses, most of the damage is caused by only a dozen or so.

Transmitting a Virus   Consider this typical example. A programmer secretly inserts a few viral instructions into a game called Kriss-Kross, which she then offers free to others via the Internet. Any takers download the game to their own computers. Now, each time a user runs Kriss-Kross—that is, loads it into memory—the virus is loaded too. The virus stays in memory, infecting any other program loaded until the computer is turned off again. The virus now has spread to other programs, and the process can be repeated again and again. In fact, each newly infected program becomes a virus carrier. Although many viruses are

Figure 8-4 An example of a virus invasion.

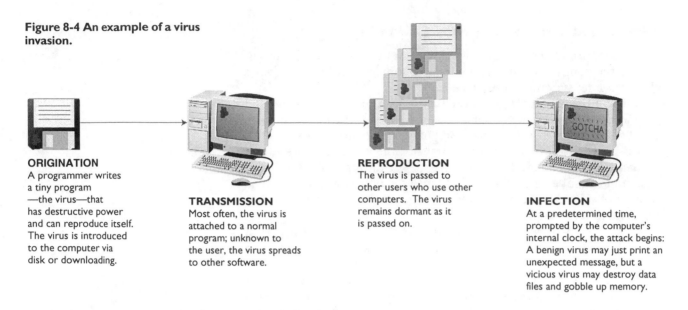

ORIGINATION
A programmer writes a tiny program —the virus—that has destructive power and can reproduce itself. The virus is introduced to the computer via disk or downloading.

TRANSMISSION
Most often, the virus is attached to a normal program; unknown to the user, the virus spreads to other software.

REPRODUCTION
The virus is passed to other users who use other computers. The virus remains dormant as it is passed on.

INFECTION
At a predetermined time, prompted by the computer's internal clock, the attack begins: A benign virus may just print an unexpected message, but a vicious virus may destroy data files and gobble up memory.

Figure 8-5 The Cascade virus. This virus attaches itself to the operating system and causes random letters in text to "drop" to a pile at the bottom of the screen display.

transmitted just this way via networks, the most common method is by passing diskettes from computer to computer (Figure 8-4).

Here is another typical scenario. An office worker puts a copy of a report on a diskette and slips it into her briefcase to take home. After shooing her children away from the new game they are playing on the computer, she sits down to work on the report. She does not know that a virus, borne by the kids' new software, has infected the diskette. When she takes the disk back to work, the virus is transmitted from her computer to the entire office network.

The most insidious viruses attach to the operating system. One virus, called Cascade, causes random text letters to "drop" to a pile at the bottom of the screen (Figure 8-5). Viruses attached to the operating system itself have greater potential for mischief.

A relative newcomer to the virus scene is the macro virus, which uses a program's own macro programming language to distribute itself. Unlike previous viruses, a macro virus does not infect a program; it infects a document. When you open the document that has the virus, any other documents opened in same session may get the virus too.

Damage from Viruses Most viruses remain dormant until triggered by some activity. For example, a virus called Jerusalem B activates itself every Friday the 13th and proceeds to erase any file you may try to load from your disk. Another virus includes instructions to add 1 to a counter each time the virus is copied to another disk. When the counter reaches 4, the virus erases all data files. But this is not the end of the destruction, of course; the three copied disks have also been infected.

The Concept virus, a relatively benign macro virus, refuses to let you save your document after you have made changes, saying the file is "read only." However, the Nuclear macro virus, among other things, destroys vital operating system files on any April 5th.

Prevention A word about prevention is in order. Although viruses are most commonly passed via diskettes, viruses can propagate by other means, such as local area networks, electronic mail, and the Internet. If your personal computer has a disk drive, a modem, or a network connector, it is vulnerable. Furthermore, viruses are rampant on some college campuses, a source of considerable annoyance to students. Use these commonsense approaches to new files:

- Never install a program unless the diskette comes in a sealed package.
- Be especially wary of software that arrives unexpectedly from companies with whom you have not done business.
- Use virus-scanning software to check any file or document, no matter what the source, before loading it onto your hard disk.
- If your own diskette was used in another computer, scan it to see if it caught a virus.

Although there have been isolated instances of viruses in commercial software, viruses tend to show up on free software or software acquired from friends or the Internet. Antivirus software can be installed to scan your hard disk every time you boot the computer or, if you prefer, at regularly scheduled intervals.

Personal Computer Security

One summer evening two men in coveralls with company logos backed a truck up to the building that housed a university computer lab. They showed the lab assistant, a part-time student, an authorization slip to move 23 personal computers to another lab on campus. The assistant was surprised but not shocked, since lab use was light in the summer quarter. The computers were moved, all right, but not to another lab. In another case a ring of thieves mingled with students in computer labs at various West Coast universities and stole hundreds of microprocessor chips from the campus computers.

There is an active market for stolen personal computers and their internal components. As these unfortunate tales indicate, personal computer security breaches can be pretty basic. One simple, though not foolproof, remedy is to secure personal computer hardware in place with locks and cables. Also, most personal computers have an individual cover lock that prevents access to internal components.

In addition to theft, personal computer users need to be concerned about the computer's environment. Personal computers in business are not coddled the way bigger computers are. They are designed, in fact, to withstand the wear and tear of the office environment, including temperatures set for the comfort of people. Most manufacturers discourage eating and smoking near computers and recommend some specific cleaning techniques, such as vacuuming the keyboard. The response to these recommendations is directly related to the awareness level of the users.

Several precautions can be taken to protect disk data. One is to use a **surge protector,** a device that prevents electrical problems from affecting computer data files. The computer is plugged into the surge protector, which is plugged into the outlet. Diskettes should be under lock and key. The most critical precaution, however, is to back up your files.

Prepare for the Worst: Back Up Your Files

A computer expert, giving an impassioned speech, said, "If you are not backing up your files regularly, you *deserve* to lose them." Strong words. Although organizations recognize the value of data and have procedures in place for backing up data files on a regular basis, personal computer users are not as devoted to this activity. In fact, one wonders why, with continuous admonishments and readily available procedures, some people still leave their precious files unprotected.

What Could Go Wrong?   If you use software incorrectly or simply input data incorrectly, it may be some time before the resulting erroneous data is detected. You then need to go back to the time when the data files were still acceptable. Sometimes the software itself can harm data, or a hard disk could physically malfunction, making your files inaccessible. Although none of these are too likely, they certainly do happen. It is even less likely that you would lose your hard disk files to fire or flood, but this is also possible. The most likely scenario is that you will accidentally delete some files yourself. One fellow gave a command to delete all files with the file name extension BAK—there were four of them—but accidentally typed *BAT* instead, inadvertently wiping out 57 files. (Deleted files, we should mention, can probably be recovered using utility software if the action is taken right away, before other data is written over the deleted files.) Finally, there is always the possibility of your files being infected with a virus. Experts estimate that average users experience a significant disk loss once every year.

Ways to Back Up Files   Some people simply make another copy of their hard disk files on diskette. This is not too laborious if you do so as you go along. If you are at all vulnerable to viruses, you should back up all your files on a regular basis.

A better way is to back up all your files on a tape. Backing up to a tape drive is safer and faster. You can also use software that will automatically back up all your files at a certain time of day, or on command. Sophisticated users place their files on a mirror hard disk, which simply makes a second copy of everything you put on the original disk; this approach, as you might expect, is expensive.

Keep backed-up files in a cool, dry place off-site. For those of you with a home computer, this may mean keeping copies of your important files at a friend's house; some people even use a bank safety deposit box for this purpose.

▶ Privacy: Keeping Personal Information Personal

Think about the forms you have willingly filled out: paperwork for loans or charge accounts, orders for merchandise through the mail, magazine subscription orders, applications for schools and jobs and clubs, and on and on. There may be some forms you filled out with less delight—for taxes, military draft registration, court petitions, insurance claims, or a stay in the hospital. And remember all the people who got your name and address from your check—fund-raisers, advertisers, and petitioners. These lists may not have covered all the ways you have supplied data, but you can know with certainty where it went: straight to computer files.

Passing Your Data Around

Where is that data now? Is it shared, rented, sold? Who sees it? Will it ever be deleted? Or, to put it more bluntly, is *anything* private anymore?

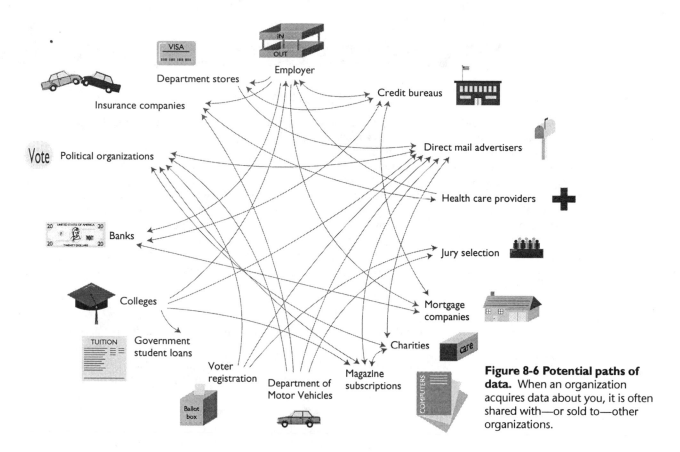

Figure 8-6 Potential paths of data. When an organization acquires data about you, it is often shared with—or sold to—other organizations.

In some cases one can only guess at the answers. It is difficult to say where your data is now, and bureaucracies are not eager to enlighten you. The data may have been moved to other files without your knowledge. In fact, much of the data is most definitely passed around, as anyone with a mailbox can attest. Even online services sell their subscriber lists, neatly ordered by zip code and computer type.

As for who sees your personal data, the answers are not comforting. Government agencies, for example, regularly share data that was originally filed for some other purpose. IRS records, for example, are compared with draft registration records to catch draft dodgers, and also with student loan records to intercept refunds to former students who have defaulted on their loans. The IRS created a storm of controversy by announcing a plan to use commercial direct-mail lists to locate tax evaders. Many people are worried about the consequences of this kind of sharing (Figure 8-6). For one thing, few of us can be certain that data about us, good or bad, is deleted when it has served its legitimate purpose.

The unfortunate fact is that, for very little money, anybody can learn anything about anybody—through massive databases. There are matters you want to keep private. You have the right to do so. Although you can do little to stop data about you from circulating through computers, there are some laws that give you access to some of it. Let us see what kind of protection is available to help preserve privacy.

Privacy Legislation

Significant legislation relating to privacy began with the **Fair Credit Reporting Act** in 1970. This law allows you to have access to and gives

NEW DIRECTIONS

TIGER TEAMS

Faced with threats on every side, some network-laced companies have chosen a proactive stance. Rather than waiting for the hacks and snoops and thieves to show up, they hire professionals to beat them to it. Called tiger teams or sometimes "intrusion testers" or "hackers for hire," these highly trained technical people are paid to try to break into a computer system before anyone else does.

Using the same kind of finesse and tricks a hacker might, tiger team members exploit the system weaknesses. Once such chinks are revealed, they can be protected. The team's first approach, typically, is to access the company's system from the Internet. The quality of security varies from company to company. Sometimes security is fairly tight; other times,

as one tiger team member put it, "It's a cakewalk."

Sometimes companies will hire one company to establish security and then hire a tiger team to try to defeat it. The company may not even alert its own employees to the tiger team activities, preferring to see whether the intrusions are detected and, if so, how employees react.

you the right to challenge your credit records. In fact, this access must be given to you free of charge if you have been denied credit. Businesses usually contribute financial information about their customers to a community credit bureau, which gives them the right to review a person's prior credit record with other companies. Before the Fair Credit Reporting Act, many people were—without explanation—turned down for credit because of inaccurate financial records about them. Because of the act, people may now check their records to make sure they are accurate.

The **Freedom of Information Act** was also passed in 1970. This landmark legislation allows ordinary citizens to have access to data about them that was gathered by federal agencies (although sometimes a lawsuit has been necessary to pry data loose).

The most significant legislation protecting the privacy of individuals is the **Federal Privacy Act** of 1974. This act stipulates that there can be no secret personnel files; individuals must be allowed to know what is stored in files about them and how the data is used, and must be able to correct it. The law applies not only to government agencies but also to private contractors dealing with government agencies. These organizations cannot obtain data willy-nilly, for no specific purpose; they must justify obtaining it.

A more recent law is the **Video Privacy Protection Act** of 1988, which prevents retailers from disclosing a person's video rental records without a court order; privacy supporters want the same rule for medical and insurance files. Another step in that direction is the **Computer Matching and Privacy Protection Act** of 1988, which prevents the government from comparing certain records in an attempt to find a match. However, most comparisons are still unregulated.

➤ The Internet: Security and Privacy Problems

Networks, whether connected to the Internet or not, pose unique security and privacy problems. Many people have access to the system, often

MAKING THE RIGHT CONNECTIONS

YOU HAVE NO PRIVACY WHATEVER

No privacy on the company e-mail, that is. Your employer can snoop into messages you send or receive even if you think you erased them. You have only erased them from their current hard drive location; copies are still in the company computer files. In fact, most companies archive all such files on tape and store them for the foreseeable future. Companies may fail to convey the message that e-mail, as a company conduit, is not private. Employees are often startled, after the fact, to discover that their messages have been invaded.

Furthermore, some people specialize in extracting deleted messages for use as evidence in court. E-mail can be a dangerous time bomb because litigators argue that, more than any other kind of written communication, e-mail reflects the real, unedited thoughts of the writer. This candid form of corporate communication increasingly is providing the most incriminating evidence used against companies in litigation.

What to do? It is certainly degrading to have something you thought was private waved in front of you as evidence of malingering. As one computer expert put it, if nothing is private, just say so. Companies have begun doing exactly that. The company policy on e-mail is—or should be—expressed in a clear, written document and routinely disseminated to all employees. However, even that step is probably insufficient. People tend to forget or get

complacent. Reminders should be given through the usual company conduits—bulletin boards, posters, and so forth.

What about the e-mail you send and receive at home—do you at least have privacy in your own home? Maybe not. You certainly cannot count on it if the

computer of the party at the other end is in an office. Further, keep in mind that messages sent across the Internet hop from computer to computer, with (depending on the service used) the sender having little say about its route. There are many vulnerable spots along the way.

from remote locations. Clearly, questions arise: If it is so easy for authorized people to get data, what is to stop unauthorized people from tapping it? Organizations must be concerned about unauthorized people intercepting data in transit, whether hackers or thieves or industrial spies.

One fundamental approach to network security is to dedicate one computer, called a **firewall**, whose sole purpose is to talk to the outside world. A firewall will provide an organization with greatly increased security because only one network computer is accessible to people outside the network, and that one computer accepts only appropriate access.

Encryption

Data being sent over communications lines may be protected by scrambling the messages—that is, putting them in code that can be broken only by the person receiving the message. The process of scrambling messages is called **encryption.** The American National Standards Institute has endorsed a process called the **Data Encryption Standard (DES)**, a standardized public key by which senders and receivers can scramble and unscramble their messages. Although the DES code is well known, companies still use it because the method makes it quite expensive to intercept coded messages. Thus, interlopers are forced to use other methods of gathering data—methods that carry greater risk of detection. Encryption software is available for personal computers. A typical package, for example, offers a variety of security features: file encryption, keyboard lock, and password protection.

Privacy Problems for Networked Employees

Although employees do not have expectations of total privacy at the office, they are often shocked when they discover that the boss has been spying on them via the network, even their comings and goings on the Internet. The boss, of course, is not spying at all, merely "monitoring." This debate has been heightened by the advent of software that lets managers check up on networked employees without their ever knowing that they are under surveillance. With a flick of a mouse button, the boss can silently pull up an employee's current computer screen.

Surveillance software is not limited to checking screens. It can also check on e-mail, count the number of keystrokes per minute, note the length of a worker's breaks, and monitor what computer files are used and for how long.

Worker associations complain that workers who are monitored suffer much higher degrees of stress and anxiety than nonmonitored workers. However, vendors defend their products by saying that they are not "spy software" but rather products designed for training, monitoring resources, and helping employees. Privacy groups are lobbying legislators at both the state and federal levels to enact legislation that requires employers to alert employees that they are being monitored.

People who feel invaded at work may be shocked to find out that they are also being watched when online—from the privacy of their homes. This time it is not the boss but the web site owners who are watching you.

You Are Being Watched

It may seem to be the ultimate in privacy invasion. When you visit a web site, it can easily collect the city you are calling from, the site from which you just came, and, of course, everything you do while you are at the site. Software can also discover and record the hardware and software you use. That's the good part. Software can even monitor a user's **click**

stream, the series of mouse clicks that link from site to site. Thus, a history of what a user chooses to view on the web can be recorded and used for a variety of purposes by managers and marketers.

If your computer is identifiable, presumably by an e-mail address, then the web site adds a record to a special file called a **cookie.** To add insult to injury, the file—actually called *cookie*—is kept right on your own computer, without your permission and probably without your knowledge. (Go ahead, check your computer's files.) The next time you show up at that web site, it checks what it knows about you on your cookie file.

In true computer industry style, however, anonymity software can now defeat the snooping software. The anonymous software, where you must begin each web session, acts as a middleman, retrieving sites and documents without revealing your identity.

Junk E-mail

Privacy invasion in the form of junk e-mail has become, unfortunately, a common event. Furthermore, it promises to get worse. The volume of junk e-mail will only soar as marketers discover how cheap it is. A postal mailing to a million people costs about $800,000, including postage and printing. Internet marketers can reach the same number of people by making a phone call and paying a few hundred dollars for time spent online. The software that makes mass advertising—called **spamming**—possible both gathers e-mail addresses and sends e-mail messages for marketers—thousands and thousands every day. One of the most annoying aspects of e-mail is that, unlike postal junk mail, which at least arrives at no cost to you, a user who pays for online usage may be paying for part of the cost of junk e-mail delivery.

Enraged spam recipients sometimes respond to the perpetrator by **flaming**, sending insulting messages in return. Experienced spammers, however, may have already abandoned the originating site and, most likely, moved to another one.

If you want to maximize your privacy and reduce your chances of getting junk e-mail, be careful where you leave your e-mail address. As noted in Chapter 7, a prime source of e-mail addresses is newsgroup messages, whose e-mail addresses will likely be gathered up and sold. Further, Internet business sites entice visitors to supply personal data that can be used for marketing and promotion. An e-mail address is their most treasured commodity.

Government Intervention?

The invasion of privacy online, especially through the Internet, may be that rare problem that, in the opinion of some communications experts, requires government intervention. Such laws would have to carefully carve out a middle ground between preserving new opportunities for the legitimate needs of business people, researchers, and investigators on the one hand, and preserving the right to privacy on the other.

➤ Ethics and Privacy

Snooping did not begin with computers. Neither did improper dissemination of personal information. But computers have elevated those problems to a much more serious level. As we have already noted, just about everything there is to know about you is already on a computer file, more likely several computer files. The thorny issues center around appropriate ethical treatment of that data by those who control it or merely have access to it. It is not unlikely that, in the course of your career, you will see personal data about other people. Consider these scenarios:

- Suppose that, as a programmer, you work on software that uses the company personnel files. Is it legitimate to look up salary data for people you know? If you see such data in the normal course of your work, is it appropriate to let those individuals know that you saw it?
- Suppose that you had access to data about bank loan applications, some of which appeared in test reports on which you are working. If someone takes these from your desktop while you are on your lunch break, is this an ethical breach on your part?
- Suppose that you are a programmer for a medical organization and, in the normal course of your work, see records about a celebrity. Is it ethical to describe the medical treatment to your friends, saying that it is a celebrity but not giving the name? Is it ethical to mention that the named celebrity uses your clinic without giving any medical details?

The above descriptions involve programmers, who are likely to see considerable private data over the course of a career. But people in many walks of life—accountants, tellers, nurses, contractors, and more—see data that resides on a computer. All of us need to respect the privacy of personal data.

The issues raised in this chapter are often the ones we think of after the fact—that is, when it is too late. Security and privacy factors are somewhat like insurance that we wish we did not have to buy. But we do buy insurance for our homes and cars and lives because we know we cannot risk being without it. The computer industry also knows that it cannot risk being without safeguards for security and privacy. As a computer user, you will share responsibility for addressing these issues.

CHAPTER REVIEW

Summary and Key Terms

- The word **hacker** originally referred to an enthusiastic, self-taught computer user, but now the term usually describes a person who gains access to computer systems illegally. Using **social engineering**, a tongue-in-cheek term for con artist actions, hackers persuade unsuspecting people to give away their passwords over the phone.

- The changing face of computer crime includes credit card fraud, data communications fraud, unauthorized access to computer files, and unlawful copying of copyrighted software.

- Prosecution of computer crime is often difficult because law enforcement officers, attorneys, and judges are unfamiliar with the issues involved. However, in 1986 Congress passed the latest version of the **Computer Fraud and Abuse Act**, and most states have passed some form of computer crime law.

- **Security** is a system of safeguards designed to protect a computer system and data from deliberate or accidental damage or access by unauthorized persons.

- The means of giving access to authorized people are divided into four general categories: (1) **what you have** (a key, badge, or plastic card); (2) **what you know** (a system password or identification number); (3) **what you do** (such as signing your name); and (4) **what you are** (by making use of **biometrics**, the science of measuring individual body characteristics such as fingerprints, voice, and retina). An **active badge**, a clip-on employee identification card with an embedded computer chip, signals its wearer's location—legal or otherwise—by sending out infrared signals, which are read by sensors sprinkled around the building.

- Loss of hardware and software is generally less of a problem than loss of data. Loss of hardware should not be a major problem, provided that the equipment is insured and a substitute processing facility is found quickly. Loss of software should not be critical, provided that the owner has taken the practical step of making backup copies. However, replacing lost data can be quite expensive.

- A **disaster recovery plan** is a method of restoring data processing operations if they are halted by major damage or destruction. Common approaches to disaster recovery include relying temporarily on manual services; buying time at a computer service bureau; making mutual assistance agreements with other companies; or forming a **consortium**, a joint venture with other organizations to support a complete computer facility used only in the event of a disaster.

- A **hot site** is a fully equipped computer facility with hardware, environmental controls, security, and communications equipment. A **cold site** is an environmentally suitable empty shell in which a company can install its own computer system.

- A disaster recovery plan should include a list of priorities identifying the programs that must be up and running first, plans for notifying employees of changes in locations and procedures, a list of needed equipment and where it can be obtained, a list of alternative computing facilities, and procedures for handling input and output data in a different environment.

- If a programmer is employed by an organization, any program written for the organization belongs to the employer. If the programmer is a consultant, however, the contract must clearly state whether it is the organization or the programmer that owns the software. Software can be copyrighted.

- Common means of protecting data are secured waste, internal controls, auditor checks, applicant screening, passwords, and built-in software protection.

- A **worm** is a program that transfers itself from computer to computer over a network, planting itself as a separate file on the target computer's disks. A **virus** is a set of illicit instructions that passes itself on to other programs with which it comes in contact. A **vaccine**, or **antivirus**, is a computer program that stops the spread of the virus and eradicates it. A **retrovirus** can fight back and may delete antivirus software.

- Personal computer security includes such measures as locking hardware in place; providing an appropriate physical environment; and using a **surge protector**, a device that prevents electrical problems from affecting computer data files.

- Files are subject to various types of losses and should be backed up on disk or tape.

- The security issue extends to the use of information about individuals that is stored in the computer files of credit bureaus and government agencies. The **Fair Credit Reporting Act** allows individuals to check the accuracy of credit information about them. The **Freedom of Information Act** allows people access to data that federal agencies have gathered about them. The **Federal Privacy Act** allows individuals access to information about them that is held not only by government agencies but also by private contractors working for the government. Individuals are also entitled to know how that information is being used. The **Video Privacy Protection Act** and the **Computer Matching and Privacy Protection Act** have extended federal protections.

- A **firewall** is a dedicated computer whose sole purpose is to talk to the outside world and decide who gains entry.

- The process of scrambling messages is called **encryption.** The American National Standards Institute has endorsed a process called the **Data Encryption Standard (DES)**, a standardized public key by which senders and receivers can scramble and unscramble their messages.

- Software can monitor a user's **click stream**, the series of mouse clicks that link from site to site, providing a history of what a user chooses to view on the Web.

- If your computer is identifiable, the web site can add a record of your activity to a **cookie** file that is stored on your computer.

- Privacy invasion in the form of junk e-mail has become a common event and will get worse because it is inexpensive. Mass advertising on the Internet is called **spamming.** Enraged spam recipients sometimes respond to the perpetrator by **flaming**, sending insulting messages in return.

- To reduce your chances of getting junk e-mail, be careful where you leave your e-mail address.

Quick Poll

Compare your answers to those of your colleagues or classmates.

1. Regarding security and privacy overall:
   - ❑ a. I can see that I need to pay more attention.
   - ❑ b. I will seek out my employer's policies to make sure I stay out of trouble.
   - ❑ c. These topics will be a key concern as I use computers.
2. Regarding viruses:
   - ❑ a. No encounters thus far; they seem to be only a moderately serious problem.
   - ❑ b. They are an occasional problem for me and for friends.
   - ❑ c. They are a major problem.
3. Regarding privacy on the Internet:
   - ❑ a. I provide no personal information. Period.
   - ❑ b. I may give my e-mail address to a reputable site, other information rarely.
   - ❑ c. They can find out anything; if I were that worried I'd just stay off the 'Net.

Discussion Questions

1. Before accepting a particular patient, a doctor might like access to a computer file listing patients who have been involved in malpractice suits. Before accepting a tenant, the owner of an apartment building might want to check a file that lists people who have previously sued landlords. Should computer files be available for such purposes?

2. Discuss the following statement: An active badge may help an organization maintain security, but it also erodes the employee's privacy.

3. Why do some people consider computer viruses important? Discuss your answer from the point of view of the professional programmer, the MIS manager, and the hacker.

Student Study Guide

Multiple Choice

1. Persuading people to tell their passwords:
   a. social engineering   c. biometrics
   b. flaming   d. encryption

2. History of a user's movements from site to site:
   a. worm   c. consortium
   b. vaccine   d. click stream

3. One safeguard against theft or alteration of data is the use of
   a. DES   c. identical passwords
   b. the Trojan Horse   d. data diddling

4. Legislation that prohibits government agencies and contractors from keeping secret personal files on individuals:
   a. Federal Privacy Act   c. Fair Credit Reporting Act
   b. Computer Abuse Act   d. Freedom of Information Act

5. Mass advertising via the Internet:
   a. hacking   c. social engineering
   b. spamming   d. flaming

6. Computer crimes are usually
   a. easy to detect   c. prosecuted
   b. blue-collar crimes   d. discovered accidentally

7. The "what you are" criterion for computer system access involves
   a. a badge   c. biometrics
   b. a password   d. a magnetized card

8. The key factor in a computer installation that has met with disaster is the
   a. equipment replacement   c. loss of hardware
   b. insurance coverage   d. loss of processing ability

9. In anticipation of physical destruction, every computer organization should have a
   a. biometric scheme   c. disaster recovery plan
   b. DES   d. set of active badges

10. A file with a record of web site activity:
    a. hot file   c. click file
    b. cookie file   d. active file

11. Networked employees may be monitored with
    a. disaster recovery plan   c. surveillance software
    b. DES   d. biometrics

12. Secured waste, auditor checks, and applicant screening all aid
    a. data security   c. built-in software protection
    b. license protection   d. piracy detection

13. The weakest link in any computer system:
    a. the people in it   c. hardware
    b. passwords   d. software

14. A device that prevents electrical problems from affecting data files:
    a. site license   c. Trojan Horse
    b. hot site   d. surge protector

15. One form of built-in software protection for data is
    a. secured waste   c. applicant screening
    b. user profiles   d. auditor checks

16. An identification card with an embedded chip to signal its wearer's location:
    a. antivirus   c. active badge
    b. site license   d. consortium

17. An empty shell in which a company may install its own computer is called a
    a. restoration site   c. cold site
    b. hot site   d. hardware site

18. A program written when the programmer is employed by an organization is owned by
    a. the programmer   c. no one
    b. the state   d. the organization

19. Security protection for personal computers includes
    a. internal components   c. locks and cables
    b. software   d. all of these

20. The secret words or numbers to be typed in on a keyboard before any activity can take place are called
    a. biometric data   c. data encryptions
    b. passwords   d. private words

21. Another name for an antivirus:
    a. vaccine   c. worm
    b. Trojan Horse   d. DES

22. Sending insulting messages to mass advertisers:
    a. surging   c. clicking
    b. flaming   d. spamming

23. A virus that replicates itself is called a
    a. bug   c. worm
    b. vaccine   d. bomb

24. A program whose sabotage depends on certain conditions is called a
    a. bug   c. worm
    b. vaccine   d. bomb

25. A person who gains illegal access to a computer system:
   a. hacker
   b. software pirate
   c. worm
   d. zapper

True/False

T   F   1. Most computer organizations cannot afford consortiums.

T   F   2. Vaccine is another name for antivirus software.

T   F   3. The Trojan Horse is an embezzling technique.

T   F   4. If a computer crime is detected, prosecution is assured.

T   F   5. Computer security is achieved by restricting physical access to the computer.

T   F   6. Fingerprints are an example of biometrics.

T   F   7. The actual loss of hardware is a major security problem due to its expense.

T   F   8. If a user is identifiable, a web site may add a record to the user's spam file.

T   F   9. A victim of mass advertising may respond by flaming.

T   F   10. Most computer crimes are not detected.

T   F   11. The science of studying individual body characteristics is called biometrics.

T   F   12. Passwords are best changed annually.

T   F   13. The spread of a vaccine is usually stopped by an antivirus.

T   F   14. Data diddling is a criminal method whereby data is modified before it goes into a computer file.

T   F   15. Although hackers have invaded corporate and government mainframes, they have thus far respected web sites.

T   F   16. A mutual aid pact with another computer facility is one possibility for a disaster recovery plan.

T   F   17. A cookie file holds records on Web activities right on the user's disk.

T   F   18. The Data Encryption Standard is a standardized list of passwords for software security.

T   F   19. By allowing a programmer also to be a computer operator, a computer organization can improve security.

T   F   20. Increasing access to networks has changed the nature of computer crime.

T   F   21. Mass advertising is called flaming.

T   F   22. Most states have passed some form of computer crime law.

T   F   23. A cold site is an environmentally suitable empty shell in which a company can install its own computer system.

T   F   24. Social engineering is a movement to improve password protection.

T   F   25. Users concerned about privacy should withhold personal information but need not worry about giving out their e-mail address.

Fill-In

1. An environmentally suitable empty shell into which a computer organization can put its computer system: _____

2. A system of safeguards to protect a computer system and data from damage or unauthorized access: _____

3. Bypassing security systems with an illicitly acquired software package is called _____

4. The field concerned with the measurement of individual body characteristics: _____

5. The name for a fully equipped computer center to be used in the event of a disaster: _____

6. What is the assurance to individuals that personal property is used properly called? _____

7. A person who gains access to a computer system illegally is called _____

8. A standardized public key by which senders and receivers can scramble and unscramble their messages: _____

9. The four categories of authorized access to a computer system:
   a. _____
   b. _____
   c. _____
   d. _____

10. The file on your own computer that has records of Web activity: _____

11. The law, passed in 1970, that allows ordinary citizens to have access to data gathered by federal agencies: _____

12. The law that prohibits government agencies and their private contractors from keeping secret personal files: _____

13. The Fair Credit Reporting Act of 1970 gives people access to this information: _____

14. Another name for mass advertising on the Internet: _____

15. Does a program belong to the employed programmer or the employing organization? _____

16. Which is potentially the least damaging type of security violation: hardware, software, or data? _____

17. The salami technique is which type of method? _____

18. Placing an illicit program within a completed program, allowing unauthorized entry: _____

19. Sending insulting messages to those who send mass advertising: _____

20. Persuading people to give away their passwords: _____

21. Another name for a vaccine: _____

22. An illegal program that transfers itself from computer to computer over a network: _____

23. A user's movements from site to site: _____

24. A device that prevents electrical problems from affecting computer files: _____

25. The name for the identification card that can track the wearer's location: _____

Answers

Multiple Choice
1. a	6. d	11. c	16. c	21. a
2. d	7. c	12. a	17. c	22. b
3. a	8. d	13. a	18. d	23. c
4. a	9. c	14. d	19. d	24. d
5. b	10. b	15. b	20. b	25. a

True/False
1. T	6. T	11. T	16. T	21. F
2. T	7. F	12. F	17. T	22. T
3. F	8. F	13. F	18. F	23. T
4. F	9. T	14. T	19. F	24. F
5. F	10. T	15. F	20. T	25. F

Fill-In
1. cold site
2. security
3. zapping
4. biometrics
5. hot site
6. privacy
7. hacker
8. Data Encryption Standard (DES)
9. a. what you have
   b. what you know
   c. what you do
   d. what you are
10. cookie
11. Freedom of Information Act
12. Federal Privacy Act
13. credit reports
14. spamming
15. the organization
16. hardware
17. embezzlement
18. trapdoor
19. flaming
20. social engineering
21. antivirus
22. worm
23. click stream
24. surge protector
25. active badge

PLANET INTERNET

Unexpected. Even so, you can easily come across sites that feature subjects you never expected to find on the Web. For example, few would expect to come across a panhandler site; he wants a handout. He prefers credit card donations but will accept cash through the mail. Been thinking about prisons lately? Probably not. But there it is, the Alcatraz prison site. An even more somber site is the World Wide Cemetery, in which you can post dedications to departed loved ones.

Not your everyday pursuit. You might whip up some interest in gold prospecting when you see all the links on the site. And speaking of riches, the Found Money site suggests that "you may be rich and not even know it!" You can check their database to see if you have any money lying around.

YOU JUST NEVER KNOW WHAT YOU'LL FIND

You never know what you might find on the Internet. If you deliberately put provocative words through a search engine, even something as tame as *strange*, you may find some of the sites returned to be disconcerting or even alarming. But it is pretty easy to stay away from such sites if you tread the beaten paths.

You didn't know you needed this. Have Cyrano write love letters for you. See the clever ArtsWire site for the Mona Lisa links. Hear what the flake man has to say about his collection of classic cereal boxes. Read the southern cooking recipes at the Grits site. Take the survey; they want to include you in their Internet demographics compilation. Finally, take a hint and write a letter to Dear Mom.

Dear Timmy,
I'll always be here when you need me. A nice card from you would make any day special.

ps: Write more often. You know how your mother worries.

A YEAR ROUND Tribute to Mom

Gold Prospecting

Cyrano Server

Internet Exercises

1. **Structured exercise.** *Begin with the AWL URL, http://hepg.awl.com/ capron/planet/ and take a tour of Alca-traz. Visit the bookstore.*
2. **Freeform exercise.** *Use the WebCrawler's Search Ticker to check out a few of its randomly selected sites.*

GRITS

"NO ONE CAN EAT JUST ONE!"

Art Room

Art News

Pet Peeves

Art Jobs

Art Stuff

Guest Book

Lessons

Art Site of the Week

Awards

AEAI

Cartoons

SUR☑EY.NET

™

Testing Your Understanding—Unit III

Computers, Chapter 8: Security and Privacy: Computers and the Internet

Pages 106–112
CHECKING YOUR COMPREHENSION

Choose the best answer for each of the following questions.

1. Based on the chapter introduction, which of the following questions should you expect to be able to answer after reading the chapter?
   a. Why do people commit computer crimes?
   b. Who commits computer crimes?
   c. How can computerized data be kept private?
   d. What ethical dilemmas does Internet access create?

2. It can be inferred from the passage that computer crimes are primarily discovered by accident because
   a. people change computers frequently.
   b. hackers warn each other when discovery is imminent.
   c. hackers use techniques that are easily covered up.
   d. people assume hackers are not actually going to damage the system.

3. The primary purpose of including the section "Some 'Bad Guy' Tricks" in the chapter is to
   a. introduce basic methods of computer crime.
   b. educate computer users about potential problems.
   c. explain sources of computer jargon.
   d. suggest ways to prevent computer crime.

Identify the following statements as true or false.

4. Only a small percentage of large corporations actually experience hackers invading their systems.

5. Most hackers use high-tech computer programs to break a computer's security.

6. Most corporations prosecute computer crime.

7. Most hackers are teenagers trying to show off.

Answer the following questions.

8. List the four broad categories of computer crime.

9. Describe the three difficulties encountered in prosecuting computer crimes.

10. List five ways to protect passwords.

Identify the following terms as they are used in the chapter.

11. miscreants

12. Computer Fraud and Abuse Act of 1986

13. social engineering

14. hacker

Discussion and Critical Thinking Questions

1. What reasons do hackers cite as justification for their actions?

2. Are there ever any cases of hacking that are justifiable?

3. Should "no harm" hacking be prosecuted? If so, what kind of punishment do you think is appropriate?

Pages 112–120
CHECKING YOUR COMPREHENSION

Choose the best answer for each of the following questions.

1. According to the passage, a disaster recovery plan is essentia in order to
   a. prevent hackers from altering data.
   b. establish computer processing quickly following a power outage.
   c. erase virus programs from computer networks.
   d. establish lawful access to computer facilities following a break-in.

2. In the section "When Disaster Strikes: What Do You Have to Lose?" the types of details given in the first paragraph can best be described as
   a. illustrations.
   b. statistical facts.
   c. reasons.
   d. descriptions.

3. In the section "Disaster Recovery Plan," the organizational pattern in the second paragraph can be best described as
   a. classification.
   b. cause-effect.
   c. enumeration.
   d. definition.

Identify the following statements as true or false.

4. Loss of computer hardware is the most devastating loss a computer-operating business will sustain.

5. Computer programmers usually maintain rights to the programs they write.

6. Although viruses are easily transmitted, they usually cause only simple, if irritating, damage to programs.

Answer the following questions.

7. List the five major types of damage that can affect hardware and software.

8. List four categories of access to a computer system.

9. List six techniques for protecting data from unwanted employee alteration.

10. List three types of back-up files.

Define each of the following terms

11. consortium

12. hot site

13. retrovirus

14. biometrics

15. worm

Discussion and Critical Thinking Questions

1. What kind of data should a college or university have backed up? What kind of disaster recovery plan would be necessary for a college or university?

2. In what ways might increased password security rules actually increase the likelihood that users will write down their passwords? What methods would both make passwords more secure and not increase the incidence of passwords being written down?

3. What types of computer systems do you think should have unlimited access?

4. Develop a recall strategy for remembering what should be included in a disaster recovery plan.

Pages 120–126
CHECKING YOUR COMPREHENSION

Choose the best answer for each of the following questions.

1. According to the passage, an employer can monitor an employee's computer use through
   a. encryption software.
   b. surveillance software.
   c. firewall computers.
   d. cookie files.

2. Which of the following best describes the tone of the section "You Have No Privacy Whatever"?
   a. complacent
   b. conspiratorial
   c. warning
   d. grateful

3. The primary purpose of the "New Directions" box on page 122 is to
    a. illustrate an innovative solution.
    b. propose an alternative theory.
    c. question an unusual case.
    d. reconcile contrasting positions.

Identify the following statements as true or false.

4. Erasing e-mail messages from your office desktop computer ensures their privacy.

5. Encryption is effective because a message using DES is almost impossible to unscramble.

6. Organizations frequently sell information to other organizations.

7. Computers have created the problem of invasion of privacy.

Match the legislation with what it regulates.

8. Fair Credit Reporting Act   a. movie rentals

9. Freedom of Information Act   b. personnel files

10. Video Privacy Protection Act   c. credit records

11. Computer Matching and Privacy   d. personal data in government files
Protection Act

12. Federal Privacy Act   e. record comparison

Answer the following questions.

13. List two kinds of software through which a user can protect Internet data and identity.

14. List two ways information is commonly passed around.

Identify each of the following terms by as either a protective, defensive system or an aggressive, invasive system.

15. firewall

16. encryption

17. click stream

18. cookie

19. spamming

20. flaming

Discussion and Critical Thinking Questions

1. What role do you think the government should play in regulating Internet privacy? Should there be local standards? National standards? International standards?

2. What criteria do you think are important in order to ensure privacy of information?

3. Should a company limit employee access to the Web during office hours?

4. What are the advantages and disadvantages of anonymous programs?

CHAPTER REVIEW

End of Chapter Analysis

Choose the best answer for each of the following questions.

1. The chapter employs all of the following techniques for making the material easier to read except
   a. marginal annotations.
   b. graphic elements.
   c. boldface.
   d. chapter outline.

2. Which of the following would probably be the most useful technique for organizing the primary concepts in the chapter in order to remember them?
   a. drawing conceptual diagrams
   b. paraphrasing the headings
   c. annotating your reactions
   d. highlighting definitions

3. The author uses which of the following types of supports in the chapter?
   a. personal experience
   b. analogies
   c. counter arguments
   d. definitions

4. The author would most probably agree with which of the following statements about the Internet?
   a. The problems encountered by viruses and data sharing outweigh the benefits of using the Internet.
   b. Workers should have unlimited access to the Internet through their office machines.
   c. Sending an encrypted message over the Internet is as safe as giving the information over a phone.
   d. The Internet provides an excellent storage location for backup data files.

Group Projects

1. In the development of an oral history of the Holocaust, the decision was made recently not to put the actual testimonies on the Internet. What issues discussed in this chapter might have contributed to this decision? Should the testimonies be available on the Internet?

2. Develop a plan for a Web-based student records system for a university, evaluating all the major areas discussed in the chapter.

3. Develop policy for college computer needs usage.

Journal Ideas

1. What policies would you put in place for how elementary-school children could use the computer in your home?

2. List all the computer systems to which you have some kind of access. What ethical issues does each raise for you? Are the dilemmas raised by each the same? Which is most problematic for you?

UNIT IV

From

Neil A. Campbell

Biology
Fourth Edition

Chapter 31:
Plant Structure and Growth

CHAPTER 31

PLANT STRUCTURE AND GROWTH

KEY CONCEPTS

- Plant biology reflects the major themes in the study of life

- A plant's root and shoot systems are evolutionary adaptations to living on land

- The many types of plant cells are organized into three major tissue systems

- Meristems generate cells for new organs throughout the lifetime of a plant: *an overview of plant growth*

- Apical meristems extend roots and shoots: *a closer look at primary growth*

- Lateral meristems add girth to stems and roots: *a closer look at secondary growth*

*P*lants are the pillars of most terrestrial ecosystems. Their photosynthesis supports their own growth and maintenance, and it feeds, directly or indirectly, an ecosystem's various consumers, including animals. Although most humans now live far from natural ecosystems and farms, our dependence on plants is evident in our lumber, fabrics, paper, medicines, and—most importantly—our food. The study of plants began when early humans learned to distinguish edible plants from poisonous ones and began to make things from wood and other plant products. Modern plant biology still has its pragmatic side—in research aimed at improving crop productivity, for example—but the pure fun of discovery is what motivates most plant scientists. Plant biology, perhaps the oldest branch of science, is driven by a combination of curiosity and need—curiosity about how plants work and a need to apply this knowledge judiciously to feed, clothe, and house a burgeoning human population.

◼ Plant biology reflects the major themes in the study of life

Plant biology is in the midst of a renaissance. New methods coupled with clever choices of experimental organisms have catalyzed a research explosion. For example, many scientists interested in the genetic control of plant development are focusing their research on *Arabidopsis thaliana*, a little weed that belongs to the mustard family. *Arabidopsis* is small enough to be grown in test tubes, and its short generation span of about six weeks makes it an excellent model for genetic studies. Plant biologists are also attracted to *Arabidopsis* by its tiny genome; the amount of DNA per cell ranks among the least of all known plants. Efforts to associate specific genetic functions with certain regions of DNA are simplified, and it is likely that researchers will map the entire *Arabidopsis* genome within this decade. Already, plant biologists have pinpointed some of the genes that control the development of flowers and have learned the functions of these genes (FIGURE 31.1). This research is just one example of what seems to be a major thrust of modern plant biology: relating processes that occur at the molecular and cellular levels to what we observe at the level of the whole plant. Once again, we see the theme of a hierarchy of structural levels, with emergent properties arising from the ordered arrangement and interactions of component parts.

The other biological themes of this book will also guide our study of plants. The structure and functions of plants

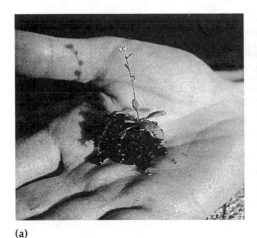

(a)

(b)

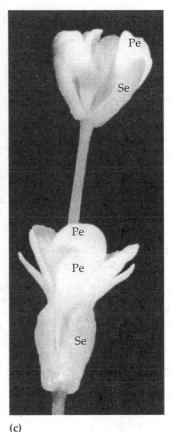

(c)

FIGURE 31.1

***Arabidopsis,* a little weed that is helping plant biologists answer big questions about the development of plant form.** (**a**) Plant biologists have made this tiny member of the mustard family one of the organisms of choice for the experimental study of how genes control plant development. Three characteristics that make *Arabidopsis* such a convenient research model are small size, a short life cycle, and a relatively small genome. Numerous laboratories are now mapping *Arabidopsis's* genome and identifying the functions of many of its genes. With the help of this model system, plant biologists hope to discover how genes and environment interact to transform a zygote into a plant. (**b**) Much of this research has centered on flower development. *Arabidopsis* normally has four whorls of flower parts: sepals (Se), petals (Pe), stamens (St), and carpels (Ca). (**c**) Researchers have identified several mutations that cause abnormal flowers to develop. This flower, for example, has an extra whorl of petals in place of stamens and an internal flower where normal plants have carpels.

are shaped by interactions with the environment on two time scales. In their long evolutionary journey from water onto land, plants became adapted by natural selection to the specific problems posed by terrestrial environments. The evolution of tissues, such as the woody tissue of trees, that can support plants against the pull of gravity is just one example. Over the short term, individual plants exhibit structural and physiological responses to environmental stimuli. As an example of how individual plants, far more than individual animals, adapt *structurally* to their environment, look at how wind has affected the growth of branches of the trees illustrated in FIGURE 31.2. Plants, like animals, also have many evolutionary adaptations in the form of *physiological* responses to short-term change. For example, the stomata of many plants—the pores of the leaf surface that function in gas exchange and transpiration—close during the hottest time of day. This response helps the plant conserve water. As we analyze the evolutionary adaptations of plants and the responses of individual plants to their environment, our main tool will be a related theme: the correlation between structure and function. We will learn, for example, how the opening and closing of stomata are consequences of the structure of the guard cells that border these pores.

In studying the structure and function of plants, comparisons with the animal kingdom are inevitable and sometimes useful. Plants and animals confront many of the same problems, which they may solve in different ways. For example, an elephant and a redwood tree support their enormous weight on land by means of very different kinds of "skeletons": bones in the elephant and wood in the tree. In some cases, plant and animal solutions to a common problem seem similar. For example, large organisms require internal transport systems to carry water and other substances between body parts, and networks of tubes have evolved in both plants and animals. But on closer examination, we will see that any anatomical similarities between plants and animals are superficial. These similar adaptations are, in the lexicon of biology, analogous, not homologous (see Chapter 23). The multicellular organization of plants evolved independently from that of animals, from unicellular ancestors with an entirely different mode of nutrition. The autotrophic/heterotrophic distinction has placed plants and animals on separate evolutionary paths. Setting the

FIGURE 31.2

The effect of the environment on plant form. The "flagging" of these firs growing on a windy ridge on Mt. Hood, Oregon, resulted partly from the mechanical disturbance of the prevailing winds inhibiting limb growth on the windward sides of the trees. This growth response reduces the number of limbs that are broken during strong winds. Although environment affects the growth and development of all organisms, environmental impact on plant form is particularly impressive. In contrast, animal form is much less plastic; wind, for example, does not alter the number, size, or placement of human limbs.

stage for our survey of plant biology, this chapter introduces the general body plan of flowering plants, beginning with external structure. We will see that the architecture of plants is dynamic, continuously shaped by the plants' genetically directed growth patterns and their responses to the environment.

■ A plant's root and shoot systems are evolutionary adaptations to living on land

Plant biologists study plant architecture on two levels: morphology and anatomy. **Plant morphology** (Gr. *morphe,* "form") is the study of the external structure of plants. The placement of leaves along a stem is an example of morphology. **Plant anatomy** is concerned with internal structure—for example, the arrangement of cells and tissues within a leaf. This section features the morphology of flowering plants, or angiosperms. (The structure of algae, mosses, ferns, and gymnosperms was covered in Unit Five, along with the evolutionary relationships of these plant groups to the angiosperms.)

Angiosperms are characterized by flowers and fruits, evolutionary adaptations that function in reproduction and the dispersal of seeds. With about 275,000 known species, angiosperms are by far the most diverse and widespread group of plants. Taxonomists split the angiosperms into two classes: **monocots,** named for their single cotyledon (seed leaf), and **dicots,** which have two cotyledons. Monocots and dicots have several other structural differences as well (FIGURE 31.3).

The basic morphology of plants reflects their evolutionary history as terrestrial organisms. The algal ancestors of plants were bathed in a solution of water and minerals, including bicarbonate, the source of CO_2 for photosynthesis in aquatic habitats. In contrast, the resources a terrestrial plant needs are divided between the soil and air, and the plant must inhabit these two very different environments at the same time. Soil provides water and minerals, but air is the main source of CO_2, and light does not penetrate far into the soil. The evolutionary solution to this separation of resources was differentiation of the plant body into two main systems: a subterranean **root system** and an aerial **shoot system** consisting of stems, leaves, and flowers (FIGURE 31.4). Neither system can live without the other. Lacking chloroplasts and living in the dark, roots would starve without sugar and other organic nutrients imported from the photosynthetic tissues of the shoot system. Conversely, the shoot system depends on water and minerals absorbed from the soil by roots. Vascular tissues, continuous throughout the plant, transport materials between roots and shoots. Each vein has two types of vascular tissue: **xylem,** which conveys water and dissolved minerals upward from roots into the shoots; and **phloem,** which transports food made in the leaves to the roots and to nonphotosynthetic parts of the shoot system. As we take closer looks at the morphology of roots and shoots, try to view these systems from the evolutionary perspective of adaptation to living on land.

The Root System

Roots anchor the plant in the soil, absorb minerals and water, conduct water and nutrients, and store food. The structure of roots is well adapted to these functions.

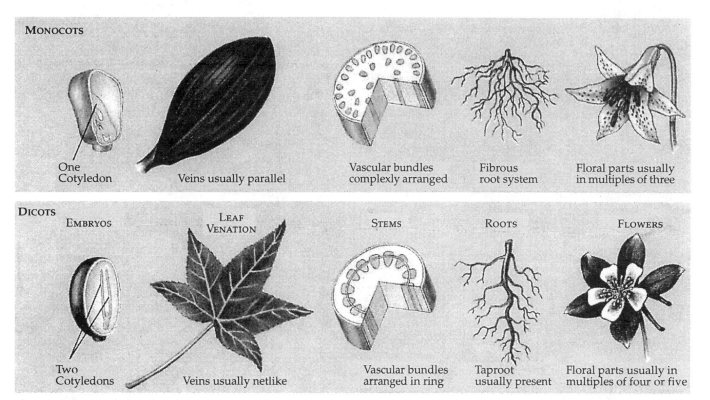

MONOCOTS

EMBRYOS	LEAF VENATION	STEMS	ROOTS	FLOWERS

One Cotyledon — Veins usually parallel — Vascular bundles complexly arranged — Fibrous root system — Floral parts usually in multiples of three

DICOTS

Two Cotyledons — Veins usually netlike — Vascular bundles arranged in ring — Taproot usually present — Floral parts usually in multiples of four or five

FIGURE 31.3

A comparison of monocots and dicots. These classes of angiosperms are named for the number of cotyledons, or seed leaves, present in the seed of the plant. Monocots include orchids, bamboos, palms, lilies, and yuccas, as well as the grasses, such as wheat, corn, and rice. A few examples of dicots are roses, beans, sunflowers, maples, and oaks.

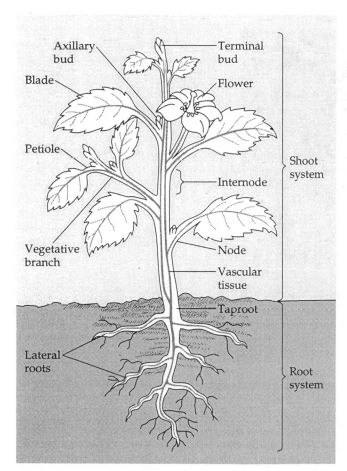

FIGURE 31.4

Morphology of a flowering plant: an overview. The plant body is divided into a root system and a shoot system, connected by vascular tissue that is continuous throughout the plant. The root system of this dicot consists of a taproot and several lateral roots. Shoots consist of stems, leaves, and flowers. The blade, the expanded portion of a leaf, is attached to a stem by a petiole. Nodes, the regions of a stem where leaves attach, are separated by internodes. At a shoot's tip is the terminal bud, the main growing point of the shoot. Axillary buds are located in the upper angles of leaves. Most of these axillary buds are dormant, but they have the potential to develop into vegetative (leaf-bearing) branches or into flowers.

Many dicots have a **taproot** system, consisting of one large, vertical root (the taproot) that produces many smaller lateral roots (see FIGURES 31.3 and 31.4). Penetrating deep into the soil, the taproot is a firm anchor, as you know if you have ever tried to pull up a dandelion. Some taproots, such as carrots, turnips, and sugar beets, are modified roots that store exceptionally large amounts of food. The plant consumes these food reserves when it flowers and produces fruit. For this reason, root crops are harvested before the plants flower.

Monocots, including grasses, generally have **fibrous root** systems consisting of a mat of threadlike roots that spread out below the soil surface. (Large monocots, including palms and bamboo, have much thicker roots—ropelike rather than threadlike.) The fibrous root system gives the plant extensive exposure to soil water and minerals and anchors it tenaciously to the ground (see FIGURE 31.3). Because their root systems are concentrated in the upper few centimeters of the soil, grasses make excellent ground cover for preventing erosion.

Although the entire root system helps anchor a plant, most absorption of water and minerals in both monocots and dicots occurs near the root tips, where vast numbers of tiny **root hairs** increase the surface area of the root tremendously (FIGURE 31.5). Mycorrhizae, symbiotic as-sociations between roots and fungi, also enhance water and mineral absorption (see FIGURE 28.13).

In addition to roots that extend from the base of the shoot, some plants have roots arising aboveground from stems or even from leaves. Such roots are said to be **adventitious** (L. *adventicius,* "not belonging to"), a term that describes any plant part that grows in an unusual location. The adventitious roots of some plants, including corn, function as props that help support stems.

The Shoot System

The shoot system consists of vegetative shoots, which bear leaves, and floral shoots, which terminate in flowers. We will postpone discussion of the structure and function of flowers until Chapter 34 and focus here on vegetative shoots. A vegetative shoot consists of a stem and the attached leaves; it may be the plant's main shoot or a side shoot, called a vegetative branch (see FIGURE 31.4).

Stems. A stem has an alternation of **nodes,** the points at which leaves are attached, and **internodes,** the stem segments between nodes (see FIGURE 31.4). In the angle formed by each leaf and the stem is an **axillary bud,** which is an embryonic side shoot. Most axillary buds are dormant; growth is usually concentrated at the apex (tip)

FIGURE 31.5
Root hairs of a radish seedling. Growing by the thousands just behind the tip of each root, the hairs cling tightly to soil particles and increase the surface area for the absorption of water and minerals by the roots.

of a shoot, where there is a **terminal bud** with developing leaves and a compact series of nodes and internodes. The presence of the terminal bud is partly responsible for inhibiting the growth of axillary buds, a phenomenon called **apical dominance.** By concentrating resources on growing taller, apical dominance is an evolutionary adaptation that increases the plant's exposure to light, especially in a location with dense vegetation. However, branching is also important for increasing the exposure of the shoot system to the environment, and under certain conditions, axillary buds begin growing. Each bud has the dual potential to give rise to either a reproductive shoot bearing flowers or a vegetative branch complete with its own terminal bud, leaves, and axillary buds. In some cases, the growth of axillary buds can be stimulated by removing the terminal bud. This is the rationale for pruning trees and shrubs and "pinching back" houseplants to make them bushy.

Modified stems with diverse functions have evolved in many plants and are often mistaken for roots (FIGURE 31.6). Stolons are horizontal stems that grow along the surface of the ground. The "runners" of strawberry plants are examples. Rhizomes, such as those of irises, are horizontal stems that grow underground. Some rhizomes end in enlarged tubers where food is stored, as in white potatoes. Bulbs, such as those of onions, are vertical, underground shoots with fleshy leaf bases modified for food storage.

Leaves. Leaves are the main photosynthetic organs of most plants, although green stems also perform photosynthesis. Leaves vary extensively in form, but they generally consist of a flattened **blade** and a stalk, the **petiole,** which joins the leaf to a node of the stem (see FIGURE 31.4). Grasses and many other monocots lack petioles; instead, the base of the leaf forms a sheath that envelopes the stem. Some monocots, including palm trees, do have petioles.

The leaves of monocots and dicots differ in how their major veins are arranged (see FIGURE 31.3). Most monocots have parallel major veins that run the length of the leaf blade. In contrast, dicot leaves generally have a multibranched network of major veins. All leaves have numerous minor cross-veins. Vascular arrangement, leaf shape, and leaf placement on the stem are among the characteristics used by plant taxonomists to help identify or classify plants (FIGURE 31.7). Although most leaves are specialized for photosynthesis, some plants have leaves that have become adapted by evolution for other functions (FIGURE 31.8).

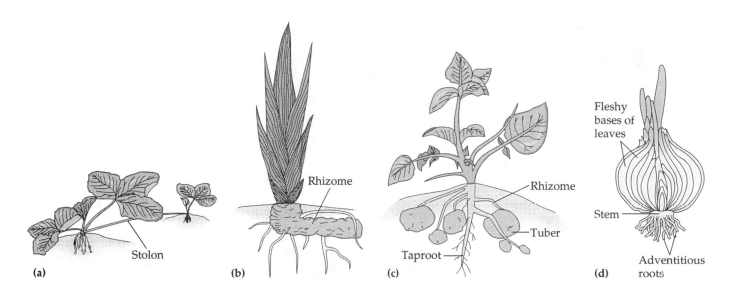

FIGURE 31.6
Modified stems. (**a**) Stolons, shown here on a strawberry plant, grow on the surface of the ground. (**b**) Rhizomes, like the one on this iris plant, are horizontal stems that grow underground. (**c**) Tubers are swollen ends of rhizomes specialized for storing food. The "eyes" arranged in a spiral pattern around the potato are clusters of buds that mark the nodes. (**d**) Bulbs are vertical, underground shoots consisting mostly of the swollen bases of leaves that store food. You can see the many layers of modified leaves attached to the short stem by slicing an onion bulb lengthwise.

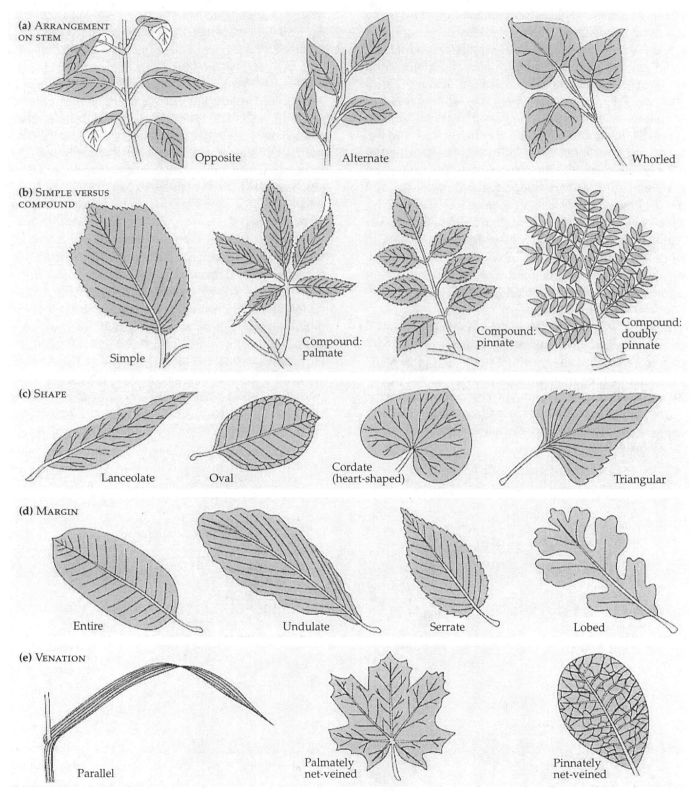

FIGURE 31.7

A survey of leaf morphology.

(a) Leaves are arranged on the stem in a variety of patterns. If each node has a pair of leaves 180° apart, the leaves are said to be opposite. The leaf placement is alternate when each node has a single leaf and the leaves of adjacent nodes point in different directions. If a node has three or more leaves attached, the arrangement is termed whorled. (b) A leaf is said to be simple if it has a single, undivided blade. If the blade is divided into several leaflets, then the leaf is compound. (You can distinguish a compound leaf from a stem with several closely spaced simple leaves by examining the locations of axillary buds. There is no bud at the base of a leaflet, but there is an axillary bud where the petiole of the compound leaf joins the stem.) (c–e) Leaves also vary in shape, in the contour of their margins, and in their pattern of veins.

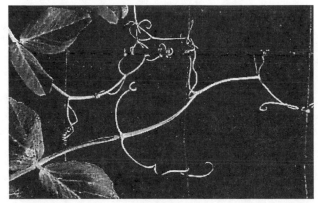

(a)

(c)

(b)

(d)

FIGURE 31.8

Modified leaves. (a) The tendrils used by this pea plant to cling to supports are modified leaflets. (b) The spines of cacti, such as this prickly pear, are actually leaves, and photosynthesis is carried out mainly by the fleshy green stems. (c) Most succulents, such as ice plant, have leaves modified for storing water. (d) In many plants, brightly colored leaves help attract pollinators to the flower. The red "petals" of the poinsettia are actually leaves that surround a group of flowers.

So far we have examined the structural organization of the whole plant as we see it with the unaided eye. We can now dissect the plant and explore its microscopic organization.

■ The many types of plant cells are organized into three major tissue systems

In this section, an introduction to plant anatomy, you will learn how the structural specializations of plant cells enable them to perform certain functions. You will also learn how these cells are organized into three main tissue systems and how these tissues are arranged in roots, stems, and leaves. FIGURE 31.9 will help you review the general structure of plant cells before you proceed to the following survey of specific cell types.

Types of Plant Cells

What distinguishes a multicellular organism from a colony of cells is a division of labor among cells differing in structure and function. As you consider each major

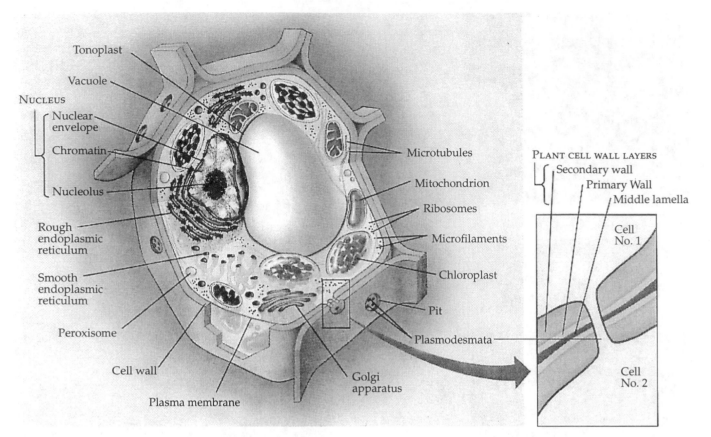

FIGURE 31.9

Plant cell structure: a review. A plant cell consists of a protoplast enclosed in a cell wall. The protoplast—the whole cell, excluding the cell wall—is bounded by the plasma membrane. Outside the plasma membrane is the primary cell wall and in some plants a secondary cell wall. Between the primary walls of adjacent plant cells is the middle lamella, a sticky layer that cements the cells together. The protoplasts of neighboring cells are generally connected by plasmodesmata, cytoplasmic channels that pass through pores in the walls. The plasmodesmata may be concentrated in areas called pits, where the distance between adjacent protoplasts is narrowed. When mature, most living plant cells have a large central vacuole that occupies as much as 90% of the volume of the protoplast. A membrane called the tonoplast separates the contents of the vacuole from the thin layer of cytoplasm, in which the mitochondria, plastids, and other organelles are located. Within the vacuole is the cell sap, a complex aqueous solution that helps the vacuole play an important role in maintaining the turgor, or firmness, of the cell.

type of plant cell, notice the structural adaptations that make specific functions possible. In some cases, we will find distinguishing characteristics within the **protoplast,** the contents of the cell exclusive of the cell wall. For example, only the protoplasts of photosynthetic cells contain chloroplasts. But also notice that modifications of cell walls are important in how the specialized cells of a plant function.

Parenchyma Cells. Because they are the least specialized of all plant cells, **parenchyma cells** are often depicted as "typical" plant cells (FIGURE 31.10a). Mature parenchyma cells have primary walls that are relatively thin and flexible. Most parenchyma cells lack secondary walls. The protoplast generally has a large central vacuole.

Parenchyma cells perform most of the metabolic functions of the plant, synthesizing and storing various organic products. For example, photosynthesis occurs within the chloroplasts of mesophyll cells, the parenchyma cells in the leaf. Some parenchyma cells in stems and roots have colorless plastids that store starch. The fleshy tissue of most fruit is composed mostly of parenchyma cells.

Developing plant cells of all types usually have the generalized structure of parenchyma cells before specializing further in structure and function. Mature parenchyma cells do not generally undergo cell division, but most of them retain the ability to divide and differentiate into other types of plant cells under special conditions—during the repair and replacement of organs after injury

Parenchyma cell   Cell wall   Collenchyma cell

Fiber cells (sclerenchyma)

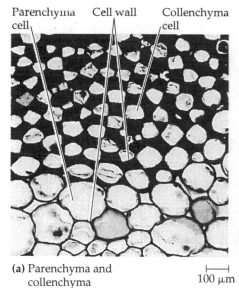
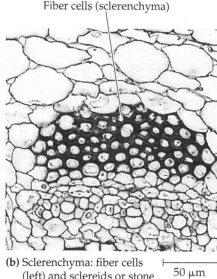
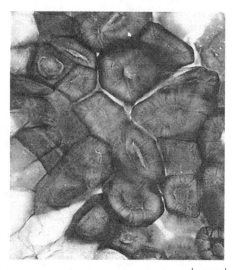

(a) Parenchyma and collenchyma   100 μm

(b) Sclerenchyma: fiber cells (left) and sclereids or stone cells (right)   50 μm

10 μm

FIGURE 31.10

Types of plant cells. (**a**) Parenchyma cells are relatively unspecialized, with thin, flexible primary walls. These cells carry on most of the plant's metabolic functions. Collenchyma cells have unevenly thickened primary walls and provide support to parts of the plant that are still growing. (**b**) Sclerenchyma cells, specialized for support, have secondary walls hardened with lignin and may be dead (lacking protoplasts) at functional maturity. The fiber cells in the left micrograph are elongated sclerenchyma cells. Sclereids (right) are irregularly shaped sclerenchyma cells with very thick, lignified secondary walls. (**c**) The water-conducting cells of xylem include tapered tracheids (left) and vessel elements arranged end to end, forming vessels (right). Both cell types have secondary walls and are dead at functional maturity. In gymnosperms, tracheids have the dual functions of water transport and structural support. In most angiosperms, both vessel elements and tracheids conduct water, and support is provided mainly by fiber cells. (**d**) The food-conducting cells of phloem are sieve-tube members, which are arranged end to end with porous walls (sieve plates) between them. (In the transverse section on the right, two sieve-tube members, including the labeled one, are sectioned through sieve plates.) The cells are living at functional maturity, but lack nuclei. Alongside each sieve-tube member is a nucleated companion cell. (All LMs.)

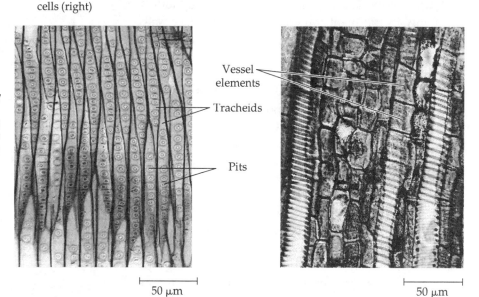

Vessel elements

Tracheids

Pits

(c) Xylem showing vessel elements and tracheids in longitudinal (left) and transverse (right) sections   50 μm   50 μm

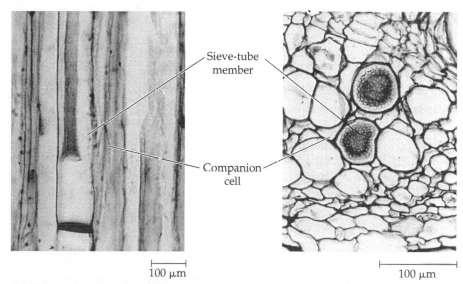

Sieve-tube member

Companion cell

(d) Phloem showing sieve-tube members and companion cells in longitudinal (left) and transverse (right) sections   100 μm   100 μm

to the plant, for instance. It is even possible in the laboratory to regenerate an entire plant from a single parenchyma cell.

Collenchyma Cells. Compared to parenchyma cells, **collenchyma cells** have thicker primary walls, though the walls are unevenly thickened (FIGURE 31.10a). Grouped in strands or cylinders, collenchyma cells help support young parts of the plant. Young stems, for instance, often have a cylinder of collenchyma just below their surface. Because they lack secondary walls and the hardening agent lignin is absent in their primary walls, collenchyma cells provide support without restraining growth. Unlike sclerenchyma cells, which we discuss next, mature, functioning collenchyma cells are living and elongate with the stems and leaves they support.

Sclerenchyma Cells. Also functioning as supporting elements in the plant, but with thick secondary walls strengthened by lignin, **sclerenchyma cells** are much more rigid than collenchyma cells. Mature sclerenchyma cells cannot elongate, and they occur in regions of the plant that have stopped growing in length. So specialized are sclerenchyma cells for support that many lack protoplasts at functional maturity, the stage in a cell's development when it is fully specialized for its function. Thus, at functional maturity a sclerenchyma cell may actually be dead, its rigid wall serving as scaffolding to support the plant.

The two forms of sclerenchyma cells are **fibers** and **sclereids** (FIGURE 31.10b). Long, slender, and tapered, fibers usually occur in bundles. Some plant fibers are used commercially, such as hemp fibers for making rope and flax fibers for weaving into linen. Sclereids are shorter than fibers and irregular in shape. Nutshells and seed coats owe their hardness to sclereids, and sclereids scattered among the soft parenchyma tissue give the pear fruit its gritty texture.

Tracheids and Vessel Elements: Water-Conducting Cells. The water-conducting elements of xylem are elongated cells of two types: **tracheids** and **vessel elements** (FIGURE 31.10c). Both types of cells are dead at functional maturity, but they produce secondary walls before the protoplast dies. In parts of the plant that are still elongating, the secondary walls are deposited unevenly in spiral or ring patterns that enable them to stretch like springs as the cell grows. Like the wire that reinforces the wall of a garden hose, these wall thickenings strengthen the water-conducting cells of the plant. Tracheids and vessel elements that form in parts of the plant that are no longer elongating usually have secondary walls with **pits,** thinner regions where only primary walls are present. A tracheid or vessel element

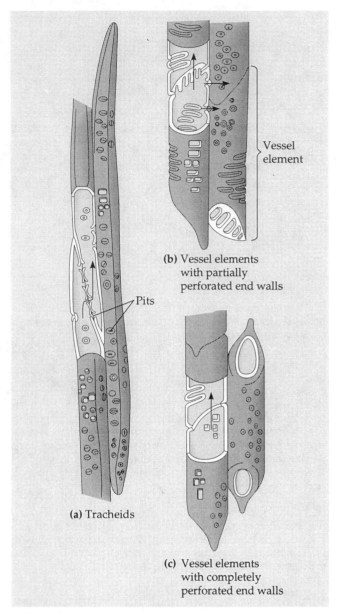

(b) Vessel elements with partially perforated end walls

Pits

(a) Tracheids

(c) Vessel elements with completely perforated end walls

FIGURE 31.11
Water-conducting cells of xylem. Arrows indicate the flow of water. (**a**) Tracheids are spindle-shaped cells with pits through which water flows from cell to cell. (**b**) Vessel elements are individual cells linked together end to end, forming long tubes, or xylem vessels. Water streams from element to element through perforated end walls. Water can also migrate laterally between neighboring vessels through pits. (**c**) Resistance to water flow in some xylem vessels is lowered by the complete perforation of walls between the vessel elements.

completes its differentiation when its protoplast disintegrates, leaving behind a nonliving conduit through which water can flow (FIGURE 31.11).

Tracheids are long, thin cells with tapered ends. Water moves from cell to cell mainly through pits. Because their secondary walls are hardened with lignin, tracheids function in support as well as water transport.

Vessel elements are generally wider, shorter, thinner-walled, and less tapered than tracheids. Vessel elements are aligned end to end, forming long micropipes, the **xylem vessels.** The end walls of vessel elements are perforated, enabling water to flow freely through xylem vessels.

Sieve-Tube Members: Food-Conducting Cells. Sucrose, other organic compounds, and some mineral ions are transported within the phloem of a plant through tubes formed by chains of cells called **sieve-tube members** (see FIGURE 31.10d). In contrast to the water-conducting cells of xylem, sieve-tube members are alive at functional maturity, although their protoplasts lack such organelles as the nucleus, ribosomes, and a distinct vacuole. In angiosperms, the end walls between sieve-tube members, called **sieve plates,** have pores that presumably facilitate the flow of fluid from cell to cell along the sieve tube.

Alongside each sieve-tube member is at least one **companion cell,** which is connected to the sieve-tube member by numerous plasmodesmata. The nucleus and ribosomes of the companion cell may serve not only that cell but also the adjacent sieve-tube member, which has no nucleus or ribosomes of its own. In some plants, companion cells also help load sugar produced in the mesophyll into the sieve-tube members of leaves.

The Three Tissue Systems of a Plant

The cells of a plant are organized into three tissue systems: the dermal, vascular, and ground tissue systems. Each tissue system is continuous throughout the plant body, although the specific characteristics of the tissues and their spatial relationships to one another vary in different organs of the plant (FIGURE 31.12). Here, we survey the three tissue systems as they occur in a young, nonwoody plant.

The **dermal tissue system,** or **epidermis,** is generally a single layer of tightly packed cells that covers and protects all young parts of the plant—the "skin" of the plant. In addition to the general function of protection, the epidermis has more specialized characteristics consistent with the function of the particular organ it covers. For example, the root hairs so important in the absorption of water and minerals are extensions of epidermal cells near the tips of roots. The epidermis of leaves and most stems secretes a waxy coating called the **cuticle** that helps the aerial parts of the plant retain water, an important adaptation to living on land.

The continuum of xylem and phloem throughout the plant forms the **vascular tissue system,** which functions in transport and support. The specific organization of vascular tissue in stems and roots is discussed in the next section.

The **ground tissue system** makes up the bulk of a young plant, filling the space between the dermal and

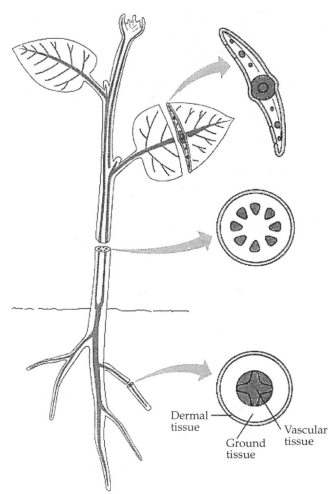

FIGURE 31.12

The three tissue systems. The dermal tissue system, or epidermis, is a single layer of cells that covers the entire body of a young plant. The vascular tissue system is also continuous throughout the plant, but it is arranged differently in each organ. The ground tissue system is located between the dermal tissue and vascular tissue in each organ.

vascular tissue systems. Ground tissue is predominantly parenchyma, but collenchyma and sclerenchyma are also commonly present. Among the diverse functions of ground tissue are photosynthesis, storage, and support.

Learning how a plant grows will help you understand how the tissue systems are organized in the different plant organs. We focus on plant growth in the next three sections.

■ Meristems generate cells for new organs throughout the lifetime of a plant: *an overview of plant growth*

From season to season and from year to year, the growth of plants alters our surroundings—yards, campuses, parks, vacant lots, woods, and the other landscapes in our communities. The growth of a plant from a seed is a fascinating transformation. The early stages of this growth—germination of the seed and emergence of the seedling—are among the topics of Chapter 34. Here, we will learn how plants continue to grow after their shoot and root systems are established.

Most plants continue to grow as long as they live, a condition known as indeterminate growth. Most animals, in contrast, are characterized by determinate growth; that is, they cease growing after reaching a certain size. While whole plants usually show indeterminate growth, certain plant organs, such as leaves and flowers, exhibit determinate growth.

Indeterminate growth does not imply immortality. Most plants probably have lifespans that are genetically programmed; such plants have a fixed longevity even when grown in constant, favorable conditions. Other plants have lifespans that are environmentally determined; if the plants are grown under controlled temperature and light conditions and are protected from disease, they may live much longer than they typically do in natural environments. Plants known as **annuals** complete their life cycle—from germination through flowering and seed production to death—in a single year or less. Many wildflowers are annuals, as are the most important food crops, including the cereal grains and legumes. A plant is called a **biennial** if its life generally spans two years. Flowering usually occurs during the second year, after a year of vegetative growth. Beets and carrots are biennials, but we rarely leave them in the ground long enough to see them flower. Plants that live many years, including trees, shrubs, and some grasses, are known as **perennials.** Some of the buffalo grass of the North American plains is believed to have been growing for 10,000 years from seeds that sprouted at the close of the last ice age.

Plants have the capacity for indeterminate growth because they have perpetually embryonic tissues called **meristems** in their regions of growth. Meristematic cells are unspecialized, and they divide to generate additional cells. Some of the products of this division remain in the meristematic region to produce still more cells, while others become specialized and are incorporated into the tissues and organs of the growing plant. Cells that remain as wellsprings of new cells in the meristem are called initials; those that are displaced from the meristem and are then destined to specialize within a developing tissue are called derivatives.

The pattern of plant growth depends on the locations of the meristems (FIGURE 31.13). **Apical meristems,** located at the tips of roots and in the buds of shoots, supply cells for the plant to grow in length. This elongation, called **primary growth,** enables roots to ramify throughout the soil and shoots to increase their exposure to light

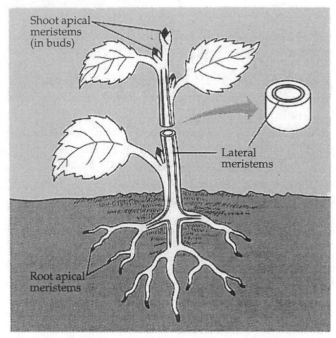

FIGURE 31.13

Locations of major meristems: An overview of plant growth. Meristems are self-renewing populations of cells that divide and provide cells for plant growth. Apical meristems, located near the tips of roots and shoots, are responsible for primary growth, or growth in length. Woody plants also have lateral meristems that function in secondary growth, which adds girth to roots and shoots.

and carbon dioxide. In herbaceous (nonwoody) plants, only primary growth occurs. In woody plants, however, there is also **secondary growth,** a progressive thickening of the roots and shoots formed earlier by primary growth. Secondary growth is the product of **lateral meristems,** cylinders of dividing cells extending along the length of roots and shoots. These lateral meristems replace the epidermis with a secondary dermal tissue that is thicker and tougher, and they also add layers of vascular tissue. Wood is the secondary xylem that accumulates over the years.

In woody plants, primary and secondary growth occur at the same time, but in different locations. Primary growth is restricted to the youngest parts of the plant—the tips of roots and shoots, where the apical meristems are located. The lateral meristems develop in slightly older regions of the roots and shoots, some distance away from the tips. There, secondary growth adds girth to the organs. The oldest region of a root or shoot—the base of a tree branch, for example—has the greatest accumulation of secondary tissues formed by the lateral meristems. Each growing season, primary growth produces young extensions of roots and shoots, while secondary growth thickens and strengthens the older parts of the plant. Closer study of primary and secondary growth in the next two sections will help you understand the morphology and anatomy of plants.

◼ Apical meristems extend roots and shoots: *a closer look at primary growth*

Primary growth produces what is called the **primary plant body,** which consists of the three tissue systems: dermal, vascular, and ground tissues (see FIGURE 31.12). A herbaceous plant and the youngest parts of a woody plant represent the primary plant body. Although apical meristems are responsible for the extension of both roots and shoots, there are important differences in the primary growth of these two kinds of organs.

Primary Growth of Roots

Primary growth pushes roots through the soil. The root tip is covered by a thimblelike **root cap,** which protects the delicate meristem as the root elongates through the abrasive soil. The cap also secretes a polysaccharide slime that lubricates the soil around the growing root tip. Growth in length is concentrated near the root's tip, where three zones of cells at successive stages of primary growth are located. From the root tip upward, they are the zone of cell division, the zone of elongation, and the zone of maturation. These regions grade together, with no sharp boundaries (FIGURE 31.14).

The **zone of cell division** includes the apical meristem and its derivatives, called primary meristems. The apical meristem, at the heart of the zone of cell division, produces the cells of the primary meristems and also replaces cells of the root cap that are sloughed off. Near the center of the apical meristem is the **quiescent center,** a population of cells that divide much more slowly than the other meristematic cells. Cells of the quiescent center are relatively resistant to damage from radiation and toxic chemicals, and they may function as reserves that can be recruited to restore the meristem if it is somehow damaged. In experiments where part of the apical meristem is removed, cells of the quiescent center become more mitotically active and produce a new meristem. Just above the apical meristem, the products of its cell division form three concentric cylinders of cells that continue to divide for some time. These are the primary

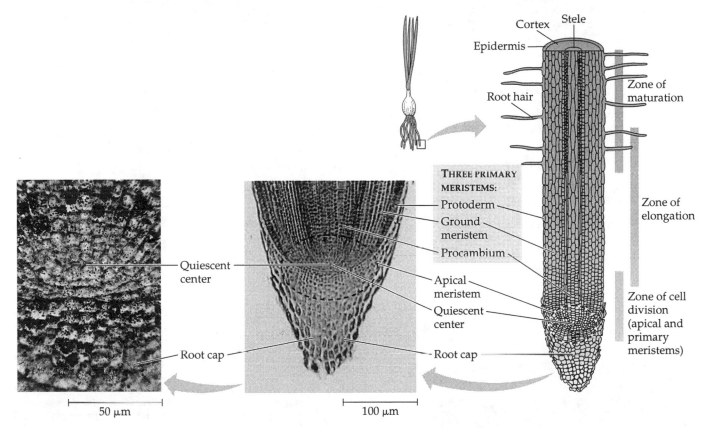

FIGURE 31.14

Primary growth of a root. Mitosis is concentrated in the zone of cell division, where the apical meristem and its products, the three primary meristems, are located. The apical meristem also maintains the root cap by generating new cells that replace those that are sloughed off (right LM). If the apical meristem is damaged, its quiescent center is activated and restores the meristem by means of cell division. Most lengthening of the root is concentrated in the zone of elongation. Cells become functionally mature in the zone of maturation. The zones of the root grade into one another without sharp boundaries. The far left micrograph of the apical meristem shows "hot spots" of cell division. This root was grown in a solution containing radioactive nucleotides, which are incorporated into the DNA of dividing cells. With the technique of autoradiography (see p. 30), the radioactive DNA exposes photographic film placed over the sectioned root, producing the black dots in the micrograph.

meristems—the **protoderm, procambium,** and **ground meristem**—which will produce the three primary tissue systems of the root: dermal, vascular, and ground tissues.

The zone of cell division blends into the **zone of elongation.** Here the cells elongate to more than ten times their original length. Although the meristem provides the new cells for growth, the elongation of cells is mainly responsible for pushing the root tip, including the meristem, ahead. The meristem sustains growth by continuously adding cells to the youngest end of the zone of elongation. Even before they finish elongating, the cells of the root begin to specialize in structure and function where the zone of elongation grades into the **zone of maturation.** In this latter region of the root, the three tissue systems produced by primary growth complete their differentiation.

Primary Tissues of Roots. The three primary meristems give rise to the three primary tissues of roots, shown in FIGURE 31.15. The protoderm, the outermost primary meristem, gives rise to the epidermis, a single layer of cells covering the root. Water and minerals that enter

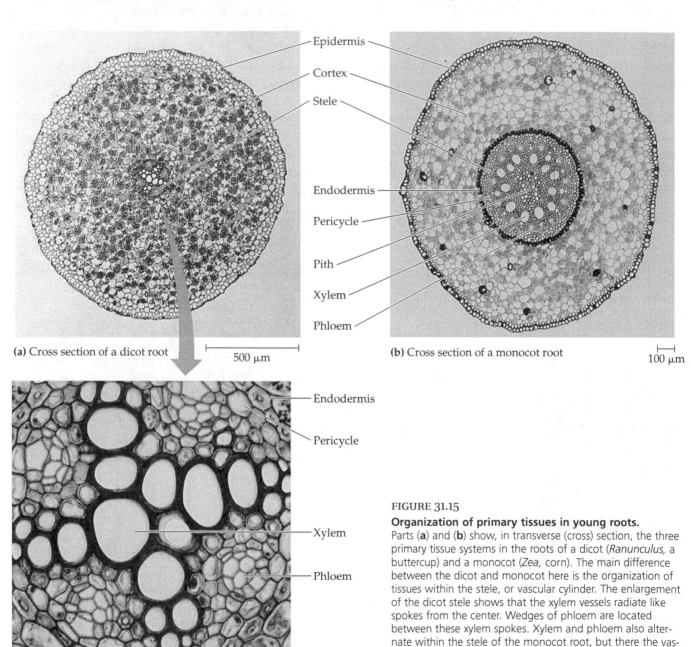

(a) Cross section of a dicot root — 500 μm

(b) Cross section of a monocot root — 100 μm

Epidermis
Cortex
Stele
Endodermis
Pericycle
Pith
Xylem
Phloem

Endodermis
Pericycle
Xylem
Phloem

50 μm

FIGURE 31.15

Organization of primary tissues in young roots.
Parts (**a**) and (**b**) show, in transverse (cross) section, the three primary tissue systems in the roots of a dicot (*Ranunculus,* a buttercup) and a monocot (*Zea,* corn). The main difference between the dicot and monocot here is the organization of tissues within the stele, or vascular cylinder. The enlargement of the dicot stele shows that the xylem vessels radiate like spokes from the center. Wedges of phloem are located between these xylem spokes. Xylem and phloem also alternate within the stele of the monocot root, but there the vascular tissues surround a core of parenchyma cells called the pith. In both dicots and monocots, the stele is circled by the endodermis, the innermost region of cells of the cortex. Just inside the endodermis is the pericycle, a layer of cells with the potential to divide and give rise to lateral roots. (All LMs.)

the plant from the soil must cross the epidermis. The root hairs enhance this process by greatly increasing the surface area of epidermal cells.

The procambium gives rise to a central vascular cylinder, or **stele,** where xylem and phloem develop. The specific arrangement of the two vascular tissues varies. In most dicots, the xylem cells radiate from the center of the stele in two or more spokes, with phloem developing in the wedges between the spokes. The stele of a monocot generally has a central core of parenchyma cells, often called the **pith,** which is ringed by vascular tissue with an alternating pattern of xylem and phloem.

Between the protoderm and procambium is the ground meristem, which gives rise to the ground tissue system. The ground tissue, which is mostly parenchyma, fills the **cortex,** the region of the root between the stele and epidermis. Ground tissue cells of the root store food, and their plasma membranes are active in the uptake of minerals that enter the root with the soil solution. The innermost layer of the cortex is the **endodermis,** a cylinder one cell thick that forms the boundary between the cortex and the stele. The endodermis functions as a selective barrier that regulates the passage of substances from the soil solution into the vascular tissue of the stele.

An established root may sprout **lateral roots,** which arise from the outermost layer of the stele, the **pericycle** (FIGURE 31.16). Just inside the endodermis, the pericycle is a layer of cells that may become meristematic and begin dividing again. Originating as a clump of cells formed by mitosis in the pericycle, a lateral root elongates and pushes through the cortex until it emerges from the primary root. The stele of the lateral root retains its connection with the stele of the primary root, making the vascular tissue continuous throughout the root system.

Primary Growth of Shoots

The apical meristem of a shoot is a dome-shaped mass of dividing cells at the tip of the terminal bud (FIGURE 31.17). As in the root, the apical meristem of the shoot tip gives rise to the primary meristems—protoderm, procambium, and ground meristem—which will differentiate into the three tissue systems. Leaves arise as leaf primordia on the flanks of the apical meristem. Axillary buds develop from islands of meristematic cells left by the apical meristem at the bases of the leaf primordia.

Within a bud, nodes, with their leaf primordia, are crowded close together, because internodes are very short. Most of the actual elongation of the shoot occurs by the growth of slightly older internodes below the shoot apex. This growth is due to both cell division and cell elongation within the internode. In some plants, including grasses, internodes continue to elongate all along the length of the shoot over a prolonged period.

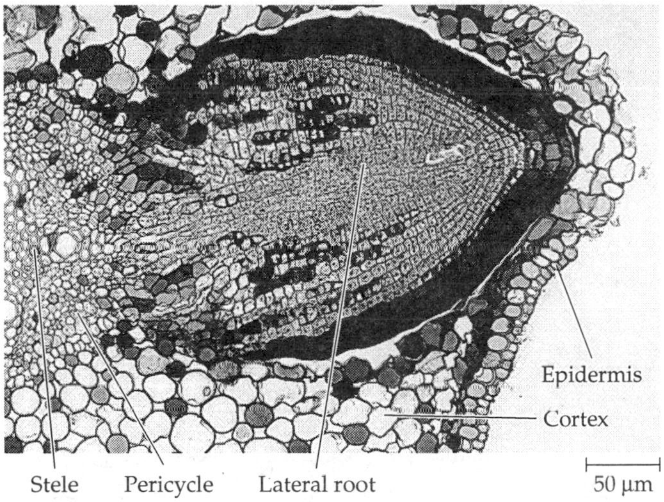

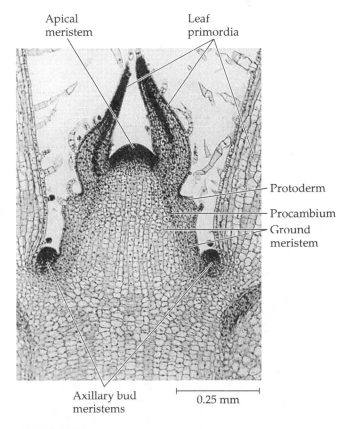

Apical meristem

Leaf primordia

Protoderm

Procambium

Ground meristem

Axillary bud meristems

0.25 mm

FIGURE 31.17
The terminal bud and primary growth of a shoot. Leaf primordia arise from the flanks of the apical dome. The apical meristem gives rise to protoderm, procambium, and ground meristem, which in turn develop into the three tissue systems. This is a longitudinal section of the shoot tip of *Coleus* (LM).

Epidermis

Cortex

Stele   Pericycle   Lateral root

50 µm

FIGURE 31.16
The formation of lateral roots. In this transverse section of a willow root, a lateral root emerges from the pericycle, the outermost layer of the stele (LM).

This is possible because these plants have meristematic regions, called intercalary meristems, at the base of each internode.

Axillary buds have the potential to form branches of the shoot system at some later time (see FIGURE 31.4). Thus, there is an important difference in how roots and shoots form lateral organs. Lateral roots originate from deep within a main root as outgrowths from the pericycle (see FIGURE 31.16). In contrast, branches of the shoot system originate from axillary buds, located at the surface of a main shoot. Only by extending from the stele can a lateral root be connected to the plant's vascular system. The vascular tissue of a stem, however, is near the surface, and branches can develop with connections to the vascular tissue without having to originate from deep within the main shoot.

Primary Tissues of Stems. Vascular tissue runs the length of a stem in several strands called **vascular bundles** (FIGURE 31.18). This arrangement contrasts with the root, where the vascular tissue forms a single stele consisting of the entire united set of vascular bundles (see FIGURE 31.15). At the transition zone where the shoot grades into the root, the vascular bundles converge to join the root stele.

Each vascular bundle of the stem is surrounded by ground tissue. In most dicots, the vascular bundles are arranged in a ring, with pith to the inside of the ring and cortex external to the ring. Both pith and cortex are part of the ground tissue system. The vascular bundles have their xylem facing the pith and their phloem facing the cortex side. The pith and cortex are connected by thin rays of ground tissue between the vascular bundles. In the stems of most monocots, the vascular bundles are scattered throughout the ground tissue rather than being arranged in a ring. The ground tissue of the stem is mostly parenchyma, but many stems are strengthened by collenchyma located just beneath the epidermis.

The protoderm of the terminal bud gives rise to the epidermis, which covers stems and leaves as part of the continuous dermal tissue system.

Tissue Organization of Leaves. The leaf is cloaked by its epidermis, with cells tightly interlocked like pieces of a puzzle (FIGURE 31.19). This epidermis, like our own skin, is a first line of defense against physical damage and

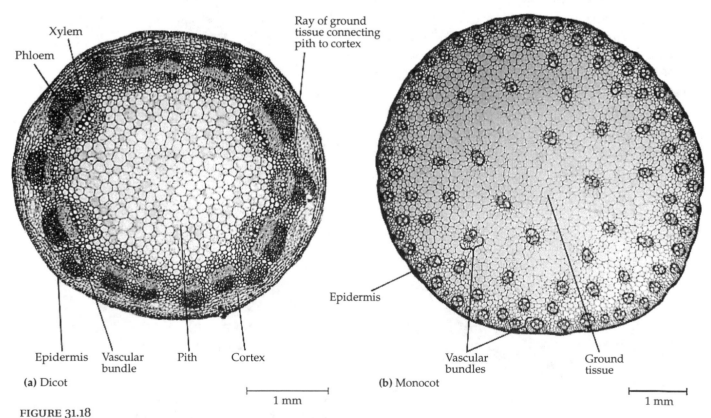

(a) Dicot

(b) Monocot

1 mm

1 mm

FIGURE 31.18

Organization of primary tissues in young stems. (*a*) A dicot stem (sunflower) with vascular bundles arranged in a ring. The ground tissue system consists of an outer cortex and an inner pith surrounded by vascular bundles. (*b*) A monocot stem (corn) with vascular bundles arranged in a complex manner throughout the ground tissue. (Both LMs.)

FIGURE 31.19

Leaf anatomy. (**a**) This cutaway drawing of a leaf illustrates the organization of the three tissue systems: dermal tissue (epidermis), vascular tissue, and ground tissue (mesophyll, consisting of palisade parenchyma and spongy mesophyll). (**b**) This surface view of a *Tradescantia* leaf shows the cells of the epidermis and the stomata with their guard cells (LM). The lower leaf surface generally has more stomata than the upper surface, an adaptation that helps reduce water loss by transpiration. (**c**) Palisade and spongy regions of mesophyll are present within the leaf of a lilac, a dicot (LM).

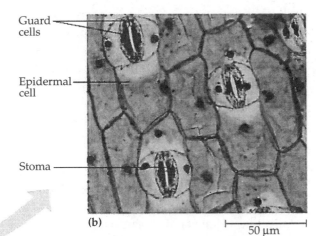

(b)

50 µm

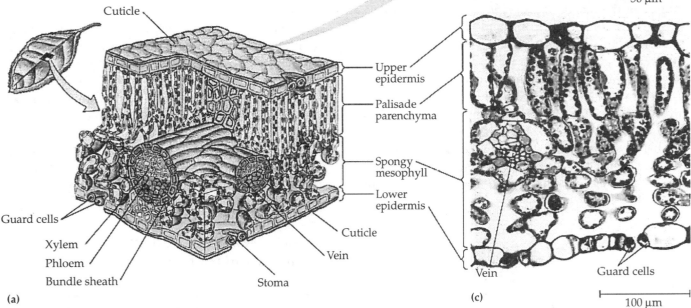

(a)

(c)

100 µm

pathogenic organisms. Also, the waxy cuticle of the epidermis is a barrier to the loss of water from the plant. The epidermal barrier is interrupted only by the **stomata,** tiny pores flanked by specialized epidermal cells called **guard cells.** Each stoma is actually a gap between a pair of guard cells. The stomata allow gas exchange between the surrounding air and the photosynthetic cells inside the leaf. Stomata are also the major avenues for the loss of water from the plant by evaporation, a process called **transpiration.**

The ground tissue of a leaf, sandwiched between the upper and lower epidermis, is the **mesophyll** (Gr. *mesos,* "middle," and *phyll,* "leaf"). It consists mainly of parenchyma cells equipped with chloroplasts and specialized for photosynthesis. The leaves of many dicots have two distinct regions of mesophyll. On the upper half of the leaf are one or more layers of palisade parenchyma, made up of cells that are columnar in shape. Below the palisade region is the spongy mesophyll, which gets its name from the labyrinth of air spaces through which carbon dioxide and oxygen circulate around the irregularly

shaped cells and up to the palisade region. The air spaces are particularly large in the vicinity of stomata, where gas exchange with the outside air occurs. In most plants, stomata are more numerous on the bottom surface of a leaf than on top. This adaptation minimizes water loss, which occurs more rapidly through stomata on the sunny upper side of a leaf. Once again, it helps to view the functional structure of plants in the evolutionary context of adaptation to land.

The vascular tissue of a leaf is continuous with the xylem and phloem of the stem. Leaf traces, which are branches from vascular bundles in the stem, pass through petioles and into leaves. Within a leaf, veins subdivide repeatedly and branch throughout the mesophyll. This brings xylem and phloem into close contact with the photosynthetic tissue, which obtains water and minerals from the xylem and loads its sugars and other organic products into the phloem for shipment to other parts of the plant. The vascular infrastructure also functions as a skeleton that supports the ground tissue (mesophyll) of the leaf.

Modular Shoot Construction and Phase Changes During Development. Serial development of nodes and internodes within the shoot apex, followed by elongation of the internodes, produces a shoot having a modular construction—a series of segments, each consisting of a stem, one or more leaves, and an axillary bud associated with each leaf (FIGURE 31.20). The development of this modular morphology should not be confused with the development of the segmented anatomy of certain animals such as earthworms. In animal development, the rudiments of all organs form in the embryo. Plants, in contrast, add organs at their tips for as long as they live. Unlike the segments of an earthworm, which are all the same age, the modules of a plant vary in age in proportion to their distance from an apical meristem.

From what you have learned so far about the shoot apex and primary growth, it would seem as if the meristem lays down a series of identical modules for as long as the shoot lives. In fact, the apical meristem can change from one developmental phase to another during its history. One of these phase changes is a gradual transition from a juvenile vegetative (leaf-producing) state to a mature vegetative state. Modification of leaf morphology is usually the most obvious sign of this phase change: The leaves of juvenile versus mature shoot modules differ in shape and other features. Once the meristem has laid down juvenile nodes and internodes, they retain that status even as the shoot continues to elongate and the meristem eventually changes to the mature phase. If axillary buds give rise to branches, those shoots reflect the developmental phase of the main shoot modules from which they arise. The juvenile-to-mature phase transition is another case where it is misleading to compare plant and animal development. In an animal, this transition occurs at the level of the entire organism. In plants, phase changes during the history of apical meristems can result in juvenile and mature regions coexisting along the axis of a shoot.

In some cases, a shoot apex undergoes a second phase transition from a mature vegetative state to a reproductive (flower-producing) state. Unlike vegetative growth, which is self-renewing, the production of a flower by an apical meristem terminates primary growth of that shoot tip; the apical meristem is consumed in the production of the flower's organs.

In Chapter 34, we will study flower development in more detail, and in Chapter 35, we will examine how this phase change from vegetative growth of a shoot to the reproductive growth of flowering is controlled.

◾ Lateral meristems add girth to stems and roots: *a closer look at secondary growth*

Most vascular plants undergo secondary growth, increasing in girth as well as length. The **secondary plant body** consists of the tissues produced during this secondary growth in diameter. Two lateral meristems function in secondary growth: the **vascular cambium,** which produces secondary xylem and phloem; and the **cork cambium,** which produces a tough, thick covering for stems and roots that replaces the epidermis. Secondary growth occurs in all gymnosperms. Among angiosperms, secondary growth takes place in most dicot species but is rare in monocots.

Secondary Growth of Stems

Vascular Cambium. The vascular cambium forms from parenchyma cells that develop the capacity to divide; that is, the cells become meristematic. This transition to meristematic activity takes place in a layer between the primary xylem and primary phloem of each vascular bundle and in the rays of ground tissue between the bundles (FIGURE 31.21). The cambium within the vascular bundle is called fasicular cambium; the portion of the cambium in the rays between vascular bundles is

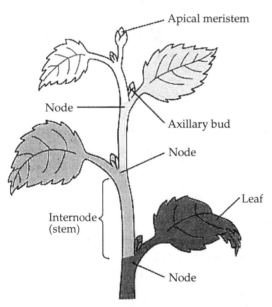

FIGURE 31.20
Modular construction of a shoot. Primary growth lays down a series of segments (different colors in this drawing), each consisting of a node with one or more leaves, an axillary bud in the axil of each leaf, and an internode. Miniature modules develop within the apical meristem and then grow, pushing the apex onward, where it forms the next module, and so on. This serial addition of segments at the growing end of the shoot contrasts with the development of segmentation in certain animals, in which all the segments form at about the same time in the embryo. (Imagine if our arms and legs were different ages, like the appendages of a plant!)

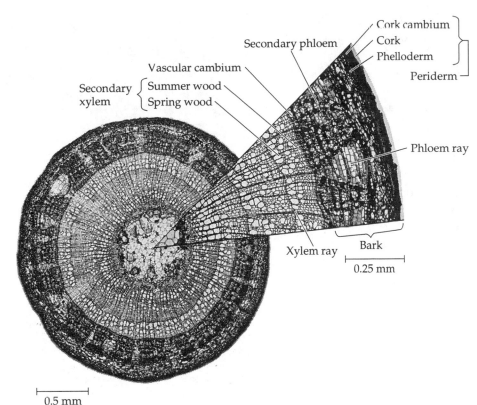

Secondary phloem

Cork cambium
Cork
Phelloderm
Periderm

Vascular cambium

Secondary xylem { Summer wood / Spring wood

Phloem ray

Xylem ray   Bark

0.25 mm

0.5 mm

FIGURE 31.21
Anatomy of a woody dicot stem. A few years of secondary growth are apparent as growth rings in this transverse section of a stem from *Tilia,* the American linden (basswood). At the boundary of one season's growth to the next, notice the spring wood and summer wood. Vascular cambium produces the secondary growth. Secondary xylem and secondary phloem are derived from fusiform initials, cambium cells that develop within the vascular bundles. The cambium cells that develop in the intervening rays of ground tissue are called ray initials; they give rise to the xylem and phloem rays, structures that function in radial transport and storage. A second lateral meristem, the cork cambium, produces cork cells to its outside and phelloderm cells to its inside. Together, the cork cambium and its derivatives, cork and phelloderm, make up the periderm, which is the protective covering of the secondary plant body. The bark consists of all tissues external to the vascular cambium. (Both LMs.)

called interfasicular cambium. Together, the meristematic bands in these fasicular and interfasicular regions give rise to the vascular cambium as a continuous cylinder of dividing cells surrounding the primary xylem and pith of the stem.

The meristematic cells of the interfasicular cambium are called **ray initials.** They produce radial files of parenchyma cells known as **xylem rays** and **phloem rays,** which function as living avenues for the lateral transport of water and nutrients and in the storage of starch and other reserves. The cambium cells within the vascular bundles (fasicular cambium) are the **fusiform initials,** a name that refers to the shape of these cells, which have tapered (fusiform) ends and are elongated along the axis of the stem. Fusiform initials produce new vascular tissue, forming secondary xylem to the inside of the vascular cambium and secondary phloem to the outside (FIGURE 31.22).

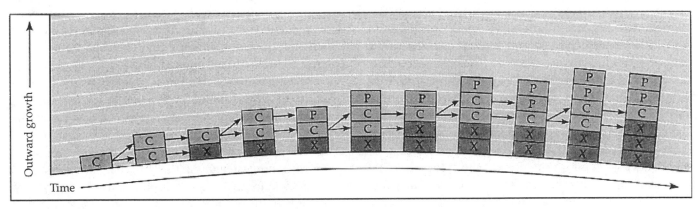

FIGURE 31.22
Production of secondary xylem and phloem by the vascular cambium. This diagram traces the file of cells that develops from the meristematic activity of a single fusiform initial of the vascular cambium as viewed in transverse section. The cambium cell (C) gives rise to xylem (X) on the inside and phloem (P) on the outside. Each time an initial divides, one daughter cell retains its status as an initial, and the other, the derivative, differentiates into a xylem or phloem cell. As layers of xylem are added, the position of the cambium becomes more distant from the center of the stem.

Outward growth

Time

As secondary growth continues over the years, layer upon layer of secondary xylem accumulates, producing what we call wood. Wood consists mainly of tracheids, vessel elements (in angiosperms), and fibers. These cells, dead at functional maturity, have thick, lignified walls that give wood its hardness and strength. In temperate regions of the world, secondary growth in perennial plants is interrupted each year when the vascular cambium becomes dormant during winter. When secondary growth resumes in the spring, the first tracheids and vessel elements to develop usually have relatively large diameters and thin walls compared to the secondary xylem produced later in the summer. Thus, it is usually possible to distinguish spring wood from summer wood (see FIGURE 31.21). The annual growth rings that are evident in cross sections of most tree trunks in temperate regions result from this yearly activity of the vascular cambium: cambium dormancy, spring wood production, and summer wood production. The boundary between one year's growth and the next is usually quite conspicuous, sometimes allowing us to estimate the age of a tree by counting its annual rings.

The secondary phloem, external to the vascular cambium, does not accumulate as extensively over the years as the secondary xylem does. As a tree grows in girth, the older (outermost) secondary phloem, and all tissues external to it, develop into bark, which eventually splits and sloughs off the tree trunk.

Cork Cambium. During secondary growth, the epidermis produced by primary growth splits, dries, and falls off the stem. It is replaced by new protective tissues produced by the cork cambium, a cylinder of meristematic tissue that first forms in the outer cortex of the stem (see FIGURE 31.21). As initials in the cork cambium divide, they give rise to parenchyma cells called **phelloderm** to their inside and **cork cells** to their outside. As the cork cells mature, they deposit a waxy material called suberin in their walls and then die. The cork tissue then functions as a barrier that helps protect the stem from physical damage and pathogens. And because cork is waxy, it impedes water loss from the stems. Together, the layers of cork plus the cork cambium and phelloderm make up the **periderm.** This is the protective coat of the secondary plant body that replaces the epidermis of the primary body. The term **bark,** more inclusive than periderm, refers to all tissues external to the vascular cambium. Thus, in an outward direction, bark consists of phloem, phelloderm, cork cambium, and cork. Put another way, bark is phloem plus periderm (FIGURE 31.23).

Unlike the vascular cambium, which grows in diameter, the original cork cambium is a cylinder of fixed size.

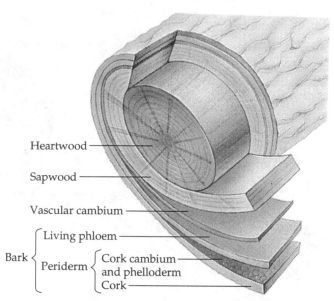

Heartwood

Sapwood

Vascular cambium

Bark { Living phloem

Periderm { Cork cambium and phelloderm

Cork

FIGURE 31.23

Anatomy of a tree trunk. Beginning at the center of the tree and tracing outward, we can distinguish several zones. Heartwood and sapwood both consist of secondary xylem. Heartwood is older and no longer functions in water transport; the lignified walls of its dead cells form a central column that supports the tree. This wood owes its rich color to resins and other compounds that clog the cell cavities and help protect the core of the tree from fungi and insects. Sapwood is so named because its secondary xylem cells still function in the upward transport of water and minerals (xylem sap). Since each new layer of secondary xylem has a larger circumference, secondary growth enables the xylem to transport more sap each year, providing water and minerals to an increasing number of leaves.

After a few weeks of cork production, the cork cambium loses its meristematic activity, and its remaining cells differentiate into cork. Expansion of the stem splits the original periderm. How is it renewed to keep pace with continued secondary growth? New cork cambium forms deeper and deeper in the cortex. Eventually, no cortex is left, and the cork cambium then develops from parenchyma cells in the secondary phloem.

Only the youngest secondary phloem, which is internal to the cork cambium, functions in sugar transport. The older secondary phloem, outside the cork cambium, dies and helps protect the stem until it is sloughed off as part of the bark during later seasons of secondary growth. Spongy regions in the bark called **lenticels** make it possible for living cells within the trunk to exchange gases with the outside air for cellular respiration.

The result of many years of secondary stem growth can be seen by examining an old tree trunk in cross section (see FIGURE 31.23). FIGURE 31.24 will help you review the relationships among the primary and secondary tissues of a woody plant.

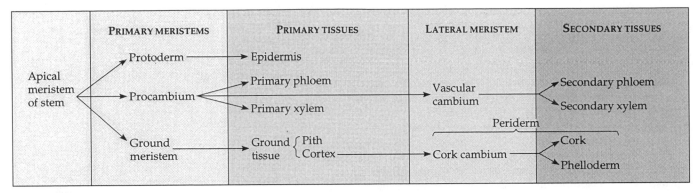

FIGURE 31.24

A summary of primary and secondary growth in a woody stem.

Secondary Growth of Roots

The two lateral meristems, vascular cambium and cork cambium, also develop and produce secondary growth in roots. The vascular cambium forms within the stele and produces secondary xylem to its inside and secondary phloem to its outside. As the stele grows in diameter, the cortex and epidermis are split and shed. A cork cambium forms from the pericycle of the stele and produces the periderm, which becomes the secondary dermal tissue. Unlike the primary epidermis of a younger root, periderm is impermeable to water. Therefore, it is only the youngest roots, those representing the primary plant body, that absorb water and minerals from the soil. Older roots, with secondary growth, function mainly to anchor the plant and to transport water and solutes between the younger roots and the shoot system.

Over the years, the root becomes more woody, and annual rings are usually evident in the secondary xylem.

The tissues external to the vascular cambium form a thick, tough bark. After extensive secondary growth, old stems and old roots are quite similar.

*   *   *

In dissecting the plant to examine its parts, as we have done in this chapter, we must remember that the whole plant functions as an integrated organism. In the following chapters, you will learn more about how materials are transported within the plant, how plants obtain nutrients, how plants reproduce and develop, and how the various functions of the plant are coordinated. Your understanding of the working plant will be enhanced by remembering that structure fits function and that interactions with the environment affect the anatomy and physiology of plants.

REVIEW OF KEY CONCEPTS (with page numbers and key figures)

- Plant biology reflects the major themes in the study of life (pp. 144–146)
  - Plants are the main producers in most terrestrial ecosystems.
  - A plant is adapted to living on land through evolution and through individual response to the environment.
- A plant's root and shoot systems are evolutionary adaptations to living on land (pp. 146–151, FIGURE 31.4)
  - Based on differences in anatomy, the angiosperms can be divided into two classes: monocots and dicots.
  - Differentiation of the plant body into an underground root system and an aerial shoot system is an adaptation to terrestrial life.
  - Vascular tissues integrate the parts of the plant body. Water and minerals move up from the roots in the xylem; sugar travels to nonphotosynthetic parts in the phloem.

- The structure of roots is adapted to anchor the plant, absorb and conduct water and minerals, and store food. Tiny root hairs near the root tips enhance absorption.
  - The shoot system consists of stems, leaves, and flowers.
  - Leaves are attached by their petioles to the nodes of stems. Axillary buds that are stimulated to grow may become flowers or vegetative branches. Stolons, rhizomes, and bulbs are modified stems.
- The many types of plant cells are organized into three major tissue systems (pp. 151–155, FIGURES 31.10, 31.12)
  - Parenchyma cells are the least specialized plant cells, peforming general metabolic and storage functions. They retain the ability to divide and differentiate into other cell types under certain conditions.
  - Collenchyma cells support young parts of the plant shoot without restraining growth.

- Sclerenchyma cells, fibers and sclereids, are supportive cells with thick, lignified secondary walls. Many lack protoplasts; thus, at maturity they are unable to elongate.
- Water-conducting xylem tissue is composed of elongated tracheid and vessel element cells that are dead at functional maturity. Tracheids are long, thin, tapered cells with lignified secondary walls that function in support and permit water flow through pits. The wider, shorter, and thinner-walled vessel elements have perforated ends through which water flows freely.
- Sieve-tube members are living cells that form phloem tubes for the transport of sucrose and other organic nutrients. Each sieve-tube member is connected to one or more companion cells by plasmodesmata.
- Plant tissues are arranged into three continuous systems. The dermal tissue system, or epidermis, is an external layer of tightly packed cells that functions in protection. The vascular tissue system, consisting of xylem and phloem, provides transport and support. The predominantly parenchymous ground tissue system functions in organic synthesis, storage, and support.

- Meristems generate cells for new organs throughout the lifetime of a plant: *an overview of plant growth* (pp. 155–156, FIGURE 31.13)
  - Because they possess permanently embryonic meristems, plants, unlike animals, show indeterminate growth.
  - Apical meristems at root tips and shoot buds initiate primary growth (growth in length) and the formation of the three tissue systems. Lateral meristems are responsible for secondary growth (growth in thickness).

- Apical meristems extend roots and shoots: *a closer look at primary growth* (pp. 157–162, FIGURES 31.14–31.19)
  - Primary growth produces the primary plant body, which consists of the three tissue systems.
  - Root tips, protected by the root caps, grow and develop by the activities of cells in the zones of cell division, elongation, and maturation.
  - Just behind the apical meristem in the zone of cell division are the three primary meristems of the root. The protoderm gives rise to the epidermis, the procambium forms the central vascular stele, and the ground meristem produces the ground tissue of the cortex. Subsequent lateral roots arise from the pericycle of the stele.
  - The elongation of shoots comes from the dome-shaped apical meristem at the top of the terminal bud. Leaf primordia arise from the sides of the apical dome, and axillary buds arise from residual islands of meristematic cells at the bases of leaf primordia.
  - In contrast to the single stele of the root, the vascular tissue of stems runs in vascular bundles surrounded by ground tissue in characteristic patterns that differ between monocots and dicots.
  - Leaves are covered with a waxy epidermis. Pairs of guard cells flank openings called stomata, through which gas exchange and transpiration occur. Between the upper and lower epidermis, the ground tissue, or mesophyll, consists mainly of parenchyma cells equipped with chloroplasts for photosynthesis. A strand of vascular tissue called the leaf trace connects the veins of the leaf with the vascular tissue of the stem.

- The shoot is a series of modules, each consisting of a node with leaves, an axillary bud, and an internode. Phase changes in the development of the shoot tip alter the morphology of modules.

- Lateral meristems add girth to stems and roots: *a closer look at secondary growth* (pp. 162–165, FIGURE 31.24)
  - Secondary growth produces the secondary plant body, the tissues that cause an increase in diameter.
  - The increase in the girth of stems and roots is due to secondary production of new cells by the vascular cambium and the cork cambium, two lateral meristems.
  - The vascular cambium, a continuous cylinder of meristematic cells, produces secondary xylem internally and secondary phloem externally.
  - The cork cambium, a meristematic cylinder in the outer cortex of the stem, produces waxy cork cells externally and phelloderm (a parenchyma) internally. The cork cambium, phelloderm, and cork make up the periderm, which replaces the epidermis that sloughs off during secondary growth. Secondary phloem gives rise to new cork cambium after the original cortex is shed. Bark consists of phloem plus periderm.
  - In roots, the vascular cambium arises between the xylem and phloem of the stele and functions similarly to that in stems. Cork cambium, produced from the pericycle of the stele, forms the periderm that replaces cortex and epidermis.

SELF-QUIZ

1. Which structure is *incorrectly* paired with its tissue system?
   a. root hair—dermal tissue
   b. mesophyll—ground tissue
   c. guard cell—dermal tissue
   d. companion cell—ground tissue
   e. tracheid—vascular tissue

2. The lateral roots of a young dicot originate from the
   a. pericycle of the taproot
   b. endodermis of fibrous roots
   c. meristematic cells of the protoderm
   d. vascular cambium
   e. root cortex

3. A sieve-tube member would likely lose its nucleus in which zone of growth in a root?
   a. zone of cell division
   b. zone of elongation
   c. zone of maturation
   d. root cap
   e. quiescent center

4. Vessel elements of the primary plant body originate from the
   a. protoderm
   b. procambium
   c. ground meristem
   d. xylem rays
   e. cork cambium

5. Which of the following is *not* a correctly stated difference between monocots and dicots?
   a. parallel veins in monocots; branching, netlike venation in dicot leaves
   b. vascular bundles scattered in monocot stems; central vascular stele in dicot stems
   c. flower parts in threes in monocots; flower parts in multiples of four or five in dicots
   d. usually only primary growth in monocots; secondary growth in many dicots
   e. one cotyledon in monocots; two cotyledons in dicots

6. Ivy (*Hedera helix*) undergoes a gradual change from a juvenile vegetative state to a mature vegetative state. This results in mature leaves on upper branches having a different shape than juvenile leaves on lower branches. If the phase of the axillary buds is fixed, then the lateral buds of lower branches can develop to form _____ branches, and the lateral buds of upper branches can develop to form _____ branches.
   a. only juvenile; only mature
   b. only mature; only juvenile
   c. juvenile or mature; only juvenile
   d. only mature; juvenile or mature
   e. juvenile or mature; only mature

7. Wood consists mostly of
   a. bark
   b. periderm
   c. secondary xylem
   d. secondary phloem
   e. cork

8. Which of the following is not part of an older tree's bark?
   a. cork
   b. cork cambium
   c. lenticels
   d. secondary xylem
   e. secondary phloem

9. Each module of a primary plant body's shoot system consists of a
   a. stem, leaf, and axillary bud
   b. stem, axillary bud, and apical bud
   c. leaf, flower, and stem
   d. stem, flower, and axillary bud
   e. node, internode, and apical bud

10. Which of the following cell types or structures is *incorrectly* paired with its meristematic origin?
    a. epidermis—protoderm
    b. stele—procambium
    c. cortex—ground meristem
    d. secondary phloem—cork cambium
    e. three primary meristems—apical meristem

CHALLENGE QUESTIONS

1. If you were to live for the next several decades in a treehouse built on the large, lower branches of a tree, would you gain much altitude as the tree grew? Explain your answer.

2. Starting at the surface of a tree trunk and working to the center, describe the structure and function of the tissue layers.

3. Describe some important differences in the growth and development of plants and animals.

4. Choose three specialized types of plant cells and describe how their structures are adapted for their specific functions.

SCIENCE, TECHNOLOGY, AND SOCIETY

1. Make a list of the plants and plant products you use in a typical day. How do you use these various plant products? Do you think the number of plants and plant products used in everyday life has increased or decreased in the last century? Do you think the number is likely to increase or decrease in the future? Why?

2. On your next trip to the grocery store, take a notepad and list the types of produce (fruits and vegetables) in one column and the parts of plants they represent in a parallel column.

FURTHER READING

Bolz, D. M. "A World of Leaves: Familiar Forms and Surprising Twists." *Smithsonian*, April 1985. A delightful article on the adaptations of leaves, featuring exquisite photographs.

Dale, J. "How Do Leaves Grow?" *BioScience*, June 1992. Using new techniques of molecular and cell biology, researchers are answering long-standing questions about plant structure and growth.

Galston, A. W. *Life Processes of Plants*. New York: W. H. Freeman, 1994. Plant structure and physiology, with an emphasis on interactions with light.

Gillis, A.M. "Using a Mousy, Little Flower to Understand Flamboyant Ones." *BioScience*, May 1995. The value of *Arabidopsis* as a model for developmental genetics.

Kaplan, D. R., and W. Hagemann. "The Relationship of Cell and Organism in Vascular Plants: Are Cells the Building Blocks of Plant Form?" *BioScience*, November 1991. Important differences in how plants and animals are organized.

Meyorowitz, E. M. "The Genetics of Flower Development." *Scientific American*, November 1994. The value of mutations in research.

Moore, R., W. D. Clark, and K. R. Stern. *Botany*. Dubuque, IA: W. C. Brown, 1995. An excellent introduction to plant biology.

Poethig, R. S. "Phase Change and the Regulation of Short Morphogenesis in Plants." *Science*, November 16, 1990. The molecular and cellular basis of shoot development.

Testing Your Understanding—Unit IV

Biology, **Chapter 31: Plant Structure and Growth**

Pages 144–151
CHECKING YOUR COMPREHENSION

Choose the best answer for each of the following questions.

1. Scientists are interested in the plant *arabidopsis thaliana* because
   a. it contains a great diversity and quantity of DNA.
   b. its size makes it easy to study with the unaided eye.
   c. it germinates and reproduces in only about six weeks.
   d. mutation occurs spontaneously in about half of the plants.

2. The introductory section of the chapter suggests that the primary organization of the chapter will
   a. compare plants to animals.
   b. move from external to internal structures.
   c. outline new research methods.
   d. categorize common plants and vegetables.

3. The primary purpose of figure 31.2 is to
   a. compare plant and animal reactions to the environment.
   b. outline the concept of plant morphology.
   c. demonstrate the importance of a taproots system.
   d. illustrate structural adaptation of plants.

Identify the following statements as true or false.

4. Potatoes are part of the root system.

5. Analogies between animals and plants reveal essential similarities.

6. Monocots usually have 3, 5, or 7 flower petals.

7. Roots provide the primary mechanism for photosynthesis.

Answer the following questions.

8. Identify the four primary purposes of roots.

9. Identify five primary ways in which leaves are differentiated.

10. Identify two recall strategies which would help you remember the answers to questions 8 and 9 and describe why they would be effective.

11. Draw a plant and label the following parts: roots, veins, nodes, internode, terminal bud, axillary bud, blade, petiole, rhizomes. What method of vocabulary building are you using in answering this question?

Discussion and Critical Thinking Questions

1. Using the information in this section of the chapter, identify as much as possible about the shoots and roots of the following items on a salad bar: lettuce, celery, carrot, radish, onion.

2. How might research into plant morphology and anatomy increase or decrease human dependence on plants?

3. If statistical information were added to this section of the chapter as additional evidence, where do you think it would be the most useful?

Pages 151–156
CHECKING YOUR COMPREHENSION

Choose the best answer for each of the following questions.

1. Which of the following best describes the purpose of the first paragraph under the heading "The many types of plant cells are organized into three major tissue systems"?
   a. categorize function
   b. propose a hypothesis
   c. summarize alternative explanations
   d. outline key concepts

2. Which of the following would be the most useful items to scan when pre-reading this section?
   a. headings and boldface words
   b. first and last paragraphs
   c. longest paragraph
   d. review of key concepts

3. The primary function of Figure 31.12 is to
   a. introduce information in addition to text material.
   b. refute text material.
   c. compare and contrast alternative categories.
   d. illustrate and summarize text material.

Identify the following statements as true or false.

4. Water flows through both end walls and pits in cells.

5. The primary purpose of sclerenchyma cells is to conduct water.

6. The locations of the tissue systems are determined by the function of the plant parts.

Answer the following questions.

7. Identify the five types of plant cells.

8. Identify the three tissue systems of plants.

9. List the three possible life spans of plants.

Define each of the following terms.

10. protoplast

11. parenchyma cells

12. sclereids

13. epidermis

14. meristems

Discussion and Critical Thinking Questions

1. Evaluate the reading difficulty of this passage. What factors should be considered in making your assessment?

2. What factors should you consider in combining annuals, biennials, and perennials in the same flower bed?

3. What information is needed to determine what type of plants would grow best in different climates?

Pages 157–165
CHECKING YOUR COMPREHENSION

Choose the best answer for each of the following questions.

1. Which of the following statements is true of the vascular systems of roots and stems?
   a. Roots usually form lateral vascular systems while shoots usually form primary vascular systems.
   b. The vascular systems of roots are in a circle while those in a stem are scattered throughout the ground tissue.
   c. The vascular systems of roots are deeper within the tissue than the vascular systems of stems.
   d. The primary purpose of the vascular systems of both roots and stems is to form a skeletal system of support.

2. Which of the following sets of words would be best to highlight in the following paragraph?

   In some cases, a shoot apex undergoes a second phase transition from a mature vegetative state to a reproductive (flower-producing) state. Unlike vegetative growth, which is self-renewing, the production of a flower by an apical meristem terminates primary growth of that shoot tip; the apical meristem is consumed in the production of the flower's organs.

   a. shoot apex undergoes transitions apical meristem consumed flower
   b. vegetative reproductive terminates flower
   c. second transition vegetative flower-producing terminates primary growth
   d. second phase production flower terminates shoot tip

3. Which of the following best describes the organizational pattern of the first paragraph under the heading "Cork Cambium"?
   a. chronological
   b. comparison
   c. cause-effect
   d. enumeration

Identify the following statements as true or false.

4. The primary purpose of the first paragraph under "Lateral meristems add girth to stems and roots" is to define secondary growth.

5. The pith has its origins in the protoderm.

6. The epidermis of a leaf is an unbroken layer of interlocking cells.

7. Older roots usually do not absorb much water or minerals from the soil.

Based on similarity of word parts, identify another term from the chapter which is related to each given term.

8. endoderm

9. angiosperms

10. procambium

11. monocot

Fill in the following outline of the section "Apical meristems extend roots and shoots."

    I. Primary growth
        A.
           1.
              a. root cap
              b.
              c.
              d.
           2. Tissue types
              a.
              b.
              c.
        B. Shoots
           1.
              a.
              b.
           2.
              a.
              b.
              c.
              d. epidermis
           3.
           4. Modular shoot construction
           5.

Discussion and Critical Thinking Questions

1. What is the basis for the differences between trees and grass?

2. Describe important differences in growth and development of plants and animals. What parts of animals grow/develop most similarly to plants? How does the function of these parts affect their growth and development?

3. To make plants fuller, gardeners often pinch the tops off of plants. Conversely, they often pinch lateral branches off tomato plants to achieve larger tomatoes. Identify where in the chapter you would find information to explain the biological reasons for these actions.

4. Environmentalists say that there would be no problem with endangered species of trees if wood could be harvested internally. Why do you think they say this?

CHAPTER REVIEW

End of Chapter Analysis

Choose the best answer for each of the following questions.

1. Which of the following strategies would be most useful in reading and studying this chapter?
    a. scanning
    b. paraphrasing
    c. highlighting
    d. reading notebook

2. After reading the chapter, you should be able to answer all of the following questions except which one?
    a. What is the function of meristems?
    b. What mechanism enables water to be dispersed through plant veins?
    c. How are plant tissue systems organized?
    d. Why have land-based plants evolved as they have?

3. The "Further Reading" section at the end of the chapter gives bibliographical citations and brief descriptions of the articles. The article which seems to have been intended for a non-scholarly audience was written by
   a. Bolz
   b. Dale
   c. Meyorowitz
   d. Poethig

Group Projects

1. Using Figure 31.24 as a model, develop a chart outlining the primary and secondary growth of a woody root.

2. Create a glossary of twenty terms from the chapter organized from external to internal parts of a plant.

Journal Ideas

1. Using information from the chapter as your source, create twelve entries in a journal recording the growth and development of a plant, written from the perspective of the plant.

2. Choose any one plant or tree with which you are familiar. If you had the capacity to make genetic changes to it, what kind of changes would you make? Why?

UNIT V

From

Joseph A. DeVito

The Interpersonal Communication Book

Eighth Edition

Unit 21:
Friends and Lovers

UNIT

21

Friends and Lovers

Unit Topics

Unit Objectives

After completing this unit, you should be able to:

Friends
The Nature of Friendship
The Needs of Friendship
Stages and Communication in Friendship
      Development
Cultural Differences in Friendship
Gender Differences in Friendship

1. Define *friendship* and its three types

2. Identify the three stages of friendship development and characterize the communications at each stage

3. Describe the cultural and gender differences in friendship

Lovers
The Nature of Love
Types of Love
Cultural Differences in Loving
Gender Differences in Loving

4. Identify the major elements that make up love

5. Define *ludus, storge, mania, pragma, eros,* and *agape*

6. Describe the cultural and gender differences in loving

EXPERIENTIAL LEARNING VEHICLES

Vehicle Nos. 23, "Friendship Behaviors," pp. 466–467, and 24, "The Television Relationship," pp. 467–468, are useful for illustrating the role of interpersonal communication in friendship and love.

Of all the interpersonal relationships you have, no doubt the most important are those with your friends, lovers, and family. In this unit, we cover friends and lovers and in the next, family. The combination of friends and lovers in one unit seems especially appropriate because many people see love as a natural progression from friendship. Both relationships also serve many of the same functions: for example, lessening loneliness and providing excitement and security.

Friends

Friendship has engaged the attention and imagination of poets, novelists, and artists of all kinds. In television, our most influential mass medium, friendships have become almost as important as romantic pairings. Friendship now engages the attention of a range of interpersonal communication researchers. Table 21.1 presents a selection of findings to illustrate the range of topics addressed. In reviewing the table, consider why the results were obtained and what implications they may have for developing, maintaining, and repairing friendship relationships.

Throughout your life, you will meet many people, but out of this wide array you'll develop relatively few relationships you would call friendships. Yet despite the low number of friendships you may form, their importance is great.

Table 21.1	A Selection of Research Findings on Friendship

As you read through these findings, consider whether they seem consistent with your own friendship experience. These findings were taken from the extensive literature review in Blieszner and Adams (1992).

1. Young single men see their friends more often than young married men do (Farrell and Rosenberg 1981).
2. Women are more expressive in their friendships than are men. Men talk about business, politics, and sports, whereas women talk about feelings and relationship issues (Fox, Gibbs, and Auerbach 1985).
3. When women were asked about the most important benefit they derive from their friendships, conversation was highlighted and included listening in a supportive way, enhancing feelings of self-esteem, and validating their experiences (Johnson and Aries 1983).
4. Men and women did not differ in their rankings of the characteristics of personal relationships with friends (Albert and Moss 1990).
5. Similarity in personality was not found to be a strong basis for selecting friends, but similarity of needs and beliefs was (Henderson and Furnhan 1982). Friends with dissimilar attitudes were preferred in recent friendships, whereas in established friendships similar attitudes were preferred (McCarthy and Duck 1976).
6. The average number of friends of college students varies from 2.88 to 9.1 (Blieszner and Adams 1992); for older persons, the average varies between 1 and 12.2 (Adams 1987).

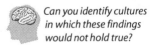 *Can you identify cultures in which these findings would not hold true?*

The Nature of Friendship

Friendship is an interpersonal relationship between two persons that is mutually productive and characterized by mutual positive regard.

Friendship is an interpersonal relationship; communication interactions must have taken place between the people. The interpersonal relationship involves a "personalistic focus" (Wright 1978, 1984). Friends react to each other as complete persons, as unique, genuine, and irreplaceable individuals.

Friendships must be mutually productive; this qualifier emphasizes that, by definition, they cannot be destructive either to oneself or to the other person. Once destructiveness enters into a relationship, it can no longer be characterized as friendship. Lover relationships, marriage relationships, parent-child relationships, and just about any other possible relationship can be either destructive or productive. But friendship must enhance the potential of each person and can only be productive.

Friendships are characterized by mutual positive regard. Liking people is essential if we are to call them friends. Three major characteristics of friends—trust, emotional support, and sharing of interests (Blieszner and Adams 1992)—testify to this positive regard.

The closer friends are the more *interdependent* they become; that is, when friends are especially close, the actions of one will impact more significantly on the other than they would if the friends were just casual acquaintances. At the same time, however, the closer friends are the more *independent* they are of, for example, the attitudes and behaviors of others. Also, they are less influenced by the societal rules that govern more casual relationships (see Unit 1 on the developmental definition of interpersonal communication). Close friends are likely to make up their own rules for interacting with each other; they decide what they will talk about and when, what they can say to each other without offending and what they can't, when and for what reasons you can call the other person, and so on.

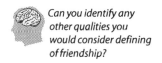 *Can you identify any other qualities you would consider defining of friendship?*

In North America, friendships clearly are a matter of choice; you choose—within limits—who your friends will be. The density of the cities and the ease of communication and relocation makes friendships voluntary, a matter of choice. But, in many parts of the world—small villages miles away from urban centers, where people are born, live, and die without venturing much beyond their birthplace, for example—relationships are not voluntary. In these cases, you simply form relationships with those in your village. Here you do not have the luxury of selecting certain people to interact with and others to ignore. You must interact with and form relationships with members of the community simply because these people are the only ones you come into contact with regularly (Moghaddam, Taylor, and Wright 1993).

Three Types of Friendships   Not all friendships are the same. But how do they differ? One way of answering this question is by distinguishing among the three major types of friendship: reciprocity, receptivity, and association (Reisman 1979, 1981).

The friendship of **reciprocity** is the ideal type, characterized by loyalty, self-sacrifice, mutual affection, and generosity. A friendship of reciprocity is based on equality: each individual shares equally in giving and receiving the benefits and rewards of the relationship. In the friendship of **receptivity**, in contrast, there is an imbalance in giving and receiving; one person is the primary giver and one the primary receiver. This imbalance, however, is a positive one because each person gains something from the relationship. The different needs of both the person who receives and the person who gives affection are satisfied. This is the friendship that may develop between a teacher and a student or between a doctor and a patient. In fact, a difference in status is essential for the friendship of receptivity to develop.

The friendship of **association** is a transitory one. It might be described as a friendly relationship rather than a true friendship. Associative friendships are the kind we often have with classmates, neighbors, or coworkers. There is no great loyalty, no great trust, no great giving or receiving. The association is cordial but not intense.

The definition and types of friendships may be seen in the responses of people who were asked to identify the qualities they felt were most important in a friend. The responses, presented in Table 21.2, are derived from a *Psychology Today* survey of 40,000 respondents (Parlee 1979). As you examine the list, you will find it easy to match each of these qualities to one of the types of friendship just described.

The Needs of Friendship

In the *Psychology Today* survey, the 40,000 respondents selected from a wide number of activities the ones they had shared with friends over the previous month. Table 21.3 presents the ten activities most frequently noted by these respondents. As can be appreciated from this list, friendship seems to serve the same needs that all relationships serve (lessening loneliness, providing stimulation, and encouraging self-knowledge).

You develop and maintain friendships to satisfy those needs that can only be satisfied by certain people. On the basis of your experiences or your predictions, you select as friends those who will help to satisfy your basic growth needs. Selecting friends on the basis of need satisfaction is similar to choosing a marriage partner, an employee, or any person who may be in a position to satisfy your needs. Thus, if you need to be the center of attention or to be popular, you might

 Of the three types of friendship identified in this unit—reciprocity, receptivity, and association—which type characterizes most of your friendships? Which type characterizes your closest friendships?

What do you feel are the five most important qualities of a best friend? How would your best friend answer this question about you? Which of these qualities is the most important in maintaining your friendship?

Table 21.2	The Most Frequently Mentioned Qualities of a Friend

Before reading this table, think about the qualities you look for in a friend and the qualities you offer to others as a friend. How similar are they to those noted here? The qualities are arranged in order of frequency of mention; No. 1, keeps confidences, was mentioned 89% of the time while No. 10, intelligence, was mentioned 57% of the time.

1. Keep confidences
2. Loyalty
3. Warmth, affection
4. Supportiveness
5. Frankness
6. Sense of humor
7. Willingness to make time for me
8. Independence
9. Good conversationalist
10. Intelligence

Table 21.3	The Ten Most Frequently Identified Activities Shared with Friends

Before reading this table, consider the activities you share with friends. How similar are the activities you engage in with those identified here? No. 1 = the most frequently identified activity.

1. Had an intimate talk
2. Had a friend ask you to do something for him or her
3. Went to dinner in a restaurant
4. Asked your friend to do something for you
5. Had a meal together at home or at your friend's home
6. Went to a movie, play, or concert
7. Went drinking together
8. Went shopping
9. Participated in sports
10. Watched a sporting event

select friends who allow you, and even encourage you, to be the center of attention or who tell you, verbally and nonverbally, that you are popular.

As your needs change, the qualities you look for in friendships also change. In many instances, old friends are dropped from your close circle to be replaced by new friends who better serve these new needs.

We can also look at needs in terms of the five values or rewards we seek to gain through our friendships (Wright 1978, 1984). First, friends have a **utility value.** A friend may have special talents, skills, or resources that prove useful to us in achieving our specific goals and needs. We may, for example, become friends with someone who is particularly bright because such a person might assist us in getting better grades, in solving our personal problems, or in getting a better job.

Second, friends have an **affirmation value.** A friend's behavior toward us acts as a mirror that affirms our personal value and helps us to recognize our attributes. A friend may, for example, help us to see more clearly our leadership abilities, athletic prowess, or sense of humor.

Third, friends have an **ego-support value.** By behaving in a supportive, encouraging, and helpful manner, friends help us to view ourselves as worthy and competent individuals.

Fourth, friends have a **stimulation value.** A friend introduces us to new ideas and new ways of seeing the world and helps us to expand our worldview. A friend brings us into contact with previously unfamiliar issues, concepts, and experiences—for example, modern art, foreign cultures, new foods.

Fifth, friends have a **security value.** A friend does nothing to hurt the other person or to emphasize or call attention to the other person's inadequacies or weaknesses. Because of this security value, friends can interact freely and openly without having to worry about betrayal or negative responses.

What values do you serve for your friends? What values do your friends serve for you?

Stages and Communication in Friendship Development

Friendships develop over time in stages. At one end of the friendship continuum are strangers, two persons who have just met, and at the other end are intimate friends. What happens between these two extremes?

As you progress from the initial contact stage to intimate friendship, the depth and breadth of communications increase (see Unit 15). You talk about issues that are closer and closer to your inner core. Similarly, the number of communication topics increases as your friendship becomes closer. As depth and breadth increase, so does the satisfaction you derive from the friendship.

Earlier (Unit 15), the concept of dynamic tension in relationships was discussed. It was pointed out that there is a tension between, for example, autonomy and connection—the desire to be an individual but also to be connected to another person. Interpersonal researcher William Rawlins (1983) argues that friendships are also defined by dynamic tensions. One tension is between the impulse to be open and to reveal personal thoughts and feelings on the one hand and the impulse to protect oneself by not revealing personal information on the other. There is also the tension between being open and candid with your friend and being discreet. These contradictory impulses make it clear that friendships do not follow a straight path of always increasing openness or candor. This is not to say that openness and candor do not increase as you progress from initial to casual to close friendships; they do. But the pattern does not follow a straight line; throughout the friendship development process, there are tensions that periodically restrict openness and candor.

Similarly, there are regressions that may temporarily pull the friendship back to a less intimate stage. And, of course, friendships stabilize at a level that is, ideally at least, comfortable to both persons; some friendships will remain as casual and others will remain as close. So, keep in mind that although friendship is presented in stages, the progression is not always a straight line to ever increasing intimacy.

With these qualifications in mind, we can discuss three stages of friendship development and integrate the ten characteristics of effective interpersonal communication identified earlier (Unit 8). The assumption made here is that as the friendship progresses from initial contact and acquaintanceship through casual friendship to close and intimate friendship, the qualities of effective interpersonal communication increase. However, there is no assumption made that close relationships are necessarily the preferred type or that they are better than casual or temporary relationships. We need all types.

As you read this section consider the differences between face-to-face friendships and online friendships. How do they follow similar development patterns? How do they follow different patterns?

Initial Contact and Acquaintanceship   The first stage of friendship development is obviously an initial meeting of some kind. This does not mean that what has happened prior to the encounter is unimportant—quite the contrary. Your prior history of friendships, your personal needs, and your readiness for friendship development are extremely important in determining whether the relationship will develop.

At the initial stage, the characteristics of effective interpersonal communication are usually present to only a small degree. You are guarded rather than open or expressive, lest you reveal aspects of yourself that might be viewed negatively. Because you do not yet know the other person, your ability to empathize with or to orient yourself significantly to the other is limited, and the "relationship"—at this stage, at least—is probably viewed as too temporary to be worth the effort. Because the other person is not well-known to you, supportiveness, positiveness, and equality would all be difficult to manifest in any meaningful sense. The characteristics demonstrated are probably more the result of politeness than any genuine expression of positive regard.

At this stage, there is little genuine immediacy; the people see themselves as separate and distinct rather than as a unit. The confidence that is demonstrated is probably more a function of the individual personalities than of the relationship. Because the relationship is so new and because the people do not know each other very well, the interaction is often characterized by awkwardness—for example, overlong pauses, uncertainty over the topics to be discussed, and ineffective exchanges of speaker and listener roles.

Casual Friendship   In the second stage, there is a dyadic consciousness, a clear sense of "we-ness," of togetherness; communication demonstrates a sense of immediacy. At this stage, you participate in activities as a unit rather than as separate individuals. A casual friend is one we would go with to the movies, sit with in the cafeteria or in class, or ride home with from school.

At this casual friendship stage, the qualities of effective interpersonal interaction begin to be seen more clearly. You start to express yourself openly and become interested in the other person's disclosures. You begin to own your feelings and thoughts and respond openly to his or her communications. Because you are beginning to understand this person, you empathize and demonstrate significant other-orientation. You also demonstrate supportiveness and develop a genuinely positive attitude toward both the other person and mutual communication situations. As you learn this person's needs and wants, you can stroke more effectively.

There is an ease at this stage, a coordination in the interaction between the two persons. You communicate with confidence, maintain appropriate eye contact and flexibility in body posture and gesturing, and use few adaptors signaling discomfort.

Close and Intimate Friendship   At the stage of close and intimate friendship, there is an intensification of the casual friendship; you and your friend see yourselves more as an exclusive unit, and each of you derives greater benefits (for example, emotional support) from intimate friendship than from casual friendship (Hays 1989).

Because you know each other well (for example, you know one another's values, opinions, attitudes), your uncertainty about each other has been significantly reduced—you are able to predict each other's behaviors with considerable accuracy. This knowledge makes possible significant interaction management. Similarly, you can read the other's nonverbal signals more accurately and can use these signals as guides to your interactions—avoiding certain topics at certain times or offering consolation on the basis of facial expressions.

At this stage, you exchange significant messages of affection, messages that express fondness, liking, loving, and caring for the other person. Openness and expressiveness are more clearly in evidence.

You become more other-oriented and willing to make significant sacrifices for the other person. You will go far out of your way for the benefit of this friend, and the friend in turn does the same for you. You empathize and exchange perspectives a great deal more, and you expect in return that your friend will also empathize with you. With a genuinely positive feeling for this individual, your

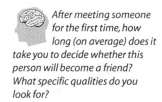 *After meeting someone for the first time, how long (on average) does it take you to decide whether this person will become a friend? What specific qualities do you look for?*

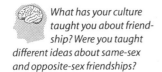

What other communication changes take place as a friendship progresses from casual to intimate? What communication changes take place when a friendship goes from intimate to casual?

supportiveness and positive stroking become spontaneous. Because you see yourselves as an exclusive unit, both equality and immediacy are in clear evidence. You view this friend as one who is important in your life; as a result, conflicts—inevitable in all close relationships—become important to work out and resolve through compromise and empathic understanding rather than through, for example, refusal to negotiate or a show of force.

You are willing to respond openly, confidently, and expressively to this person and to own your feelings and thoughts. Your supportiveness and positiveness are genuine expressions of the closeness you feel for this person. Each person in an intimate friendship is truly equal; each can initiate and each can respond; each can be active and each can be passive; each speaks and each listens.

Cultural Differences in Friendship

Your friendships and the way you look at friendships will be influenced by your culture. For example, in the United States you can be friends with someone, yet not really be expected to go much out of your way for this person. Many Middle Easterners, Asians, and Latin Americans would consider going out of their way (significantly) an absolute essential ingredient in friendship; if you are not willing to sacrifice for your friend, then this person is really not your friend (Dresser 1996).

Generally, friendships are closer in collectivist cultures than in individualistic cultures (see Unit 3). In their emphasis on the group and on cooperating, the collectivist cultures foster the development of close friendship bonds.

Members of collectivist culture are expected to help others in the group. When you help or do things for someone else, you increase your own attraction for this person (recall our discussion in Unit 16 on attraction and reinforcement) and this is certainly a good start for a friendship. Of course, the culture continues to reward these close associations. Members of individualistic cultures, on the other hand, are expected to look out for No. 1, themselves. Consequently, they are more likely to compete and to try to do better than each other—conditions that do not support, generally at least, the development of friendships. Recall as we noted earlier (Unit 3) that these characteristics are extremes; most people have both collectivist and individualistic values but have them to different degrees and that is what we are talking about here—differences in degree of collectivist and individualistic orientation.

What has your culture taught you about friendship? Were you taught different ideas about same-sex and opposite-sex friendships?

Gender Differences in Friendship

Perhaps the best-documented finding—already noted in our discussion of self-disclosure—is that women self-disclose more than do men (for example, Dolgin, Meyer, and Schwartz 1991). This difference holds throughout male and female friendships. Male friends self-disclose less often and with less intimate details than female friends do. Men generally do not view intimacy as a necessary quality of their friendships (Hart 1990).

Women engage in significantly more affectional behaviors with their friends than do males (Hays 1989). This difference, Hays notes, may account for the greater difficulty men experience in beginning and maintaining close friendships. Women engage in more casual communication; they also share greater intimacy and more confidences with their friends than do men. Communication, in all its

What do you see as the one major difference between a friendship between two women and a friendship between two men? How do same-sex friendships differ from opposite-sex friendships?

forms and functions, seems a much more important dimension of women's friendships.

When women and men were asked to evaluate their friendships, women rated their same-sex friendships higher in general quality, intimacy, enjoyment, and nurturance than did men (Sapadin 1988). Men, in contrast, rated their opposite-sex friendships higher in quality, enjoyment, and nurturance than did women. Both men and women rated their opposite-sex friendships similarly in intimacy. These differences may be due, in part, to our society's suspicion of male friendships; as a result, a man may be reluctant to admit to having close relationship bonds with another man.

Men's friendships are often built around shared activities—attending a ball game, playing cards, working on a project at the office. Women's friendships, on the other hand, are built more around a sharing of feelings, support, and "personalism." Similarity in status, in willingness to protect one's friend in uncomfortable situations, in academic major, and even in proficiency in playing Password were significantly related to the relationship closeness of male-male friends but not of female-female or female-male friends (Griffin and Sparks 1990). Perhaps similarity is a criterion for male friendships but not for female or mixed-sex friendships.

The ways in which men and women develop and maintain their friendships will undoubtedly change considerably—as will all sex-related variables—in the next several years. Perhaps there will be a further differentiation or perhaps an increase in similarities. In the meantime, given the present state of research in gender differences, we need to be careful not to exaggerate and to treat small differences as if they were highly significant. "Let us," warns one friendship researcher, "avoid stereotypes or, worse yet, caricatures" (Wright 1988).

Further, friendship researchers warn that even when we find differences, the reasons for them are not always clear (Blieszner and Adams 1992). An interesting example is the finding that middle-aged men have more friends than middle-aged women and that women have more intimate friendships (Fischer and Oliker 1983). But why is this so? Do men have more friends because they are friendlier than women or because they have more opportunities to develop such friendships? Do women have more intimate friends because they have more opportunities to pursue such friendships or because they have a greater psychological capacity for intimacy?

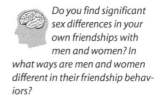

Do you find significant sex differences in your own friendships with men and women? In what ways are men and women different in their friendship behaviors?

Lovers

Of all the qualities of interpersonal relationships, none seems as important as love. "We are all born for love," noted famed British prime minister Disraeli; "It is the principle of existence and its only end." It is also an interpersonal relationship developed, maintained, and sometimes destroyed through communication.

The Nature of Love

Much research is currently devoted to identifying the ingredients of love. What makes up the love experience? What are its major parts? Here are two well-reasoned explanations.

Psychotherapist Albert Ellis has argued that love and infatuation are actually the same emotion; he claims that we use the term "infatuation" to describe relationships that did not work out and "love" to describe our current romantic relationships. Do you agree that infatuation and love are essentially the same emotion? If you disagree, in what specific ways are they different?

- ◆ Love is a combination of passion and caring (Davis 1985). Both of these emotions are looked at as clusters consisting of more specific emotions. The **passion cluster,** for example, consists of *fascination* (seen in the lovers' preoccupation with each other), *exclusiveness* (seen in their mutual commitment), and *sexual desire* (seen in their desire to touch). The **caring cluster** consists of *giving the utmost* (seen in sacrifice for the lover) and *serving as the lover's champion* or advocate (seen in support for the lover's interest and success).

- ◆ Love is a combination of intimacy, passion, and commitment (Sternberg 1986, 1988). **Intimacy** (corresponding to part of Davis's caring cluster) is the emotional aspect of love and includes sharing, communicating, and mutual support; it is a sense of closeness and connection. **Passion** is the motivational aspect (corresponding to the passion cluster) and consists of physical attraction and romantic passion. **Commitment** (corresponding to part of the caring cluster) is the cognitive aspect and consists of the decisions you make con-

INTERPERSONAL ETHICS

Gossip

Frank: father
Jeff: son
Laura: mother

Jeff: Listen, everyone. Kim told me something today that I want to tell you. I promised her I wouldn't tell anyone but I just have to tell you.

Laura: Well, maybe you shouldn't. I mean, if you promised Kim, maybe you shouldn't tell us.

Jeff: No, no, I really want to—I have to.

Frank: Your mother's right. If you promised to keep a secret, then keep it. You'll be the better person for it.

Jeff: Well, if you all promise to keep it a secret, it'll be OK.

Would it be wrong for Jeff to reveal the secret? Would your answer depend on the kind of secret? If so, what would you have to know about the secret to answer this question? What would you answer if the secret was that Kim broke up with her boyfriend yesterday for the third time this month (and they are both 14 years old)? If Kim, who has been having mental problems, plans to kill her father? If Kim, 17 years old, plans to commit suicide? If Kim is heavily into drugs?

Would your answer be different if Kim was 4 and Jeff was 5? Kim was 4 and Jeff was 32? Kim and Jeff were both 19? If the family members kept the secret confidential?

Gossip is talk about a person who is not present during the communication (Eder and Enke 1991). If you are like most people, you spend at least some of your time gossiping about others. Gossip seems universal among all cultures (Laing 1993) and among some it is a commonly accepted ritual (Hall 1993). Gossip generally occurs when two people talk about a third party and profit in some way. Among the rewards or benefits of gossip is that it helps us to make social comparisons (Leaper and Holliday 1995; Westen 1996). By hearing about others, their accomplishments and their problems, you can better see how you stand in comparison with your peers.

Another benefit is that gossip humanizes people (Westen 1996). It lets you see a little bit of the inside of people. It puts you into a network of people, cements the bonds between you (Rosnow 1977; Miller and Wilcox 1986). It gives you social status. Just think of your social standing if no one talked to you about others and, maybe more important, if no one talked about you to others. As Oscar Wilde put it, "There is only one thing in the world worse than being talked about, and that is not being talked about."

Gossip also tells you the norms of the culture or society. When a supervisor tells you that Mason took off too many Mondays and wasn't promoted because of it, you are hearing (and learning) the rules or norms of the organization. You know that you should try especially hard to avoid taking off on Mondays or you too will not get promoted.

Nevertheless, gossip does create serious problems when not managed fairly. When you tell someone your feelings for some third party, say, you expect that the conversation will be held in confidence. You do not expect it to be relayed to others, especially not to the individual discussed. If you had wanted it relayed, you probably would have done so yourself. When such a conversation is passed on without your knowledge or approval, you feel that your confidence has been betrayed.

In *Secrets* (1983), ethicist Sissela Bok identifies three kinds of gossip that she considers unethical. First, it is unethical to reveal information that you have promised to keep secret. In situations in which that is impossible (Bok offers the example of a teenager who confides a suicide plan), the information should be revealed only to those required to know it and not to the world at large.

Second, gossip is unethical when we know it to be false and pass it on nevertheless. When we try to deceive our listeners by spreading gossip we know to be false, our communications are unethical.

Third, gossip is unethical when it invades the privacy to which everyone has a right. Invasive gossip is especially unethical when the gossip can hurt the individual involved. These conditions are not easy to identify in any given instance, but they do provide us with excellent starting points for asking ourselves whether or not a discussion of another person is ethical.

◆ Under what conditions would revealing another person's secrets be ethical? Under what conditions would it be unethical? Are there times when the failure to reveal such secrets would be unethical?

◆ What is your obligation as a listener, when you hear gossip being repeated that you know to be false?

◆ Is it ethical for you to observe someone (without his or her knowledge) and report your observations to others? For example, would it be ethical to observe your communication professor on a date with a student or smoking marijuana and then report these observations back to your classmates?

◆ What ethical guidelines would you propose for revealing secrets?

[The next ethics box appears in Unit 22, page 428, and deals with developing your own ethic of interpersonal communication.]

cerning your lover. When you have a relationship characterized by intimacy only, you have essentially a **liking** relationship. When you have only passion, you have a relationship of **infatuation**. When you have only commitment, you have **empty love**. When you have all three components to about equal degrees, you have **complete or consummate love**.

Types of Love

Although there are many theories about love, the one that has captured the attention of interpersonal researchers was the proposal that there is not one, but six types of love (Lee 1976). View the descriptions of each type that follow as broad characterizations that are generally but not always true. As a preface to this discussion of the types of love, you may wish to respond to the self-test "What Kind of Lover Are You?"

Eros: Beauty and Sexuality Like Narcissus, who fell in love with the beauty of his own image, the **erotic** lover focuses on beauty and physical attractiveness, sometimes to the exclusion of qualities you might consider more important and more lasting. Also like Narcissus, the erotic lover has an idealized image of beauty that is unattainable in reality. Consequently, the erotic lover often feels unfulfilled. Not surprisingly, erotic lovers are particularly sensitive to physical imperfections in the ones they love.

Self Test

What Kind of Lover Are You?

Respond to each of the following statements with T if you believe the statement to be a generally accurate representation of your attitudes about love or F if you believe the statement does not adequately represent your attitudes about love.

_____ 1. My lover and I have the right physical "chemistry" between us.
_____ 2. I feel that my lover and I were meant for each other.
_____ 3. My lover and I really understand each other.
_____ 4. My lover fits my ideal standards of physical beauty/handsomeness.
_____ 5. I try to keep my lover a little uncertain about my commitment to him/her.
_____ 6. I believe that what my lover doesn't know about me won't hurt him/her.
_____ 7. My lover would get upset if he/she knew of some of the things I've done with other people.
_____ 8. When my lover gets too dependent on me, I want to back off a little.
_____ 9. To be genuine, our love first required caring for awhile.
_____10. I expect to always be friends with my lover.
_____11. Our love is really a deep friendship, not a mysterious, mystical emotion.
_____12. Our love relationship is the most satisfying because it developed from a good friendship.
_____13. In choosing my lover, I believed it was best to love someone with a similar background.
_____14. A main consideration in choosing my lover was how he/she would reflect on my family.
_____15. An important factor in choosing a partner is whether or not he/she would be a good parent.
_____16. One consideration in choosing my lover was how he/she would reflect on my career.
_____17. When things aren't right with my lover and me, my stomach gets upset.
_____18. Sometimes I get so excited about being in love with my lover that I can't sleep.
_____19. When my lover doesn't pay attention to me, I feel sick all over.
_____20. I cannot relax if I suspect that my lover is with someone else.
_____21. I try to always help my lover through difficult times.
_____22. I would rather suffer myself than let my lover suffer.
_____23. When my lover gets angry with me, I still love him/her fully and unconditionally.
_____24. I would endure all things for the sake of my lover.

Thinking Critically About Love

This scale is designed to enable you to identify those styles that best reflect your own beliefs about love. The statements refer to the six types of love that we discuss below: eros, ludus, storge, pragma, mania, and agape. "True" answers represent your agreement and "false" answers represent your disagreement with the type of love to which the statements refer. Statements 1–4 are characteristic of the eros lover. If you answered "true" to these statements, you have a strong eros component to

your love style. If you answered "false," you have a weak eros component. Statements 5–8 refer to ludus love, 9–12 to storge love, 13–16 to pragma love, 17–20 to manic love, and 21–24 to agapic love.

This scale comes from Hendrick and Hendrick (1990) and is reprinted by permission. (Adapted from "A Relationship: Specific Version of the Love Attitudes Scale," by C. Hendrick and S. Hendrick, 1990, from *Journal of Social Behavior and Personality* 5 (1990):239–254.) It is based on the work of Lee (1976), as is our discussion of the six types of love.

Ludus: Entertainment and Excitement   **Ludus** love is experienced as a game, as fun. The better he or she can play the game, the greater the enjoyment. Love is not to be taken too seriously; emotions are to be held in check lest they get out of hand and make trouble; passions never rise to the point where they get out of control. A ludic lover is self-controlled, always aware of the need to manage love rather than allow it to be in control. Perhaps because of this need to control love, some researchers have proposed that ludic love tendencies may reveal tendencies to sexual aggression (Sarwer, Kalichman, Johnson, Earl et al. 1993). Not surprisingly, the ludic lover retains a partner only as long as he or she is interesting and

What type of lover are you, according to this love-style test? Does this correspond to (or contradict) your self-image? Which type of love relationship (ludus, storge, mania, pragma, eros, or agape) do you think stands the best chance for survival? What type do you consider the most satisfying?

amusing. When interest fades, it is time to change partners. Perhaps because love is a game, sexual fidelity is of little importance.

Storge: Peaceful and Slow   **Storge** lacks passion and intensity. Storgic lovers do not set out to find lovers but to establish a companionable relationship with someone they know and with whom they can share interests and activities. Storgic love is a gradual process of unfolding thoughts and feelings; the changes seem to come so slowly and so gradually that it is often difficult to define exactly where the relationship is at any point in time. Sex in storgic relationships comes late, and when it comes it assumes no great importance.

Pragma: Practical and Traditional   The **pragma** lover is practical and seeks a relationship that will work. Pragma lovers want compatibility and a relationship in which their important needs and desires will be satisfied. They are concerned with the social qualifications of a potential mate even more than with personal qualities; family and background are extremely important to the pragma lover, who relies not so much on feelings as on logic. The pragma lover views love as a useful relationship, one that makes the rest of life easier. So the pragma lover asks such questions of a potential mate as "Will this person earn a good living?" "Can this person cook?" "Will this person help me advance in my career?" Pragma lovers' relationships rarely deteriorate. This is partly because pragma lovers choose their mates carefully and emphasize similarities. Another reason is that they have realistic romantic expectations.

Mania: Elation and Depression   **Mania** is characterized by extreme highs and extreme lows. The manic lover loves intensely and at the same time intensely worries about the loss of the love. This fear often prevents the manic lover from deriving as much pleasure as possible from the relationship. With little provocation, the manic lover may experience extreme jealousy. Manic love is obsessive; the manic lover has to possess the beloved completely. In return, the manic lover wishes to be possessed, to be loved intensely. The manic lover's poor self-image seems capable of being improved only by being loved; self-worth comes from being loved rather than from any sense of inner satisfaction. Because love is so important, danger signs in a relationship are often ignored; the manic lover believes that if there is love, then nothing else matters.

Can you identify a character from literature who exemplifies one of these types of lovers? What fate does each of these lovers experience?

Agape: Compassionate and Selfless   **Agape** (ah-guh-pay) is a compassionate, egoless, self-giving love. The agapic lover loves even people with whom he or she has no close ties. This lover loves the stranger on the road even though they will probably never meet again. Agape is a spiritual love, offered without concern for personal reward or gain. This lover loves without expecting that the love will be reciprocated. Jesus, Buddha, and Gandhi practiced and preached this unqualified love, agape (Lee 1976). In one sense, agape is more a philosophical kind of love than a love that most people have the strength to achieve.

Love Styles and Personality   In reading about the love styles, you may have felt that there are certain personality types who are likely to favor one type of love over another. Here are personality traits that research finds people assign to each love style. Try identifying which personality traits people think go with each of the six love styles: eros, ludus, storge, pragma, mania, and agape.

1. ____ inconsiderate, secretive, dishonest, selfish, and dangerous
2. ____ honest, loyal, mature, caring, loving, and understanding
3. ____ jealous, possessive, obsessed, emotional, and dependent
4. ____ sexual, exciting, loving, happy, optimistic
5. ____ committed, giving, caring, self-sacrificing, and loving
6. ____ family-oriented, planning, careful, hard-working, and concerned

Very likely you perceived these personality factors in the same way as did the participants in research from which these traits were drawn (Taraban and Hendrick 1995): 1 = ludus, 2 = storge, 3 = mania, 4 = eros, 5 = agape, and 6 = pragma. Note, of course, that these results do not imply that ludus lovers are inconsiderate, secretive, and dishonest. They merely mean that people *think* of ludus lovers as inconsiderate, secretive, and dishonest.

Love Styles in Combination   Each of these varieties of love can combine with others to form new and different patterns (for example, manic and ludic or storge and pragma). These six, however, identify the major types of love and illustrate the complexity of any love relationship. The six styles should also make it clear that different people want different things, that each person seeks satisfaction in a unique way. The love that may seem lifeless or crazy or boring to you may be ideal for someone else. At the same time, another person may see these same negative qualities in the love you are seeking.

Love changes. A relationship that began as pragma may develop into ludus or eros. A relationship that began as erotic may develop into mania or storge. One approach sees this as a developmental process having three major stages (Duck 1986):

♦ First stage: Initial attraction—eros, mania, and ludus.
♦ Second stage: Storge (as the relationship develops).
♦ Third stage: Pragma (as relationship bonds develop).

Love Styles and Communication   How do you communicate when you are in love? What do you say? What do you do nonverbally? How closely do the research findings describe you? According to research, you exaggerate your beloved's virtues and minimize his or her faults. You share emotions and experiences and speak tenderly, with an extra degree of courtesy, to each other; "please," "thank you," and similar politenesses abound. You frequently use "personalized communication." This type of communication includes secrets you keep from other people and messages that have meaning only within your specific relationship (Knapp, Ellis, and Williams 1980). You also create and use personal idioms—those words, phrases, and gestures that carry meaning only for the particular relationship and that say you have a special language that signifies your special bond (Hopper, Knapp, and Scott 1981). When outsiders try to use personal idioms—as they sometimes do—the expressions seem inappropriate, at times even an invasion of privacy.

You engage in significant self-disclosure. There is more confirmation and less disconfirmation among lovers than among either nonlovers or those who are going through romantic breakups. You are also highly aware of what is and is not appropriate to the one you love. You know how to reward but also how to punish each other. In short, you know what to do to obtain the reaction you want.

Among your most often used means for communicating love are telling the person face to face or by telephone (in one survey 79 percent indicated they did it this way), expressing supportiveness, and talking things out and cooperating (Marston, Hecht, and Robers 1987).

Nonverbally, you also communicate your love. Prolonged and focused eye contact is perhaps the clearest nonverbal indicator of love. So important is eye contact that its avoidance almost always triggers a "what's wrong?" response.

You grow more aware not only of your loved one but also of your own physical self. Your muscle tone is heightened, for example. When you are in love you engage in preening gestures, especially immediately prior to meeting your lover, and you position your body attractively—stomach pulled in, shoulders square, legs arranged in appropriate masculine or feminine positions.

Your speech may even have a somewhat different vocal quality. There is some evidence to show that sexual excitement enlarges the nasal membranes, which introduces a certain nasal quality into the voice (M. Davis 1973).

You eliminate socially taboo adaptors, at least in the presence of the loved one. You would curtail, for example, scratching your head, picking your teeth, cleaning your ears, and passing wind. Interestingly enough, these adaptors often return after the lovers have achieved a permanent relationship.

You touch more frequently and more intimately. You also use more "tie signs," nonverbal gestures that show that you are together, such as holding hands, walking with arms entwined, kissing, and the like. You may even dress alike. The styles of clothes and even the colors selected by lovers are more similar than those worn by nonlovers.

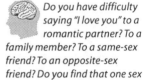
Do you have difficulty saying "I love you" to a romantic partner? To a family member? To a same-sex friend? To an opposite-sex friend? Do you find that one sex has greater difficulty saying "I love you," or are men and women equally comfortable or uncomfortable?

Cultural Differences in Loving

Although most of the research on these love styles has been done in the United States, some research has been conducted in other cultures. Here is a sampling of the research findings—just enough to illustrate that culture is an important factor in love. The test and the love styles have been found to have validity among Germans (Bierhoff and Klein 1991). Asians have been found to be more friendship oriented in their love style than are Europeans (Dion and Dion 1993b). Members of individualistic cultures (for example, Europeans) are likely to place greater emphasis on romantic love and on individual fulfillment. Members of collectivist cultures are likely to spread their love over a large network of relatives (Dion and Dion 1993a)

One study finds a love style among Mexicans characterized as calm, compassionate, and deliberate (Leon, Philbrick, Parra, Escobedo et al. 1994). In comparisons between loves styles in the United States and France, it was found that subjects from the United States scored higher on storge and mania than the French; in contrast, the French scored higher on agape (Murstein, Merighi, and Vyse 1991). Caucasian women, compared to African-American women, scored higher on mania whereas African-American women scored higher on agape. Caucasian and African-American men, however, scored very similarly; no statistically significant differences have been found (Morrow, Clark, and Brock 1995).

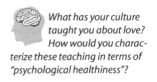
What has your culture taught you about love? How would you characterize these teaching in terms of "psychological healthiness"?

Gender Differences in Loving

In the United States, the differences between men and women in love are considered great. In poetry, novels, and the mass media, women and men are depicted as acting very differently when falling in love, being in love, and ending a love relationship. As Lord Byron put it in *Don Juan,* "Man's love is of man's life a thing apart, / 'Tis woman's whole existence." Women are portrayed as emotional, men as logical. Women are supposed to love intensely; men are supposed to love with detachment.

Women and men seem to experience love to a similar degree (Rubin 1973). However, women indicate greater love than men do for their same-sex friends. This may reflect a real difference between the sexes, or it may be a function of the greater social restrictions on men. A man is not supposed to admit his love for another man. Women are permitted greater freedom to communicate their love for other women.

Men and women also differ in the types of love they prefer (Hendrick, Hendrick, Foote, and Slapion-Foote 1984). For example, on one version of the love self-test presented earlier, men have been found to score higher on erotic and ludic love, whereas women score higher on manic, pragmatic, and storgic love. No difference has been found for agapic love.

Another gender difference frequently noted is that of romanticism. Before reading about this topic, you may wish to take the accompanying self-test, "How Romantic Are You?"

Women have their first romantic experiences earlier than men. The median age of first infatuation for women was 13 and for men 13.6; the median age for first time in love for women was 17.1 and for men 17.6 (Kirkpatrick and Caplow 1945; Hendrick, Hendrick, Foote, and Slapion-Foote 1984).

Men were found to place more emphasis on romance than women (Kirkpatrick and Caplow 1945). For example, when college students were asked the question posed in the photo caption below, approximately two-thirds of the men responded no, which seems to indicate that a high percentage were concerned with love and romance. However, less than one-third of the women responded no. Further, when men and women were surveyed concerning their view

Do you think that the love in a man and in a woman develop in essentially the same way? In a heterosexual relationship and in a homosexual relationship? How would you go about finding evidence to help answer these questions?

In an interesting study on love, men and women from different cultures were asked the following question: "If a man (woman) has all the other qualities you desired, would you marry this person if you were not in love with him (her)?" Results varied greatly from one culture to another (Levine, Sato, Hashimoto, & Verma 1994). For example, 50.4 percent of the respondents from Pakistan said, "yes," 49 percent of those from India said "yes," and 18.8 percent of those from Thailand said "yes." At the other extreme were those from Japan (only 2.3 percent said "yes."), the United States (only 3.5 percent said "yes"), and Brazil (only 4.3 percent said "yes"). How would you answer this question?

How Romantic Are You?

Indicate the extent to which you agree or disagree with each of the following beliefs. Use the following scale:

    7 = Agree strongly
    6 = Agree a good deal
    5 = Agree somewhat
    4 = Neither agree nor disagree
    3 = Disagree somewhat
    2 = Disagree a good deal
    1 = Disagree strongly

___ 1. I don't need to know someone for a period of time before I fall in love with him or her.
___ 2. If I were in love with someone, I would commit myself to him or her even if my parents and friends disapproved of the relationship.
___ 3. Once I experience "true love," I could never experience it again, to the same degree, with another person.
___ 4. I believe that to be truly in love is to be in love forever.
___ 5. If I love someone, I know I can make the relationship work, despite any obstacles.
___ 6. When I find my "true love" I will probably know it soon after we meet.
___ 7. I'm sure that every new thing I learn about the person I choose for a long-term commitment will please me.
___ 8. The relationship I will have with my "true love" will be nearly perfect.
___ 9. If I love someone, I will find a way for us to be together regardless of the opposition to the relationship, physical distance between us or any other barrier.
___ 10. There will be only one real love for me.
___ 11. If a relationship I have was meant to be, any obstacles (for example, lack of money, physical distance, career conflicts) can be overcome.
___ 12. I am likely to fall in love almost immediately if I meet the right person.
___ 13. I expect that in my relationship, romantic love will really last; it won't fade with time.
___ 14. The person I love will make a perfect romantic partner; for example, he/she will be completely accepting, loving, and understanding.
___ 15. I believe if another person and I love each other we can overcome any differences and problems that may arise.

Thinking Critically About Romanticism

To compute your romanticism score, add your scores for all 15 items. The higher your score, the stronger your romantic beliefs are. In research by Sprecher and Metts (1989), the mean score for this test was 60.45 for males and females taken together. The mean score for males was 62.55 and for females 59.10. How romantic are your beliefs compared to this research sample?

In the discussion of gender differences, research was cited showing that men are more romantic than women. The test presented above was developed for and used in that research (Sprecher and Metts 1989).

Test out the finding showing that men are more romantic by asking at least ten men and ten women to complete the scale. Compare the two groups. Are men more romantic than women? Would the finding from the Sprecher and Metts study and your findings be the same for all age groups? For example, would the same findings be obtained if you surveyed elementary school children? senior citizens? Would there be cultural differences? Test out one of your theories by surveying members of different age groups or different cultures.

From "Romantic Beliefs Scale" and "Examination of the Effects of Gender and Gender-Role Orientation," Journal of Social and Personal Relationships 6:387–411. Copyright © 1989 Sage Publications Ltd. Reprinted by permission of Sage Publications Ltd.

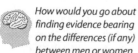

How would you go about finding evidence bearing on the differences (if any) between men or women in the breakup of friendships? For example, would a pattern similar to that found for love, be found for friendship breakups?

on love—whether it is basically realistic or basically romantic—it was found that married women had a more realistic (less romantic) conception of love than did married men (Knapp 1984).

More recent research (based on the romanticism questionnaire presented here) confirms this view that men are more romantic. For example, "Men are more likely than women to believe in love at first sight, in love as the basis for marriage and for overcoming obstacles, and to believe that their partner and relationship will be perfect" (Sprecher and Metts 1989). This difference seems to increase as the romantic relationship develops: Men become more romantic and women less romantic (Fengler 1974).

One further gender difference may be noted and that is differences between men and women in breaking up a relationship (Blumstein and Schwartz 1983; cf. Janus and Janus 1993). Popular myth would have us believe that love affairs break up as a result of the man's outside affair. But the research does not support this. When surveyed as to the reason for breaking up, only 15 percent of the men indicated that it was their interest in another partner, whereas 32 percent of the women noted this as a cause of the breakup. These findings are consistent with their partners' perceptions as well: 30 percent of the men (but only 15 percent of the women) noted that their partner's interest in another person was the reason for the breakup.

In their reactions to broken romantic affairs, women and men exhibit both similarities and differences. For example, the tendency for women and men to recall only pleasant memories and to revisit places with past associations was about equal. However, men engaged in more dreaming about the lost partner and in more daydreaming generally as a reaction to the breakup than did women.

Summary   U N I T   I N   B R I E F

A RETURN TO OBJECTIVES:

In this unit we explored friendship and love, two of our most important interpersonal relationships, and considered: (1) What is friendship? What needs does it serve? What stages does it pass through? How does friendship differ in different cultures and between men and women? (2) What is love? What are the major kinds of love? How does love vary in different cultures and between men and women?

Friendship: An interpersonal relationship (rule-governed?) between two persons that is mutually productive, and characterized by mutual positive regard.	**Love: A feeling characterized by passion and caring (Davis) and by intimacy, passion, and commitment (Sternberg)**
Types of friendships:	**Types of love:**
◆ Reciprocity	◆ Eros: Love as sensuous and erotic.
◆ Receptivity	◆ Ludus: Love as a game.
◆ Association	◆ Storge: Love as companionship.
	◆ Pragma: Love as a practical relation.
Purposes of friendships:	◆ Mania: Love as obsession and possession.
◆ Utility value	◆ Agape: Love as self-giving, altruistic.
◆ Affirmation value	
◆ Ego-support value	
◆ Stimulation value	
◆ Security value	
Culture and gender differences:	**Culture and gender differences:**
◆ Friendship demands vary between collectivist and individualistic cultures.	◆ Members of individualistic cultures are likely to place greater emphasis on romantic love than are members of collectivist cultures.
◆ Women share more and are more intimate with same-sex friends.	◆ Men score higher on erotic and ludic love; women score higher on manic, pragmatic, and storgic love.
◆ Men's friendships are built around shared activities.	◆ Men score higher on romanticism.

Testing Your Understanding—Unit V

The Interpersonal Communication Book, **Unit 21: Friends and Lovers**

Pages 178–188
CHECKING YOUR COMPREHENSION

Choose the best answer for each of the following questions.

1. Which of the following questions should you be able to answer based on prereading the unit topics and unit objectives?
   a. What are the stages of love?
   b. What are the characteristics of communication in the different types of love?
   c. What type of love is the best?
   d. How are friendships affected by cultures?

2. Which of the following statements about gender differences can be inferred from Table 21.1?
   a. Both men and women believe keeping confidences is the most important characteristic of friendships.
   b. Values are more important than personality in developing friendships.
   c. Young married women see their friends as frequently as single women do.
   d. Young adults, on average, have more friends than older adults.

3. Which of the following statements is most generally true of friendships in a collectivist culture?
   a. Competition keeps friendships exciting.
   b. Friendships are built on helping others.
   c. Close friendships are discouraged since they divide the culture.
   d. Self-disclosure is unnecessary because there are few secrets.

4. The primary purpose of the photo on page 187 is to
   a. elicit the reader's response about the relationship between male friendships and culture.
   b. explain cultural differences in how people view male friendships.
   c. illustrate gender differences in friendships.
   d. define an intimate male friendship in a particular culture.

5. In the section "Gender Differences in Friendship," the author makes the following assertion: "These differences may be due, in part, to our society's suspicion of male friendships; as a result, a man may be reluctant to admit to having close relationship bonds with another man." Which of the following assumptions is the author making?
   a. Society's concern with male friendships is bound by culture.
   b. Men are usually able to counteract society's opinions.
   c. Gender differences in friendships are generally insignificant.
   d. He and his readers are part of the same society.

Identify the following statements as true or false.

6. In North American culture, friendships are usually a matter of choice.

7. Throughout your life, the needs that motivate you to form friendships remain unchanged.

8. Friendships do not usually progress on a straight continuum between meeting and intimacy.

9. As friendships progress, the qualities of effective interpersonal communication increase

10. Differences in friendships can be most clearly understood by knowing the genders of the people involved.

Answer each of the following questions.

11. Identify the three types of friendships.

12. Identify the type of friendship which is usually associated with each of the following relationships.
   a. teacher and student
   b. classssmates
   c. coworkers
   d. doctor and patient
   e. best friends

13. Identify the five values or rewards we search for in friendships.

14. Identify the three main stages of friendship and the communication type which dominates in each.

15. Identify the three major characteristics of friendships.

From the list of types of context clues, identify the context clue that was used in defining each of the following terms in the chapter.

Term	*Context clue*
16. interpersonal relationship	formal definition
17. interdependent	indirect definition
18. collectivist culture	example
19. self-disclosure	inference

Discussion and Critical Thinking Questions

1. Maria and Isabel met when Maria was a camper and Isabel was a counselor in the same program. Isabel knew Maria's older sister, but she did not know any of the other counselors well. Maria frequently discussed her future college plans and her boyfriend with Isabel. Isabel frequently invited Maria to accompany her on program errands and played for her songs she had written. How would you evaluate this relationship in terms of type, need, and stage?

2. According to research, people tend to prefer different attitudes in new friendships, but prefer similar attitudes in long-term friendships. How do you explain the difference?

3. What kinds of problems might a cross-cultural friendship encounter?

4. The section entitled "The Needs of Friendship" is based in part on a survey of respondents to a *Psychology Today* survey. How would you evaluate the validity of *Psychology Today*?

5. What recall strategies might be helpful for remembering answers to questions 11, 13, and 14 above?

Pages 188–197
CHECKING YOUR COMPREHENSION

Choose the best answer for each of the following questions.

1. The intimacy component of love is characterized by two people
   a. finding each other fascinating
   b. making decisions based on each other
   c. communicating support for each other's interests
   d. being physically attracted to each other

2. Which of the following questions is characteristic of what a Ludic lover might ask?
   a. Is this person physically beautiful?
   b. Does my partner still fascinate me?
   c. How can I help my partner?
   d. Will my family accept this person?

3. With respect to communication, it is characteristic of people in a love relationship to
   a. make a lot of eye contact.
   b. select similar clothes.
   c. develop a private language.
   d. all of the above.

4. The primary purpose of the self-tests in this chapter is to
   a. encourage the reader to apply the concepts.
   b. suggest a mnemonic for remembering the concepts.
   c. highlight the organization of the chapter.
   d. divert the reader from the difficulties of the chapter.

Identify the following statements as true or false.

5. Each person loves in one particular way.

6. A person's personality traits are an indication of his or her type of love.

7. Research indicates that men are generally more romantic than women.

8. Although African-American and Caucasian women generally differ in their types of love, African-American and Caucasian men generally do not.

9. Most relationships break up as the result of an affair.

Answer the following questions.

10. List the six types of love.

11. Identify the three stages of development that love goes through.

12. Describe the three kinds of unethical gossip the ethicist Sissela Bok has suggested.

13. Describe three benefits of gossip.

14. Identify three gender differences in love styles.

15. Using an unabridged dictionary, find the pronunciation of storge and ludus.

Discussion and Critical Thinking Questions

1. Discuss the situation in the section entitled "Interpersonal Ethics" according to the following variables: severity of the secret, ages of the parties, relationship among family members.

2. With respect to the classifications of love relationships, what additional information should be considered in understanding and/or categorizing same-sex love relationships?

3. What do you think is the relationship between collectivist or individualist cultures and types of love?

4. Discuss the effectiveness of the self-test "How Romantic Are You?" by considering ages of respondents.

5. Choose a recent movie in which there is a love interest between characters. Analyze the characters according to style and type and stages of love.

CHAPTER REVIEW

Group Projects

1. Develop a questionnaire containing 10–15 questions that would help you determine differences between men and women in the breakup of friendships.

2. Table 21.1 contains six research findings on friendships. Using the information in the chapter, what implications would these have for love relationships?

Journal Ideas

1. In what ways is your love style different from that of your parents or another couple in the generation older than you?

2. Analyze one of your current friendships or love relationships using categories in the chapter.

Credits

Unit I

Page 4: © Melissa Zexter; p. 6: Eric Lessing/Art Resource, NY; p. 7: Fujifotos/The Image Works; p. 7: Art Wolfe/Tony Stone Images; p. 7: Les Stone/Sygma; p. 10: Sophia Smith Collection/Smith College; p. 13: © 1989 WashingtonPost Writers Group. Reprinted with permission.; p. 15: Philipp Bourseiller/Gamma-Liaison; p. 16: Philipp Bourseiller/Gamma-Liaison; p. 17: Hand colored for Addison Wesley Educational Publishers, Inc. by Cheryl Kucharzak; p. 18: Alfred Gescheidt/The Image Bank; p. 19: Courtesy of Dr. Michael E. Phelps and Dr. John Maziota, UCLA School of Medicine; p. 23: Corbis-Bettmann/Hand colored for Addison Wesley Educational Publishers, Inc. by Cheryl Kucharzak; p. 23: AP/Wide World; p. 23: Karen Garber/The Corning Leader/Sipa Press; p. 27: Photofest/Jagarts; p. 31: Carol Lee/The Picture Cube; p. 33: David Young-Wolff/Tony Stone Images; p. 39: Al Vercoutere, Malibu, CA.; p. 39: Dick Bell/Insight Magazine; p. 40: Howard Sochurek; p. 41: Howard Sochurek.

Unit II

Page 57: fabric photo, Gift of Mrs. Frederick L. Ames in the name of Frederick L. Ames, courtesy Museum of Fine Arts, Boston.

Unit III

Page 114: Courtesy of Eyedentify; p. 114: Courtesy of Technology Recognition Systems; p. 123: © James Porto/FPG

Unit IV

Page 144 © Chip Clark; p. 145: Elliot Meyerowitz, Science 254 11 October 1991: 26; p. 145: Elliot Meyerowitz and John Bowman, Development 112 1991:1-20; p. 145: Elliot Meyerowitz and John Bowman, Development 112 1991:1-20; p. 146: © David Cavagnaro/DRK; p. 148: © Dwight Kuhn; p. 151: © Dwight Kuhn; p. 151: © Kevin Shafer; p. 151: © Larry Mellichamp/Visuals Unlimited; p. 151: © E. S. Ross; p. 153: © Nels Lersten, University of Iowa; p. 153: © Bruce Iverson; p. 153: © Bruce Iverson; p. 153: © Bruce Iverson; p. 153: © Ed Reschke/Peter Arnold Inc.; p. 153: © George J. Wilder/Visuals Unlimited; p. 153: © Randy Moore; p. 157: © Carolina Biological Supply/Phototake; p. 157: Courtesy of F. A. L. Clowes; p. 158: © Ed Reschke; p. 158: © Ed Reschke; p. 158: © Carolina Biological Supply/Phototake; p. 159: © Dwight Kuhn; p. 159: © Ed Reschke; p. 160: © Ed Reschke; p. 160: © Ed Reschke; p. 161: both: © Ed Reschke/Peter Arnold, Inc.

Unit V

Page 178 Lee Snider/The Image Work; p. 187: © Jeff Greenberg/PhotoEdit; p. 195: Esbin-Anderson/The Image Works.